PRAISE FOR THE LONELY HEDONIST

"For four decades, Mike Sager has been one of our finest practitioners of feature magazine writing, picking up where the New Journalism Gods—Wolfe, Talese, Thompson, et al—left off. This latest trove of Sager's irresistible brand of social anthropology shows him in peak form, whether writing about celebrities, like J.J. Abrams and Peter Dinklage, or the usual gathering of bonafide American originals that find their way into his stories–a family-owned sex toys factory, a family farm, a weed doctor, a clown, a man who started a sex club in Beverly Hills, and more."

–Alex Belth, Editor, EsquireClassic.com

"Filled with unforgettable personalities and muscular sentences that mean business, Sager's incredible stories of celebrities, dreamers and capitalists take readers through the warped frontier of new American excess and commerce, and they locate the pain and beauty in the dark circles under America's eyes. Thankfully, Sager has a great sense of humor."

–Aaron Gilbreath, editor, Longreads.com,
author, Everything We Don't Know

"I have been a fan of Sager's work roughly since I learned to read. Whether he's profiling the actor Peter Dinklage, a professional clown, or almond farmers in California's Central Valley, Sager gives you a peek into his subject's soul. How he does it remains a mystery."

–Elon Green, contributor, Harvard University's
Neiman Storyboard, The New Yorker

PRAISE FOR MIKE SAGER

"Like his journalistic precursors Tom Wolfe and Hunter S. Thompson, Sager writes frenetic, off-kilter pop-sociological profiles of Americans in all their vulgarity and vitality. He writes with flair, but only in the service of an omnivorous curiosity. He defies expectations in pieces that lesser writers would play for satire or sensationalism... a Whitmanesque ode to teeming humanity's mystical unity."

—*The New York Times Book Review*

"Mike Sager writes about places and events we seldom get a look at—and people from whom we avert our eyes. But with Sager in command of all the telling details, he shows us history, humanity, humor, sometimes even honor. He makes us glad to live with our eyes wide open."

—*Richard Ben Cramer, Pulitzer Prize winning author of* What It Takes: The Way to the White House *and* Joe Dimaggio: The Hero's Life

"Sager plays Virgil in the Modern American Inferno... Compelling and stylish magazine journalism, rich in novelistic detail."

—*Kirkus Reviews*

"Like a silver-tongued Margaret Mead, Sager slips into foreign societies almost unnoticed and lives among the natives, chronicling his observations in riveting long-form narratives that recall a less tragic, less self-involved Hunter S. Thompson and a more relatable Tom Wolfe."

—*Performances*

"Mike Sager is the Beat poet of American journalism, that rare reporter who can make literature out of shabby reality. Equal parts reporter, ethnographer, stylist and cultural critic, Sager has for 20 years carried the tradition of Tom Wolfe on his broad shoulders, chronicling the American scene and psyche. Nobody does it sharper, smarter, or with more style."

> — *Walt Harrington, author of* Acts of Creation,
> *journalism professor, University of Illinois*
> *at Urbana-Champaign*

"I can recognize the truth in these stories—tales about the darkest possible side of wretched humanity. Sager has obviously spent too much time in flop houses in Laurel Canyon."

> — *Hunter S. Thompson, author of* Fear and Loathing
> in Las Vegas *and* Hells Angels

THE
LONELY
HEDONIST
TRUE STORIES
OF SEX, DRUGS, DINOSAURS
AND PETER DINKLAGE

The Lonely Hedonist: True Stories of Sex, Drugs, Dinosaurs and Peter Dinklage.
Mike Sager

Cover Designed by Stravinski Pierre and Siori Kitajima, SF AppWorks LLC
Interior design by Siori Kitajima, SF AppWorks LLC
Formatting by Ovidiu Vlad, SF AppWorks LLC
http://sfappworks.com

Cataloging-in-Publication data for this book
is available from the Library of Congress.

ISBN-13: 978-0-9980793-5-6
ISBN-10: 0-9980793-5-9

Published by The Sager Group LLC
info@TheSagerGroup.net
info@MikeSager.com

THE LONELY HEDONIST

TRUE STORIES OF SEX, DRUGS, DINOSAURS AND PETER DINKLAGE

BY MIKE SAGER

THE SAGER GROUP

Artifex Te Adiuva

ALSO BY MIKE SAGER

Stoned Again

The Devil and John Holmes

High Tolerance, A Novel

The Someone You're Not

Wounded Warriors

Deviant Behavior, A Novel

Revenge of the Donut Boys

Scary Monsters and Super Freaks

DEDICATION

To my friends and colleagues at The Sager Group LLC, particularly Stravinski Pierre and Jamie Ballard, and our close cousins at SFAppWorks LLC—Andrew Greenstein, Darius Zăgrean, Ovidiu Vlad, Siori Kitajima, and Laura Apetroaei. Together we harness the means of production and enable good things.

TABLE OF CONTENTS

A COLLECTION OF STORIES CHANGED MY LIFE

My new editor took a seat and curtly slapped his thigh with his palm, a sort of gavel rap calling our little meeting to order—a homey and antiquated gesture with which I would become well-acquainted over the rest my lifetime. Often the slap would be accompanied by a delighted guffaw, or the occasional snort of disbelief. But this time he was all business.

"You ever read Tom Wolfe?"

I was twenty-four. Though I had no way of knowing, I was exactly at the midpoint of my six-year stay at the *Washington Post*. It was my first real job, an intense period of learning and growing up that I have come to recognize as a sort of starter marriage, grad school, and medieval-style apprenticeship all rolled into one. I was nobody from nowhere working at one of the greatest newspapers in the world. But like any twenty-something, the monumental drama of my day-to-day narrative blotted out most of my reality. Had I any appreciation of the impossibility of my position—reportedly I was the first white male in twenty years to work his way up from copy boy to reporter—I'm sure I would have spontaneously combusted.

It was January of 1981, a period you might call the dawn of the Infotainment Era. Besides the *Post's* well-known expertise in newsgathering and investigation, the paper's Style section was distinguishing itself as a platform for great writing and writers, helping to usher in a golden age of narrative at newspapers. Under editor Shelby Coffee III, staffers like Paul Hendrickson, Myra MacPherson, Sally Quinn, and Henry Allen were combining newspaper journalism with the sensibilities of literature, bringing a glossy magazine feel to news-print. Long stories, eye-catching layouts with large photos, and stylish prose ruled the day. Not to be outdone, the other sections of the paper were following suit, evidenced by the hiring of Walt Harrington as an editor/writing coach for the Metro section, charged with elevating the features game. I'd been assigned to work with him.

Because this was a time before offices had conference rooms for intimate meetings, we sat down in a couple of chairs in front of the Formica counter that served as the portal to the *Post*'s library. Following the antiquated tradition of gallows humor that still reigned at this time before Political Correctness, some still called it the *morgue*. It was conveniently located at the junction of two of the three build-ings that opened to make the newsroom. In total we occupied an entire acre of floor space. As we sat in our chairs chatting, Harrington and I, reporters from all the different sections walked by, alone or in knots of twos and threes, many of them returning from the cafeteria downstairs, every one of them taking us in side-eyed as journos will do, every one of them wondering what was up at our meeting, I am sure. It was said that the number of full-time staff in the newsroom included nine hun-dred writers and editors. You could spend an entire day moving from desk to desk, chatting and catching up with the best and the brightest. You'd plunk your ass down on the far side of a desk, smile and say, "What's the gossip?" In the heart of the heart of the nation's capital, just a few blocks down the street from the White House, you could be sure there was plenty.

Three years into my tenure—as a copy boy, a night police reporter, and a night "rewrite man"—I was finally pulling some daylight shifts. Most of the hair on the top of my head was gone; I'd grown a beard to compensate. That the hair loss made me look a bit older sort of worked in my favor; many of my Metro colleagues were pushing thirty and beyond. Many had wives and families. With the dark circles under my eyes and my snappy wardrobe of suits and ties (my dad had always been a clothes horse), nobody was mistaking me for a kid anymore.

At the *Post* I began my (lifelong) study of the art of reporting. I like to think I learned the right way from some of the best—the stan-dards and practices, the tricks of the trade, the finer points, like the difference between *off the record* and *not for attribution*, and the way you could see people physically lean forward when you listened really hard. I could dig up documents. Find sources. Fearlessly knock on doors in the worst neighborhoods or call strangers on the phone at all hours. Wheedle my way into an office, squad room, apartment building, or factory floor. Stand toe-to-toe with the most senior official or the most heinous criminal and ask honest questions.

By far the most important lesson I'd learned was tenacity. There were no excuses. *There could be no excuses.* The boss of the Metro Section was Bob Woodward—the guy who'd broken the story of Watergate and contributed to the unseating of President Richard M. Nixon. His boss, and mine, was Ben Bradlee, the storied newsman who carried a brass-topped Hawthorne walking stick and was best buddies with President John F. Kennedy. And *his* boss was Kaye Graham, the grande dame of newspapering (read her autobiography). All around me in the newsroom were some of the finest and most experienced reporters and editors in the world, all of us striving, competing, itching to be the best. In some cases, people didn't fare very well under this system, which Bradlee called "creative tension." My close friend, Janet Cooke, won the Pulitzer Prize for a story she invented because she couldn't pin down the piece she had promised. You can read her unfortunate tale in my e-book, *Janet's World.*

When not pursuing my night duties as a cub reporter, or doing the stories I was assigned as a general assignment writer (everything from murders and protests to Sunday weather stories and car accidents to a re-act piece about insurance rates rising to unprecedented rates), I spent a lot time chasing down what they used to call "enterprise stories," articles reporters come up with outside of or ancillary to their normal work on the beat. Though I'd secured my promotion to reporter with a purely investigative story about wrongdoings taking place at the Department of Agriculture, the stories I enjoyed the most were Style-like features: bright and interesting tales and character profiles about ordinary people who weren't so much newsworthy as they were wonderfully weird or interesting or universally revealing—especially given the right research, approach, and literary care.

Yes, I admit: I began my journalism career as a wannabe fiction writer. In college, I'd minored in creative writing. Undeniably, I had a sense for words, rhythm, and poetry; I could churn out a pretty good series of sentences to read aloud in one of our rambunctious, gloves-off roundtable workshops. But by the time I was a senior in college, it became apparent (even to me) that I couldn't tell a story for shit. Or at least that I had no stories in me to tell. I was a (somewhat) innocent kid from the suburbs. Nothing much had happened in my life. I had nothing to say.

In journalism I found my answer. Armed with the raw material of other people's stories, the facts and interviews and reported emotions, the scenes, the settings, the differing points of view—I had begun to teach myself a way of cobbling together well-written and evocative pieces about true events and real people. Because I had difficulty figuring out what questions to ask my subjects before I met them, because I was kind of shy and felt awkward meeting strangers, and because in anthropology classes in college, I'd become fascinated by the work of Margaret Meade, early on I developed a particular style of reportage. At the time people liked to call it being a "fly on the wall." I preferred to think of it as literary anthropology; I was pulling up a log at the tribal fire. For the subjects of my enterprise stories, I instinctively looked for evocative and colorful material—welfare families; drug dealers; the members of a flying circus; an apartment janitor who lived the nightlife of a disco king; a grown man who was obsessed with model trains; a woman in the exurbs of Virginia who kept a menagerie of pets in her backyard, including a stallion and a male lion. For me the first rule of feature writing has always been: thou shalt not bore.

By the time Harrington arrived, I'd begun to establish myself in the newsroom as a writer with a certain amount of raw talent—hence the matchup, of course. Woodward liked to tell me he admired the way I could "spin a good yarn." But as a serious and sensitive twenty-four-year-old, it rankled to be misunderstood. A lot of research went into my "little features." Maybe I wasn't writing about Nixon's final days, but to make my stories work, I had to uncover a ton of intimate personal detail. I had to get inside peoples' minds. Every subject was like a safe to crack, only I had to use finesse and human understanding instead of

Freedom of Information requests. Not to mention the little spats I'd been getting into with my line editors, ink-stained wretches with tin ears, most of them, except for the future Pulitzer Prize winner David Maraniss, who worked as Woodward's assistant managing editor and once told me, "Sager, everything you write is either great or terrible."

So when Harrington first mentioned Tom Wolfe, I should have been overjoyed. Wolfe, of course, is the journalist who coined the term The New Journalism, which set our craft moving into a whole different space—the space I was going. Call it literary journalism, creative nonfiction, longform, what have you, Wolfe was the one that wrote the manifesto. Wolfe was the one who had made my kind of stories possible.

Except I'd never heard of Tom Wolfe or New Journalism or anything of the sort.

The next day, Harrington brought me his copy of *The New Journalism*— at Wolfe's own insistence, I would later learn, the book was no longer in print.

That night, home in bed, reading into the wee hours, I realized I wasn't alone, that my instincts were correct, and I was heading somewhere, even if I hadn't realized where.

Right in the first few pages of the introduction, Wolfe hit me right where I was living. In what I would later learn to recognize as his typical bombast, Wolfe laid it out: There were two types of journalists. There were the *scoop reporters*, who "competed with their counterparts . . . to see who could get a story first and write it fastest; the bigger the story . . . the better." And then there were these others, known as *feature writers*. "What they had in common was that they all regarded the newspaper as a motel you checked into overnight. . . to get to know 'the world,' accumulate 'experience,' perhaps work some of the fat off your style" and eventually quit and to go on to higher literary achievement. From there, Wolfe went on to describe a new type of journalism that combined rigorous research and investigation with the literary elements of a novel.

Holy shit, I thought. *That's just what these Style writers are doing. That's exactly what I'm trying to do!* I wasn't spinning yarns, despite what Woodward said. I was doing New Journalism!

Granted, I should have known. I was a lot less well-educated than some of the fancy people with whom I was working with. And I admit: I was at the age where my head was mostly up my own ass. To be fair, I'd been a history major. And for the last three years I'd been working eighty hours a week just following directions and instinct and trying not to fuck up on the big stage where I'd landed. Today I recognize the same faults in my own young students—the urge to commit art is much stronger than the urge to study the art that possesses you.

Following Wolfe's (extended) essay in *The New Journalism* was a collection of writings by other writers of whom I'd never heard of, among them Gay Talese, Hunter S. Thompson, Michael Herr, Truman Capote, Terry Southern, Norman Mailer, George Plimpton, Joan Didion, Harry Crews, Garry Willis, and more.

I stayed up all night reading. The next day I went to the bookstore and bought every collection of Wolfe's magazine stories I could find. *The Kandy-Kolored Tangerine-Flake Streamline Baby, The Pump House Gang, Radical Chic and Mau-Mauing the Flak Catchers.* And his epic full-length piece, *The Electric Kool-Aid Acid Test.*

From there I moved onto Hunter Thompson. *The Great Shark Hunt, Hell's Angels, Fear and Loathing in Las Vegas.* Next came Gay Talese—*Fame and Obscurity, Thy Neighbor's Wife.* And then Truman Capote—*In Cold Blood.*

Over the next year or so, I worked through the list provided by Professor Wolfe in his primer of the New Journalism—a manic bout of self-education brought on by the stark realization of how undereducated I really was.

Luckily a journalist's job is to start stupid and become an expert. One thing I've always been good at is starting stupid. I don't mind being wrong if I can find out how to be right. It's the same with writing stories.

Like Maraniss seemed to be implying, you have to be willing to be bad in order to get good. That's what editing is about. The readers only see the last version.

As the years passed, as I left the *Post* and went on to local magazines and then to the nationals, I continued my study of writers and writing.

I started with the forefathers of the New Journalists, the deviants and the Beats, going back to Henry Miller, Louis-Ferdinand Celene, William Burroughs, Hubert Selby Jr., Herbert Huncke, Jack Kerouac, Allen Ginsberg, and Paul Bowles. Later there would be intense periods of reading short stories, world writers, black writers, women writers, literary science fiction writers (Ray Bradbury, George Orwell), and then a revisitation of all the classics of the American cannon, the ones I never read in high school, all the Steinbecks and Hemingways and Fitzgeralds, and then even all the Shakespeares, as I'd been raised during the post-sixties educational upheaval that replaced the study of the Bard with a reading unit on "alienation"—*Black Like Me, The Painted Bird* . . . I read all of those again as well.

Meanwhile, I honed my skills on the keyboard and in the field, working as much as I could, eventually winning contract positions with *Rolling Stone*, *GQ*, and then *Esquire*.

As my career continued, and I started to be recognized for having a certain style of my own, the notion of having collections of stories floated to the top of my list of goals. Not only had reading *The New Journalism* changed my life, but along the way, I decided that I most enjoyed the work of a magazine writer—doing a number of stories every year—as opposed to that of a book writer, who spends years and years on a single story. (No doubt, during those golden years of magazine writing, the pay was better and more consistent as well.) Today, my collections are my legacy. Perhaps it is not the work of a household name, but it is a body of work nonetheless.

Now, entering my fifth decade of doing journalism, with seismic shifts taking place in the field, I offer this latest collection of my stories. With the downsizing of glossy magazines and the rise of the Internet, the nature of narrative journalism has changed considerably. There is far less money for field work, far less space in magazines, and considerably shorter attention spans (according to the endless research by the marketers, who seem to always want to give the people what they want, even when they don't know what that is). The kinds of stories I have always loved to do are harder and harder to sneak past the starting gate—I still love most the bright and interesting tales, the character profiles about ordinary people who aren't so much newsworthy as they are wonderfully weird or interesting or universally revealing—especially given the right research, approach, and literary care.

Luckily, with practice comes some precision. I need fewer words to make my point. Being willing to do the same job for much less money doesn't hurt either.

Come with me now and meet my latest collection of wonderfully fascinating people: The founder of a Beverly Hills sex club who has everything he ever wanted but misses his old life. The Montana rancher who found the most amazing dinosaur fossil ever—that may never be seen by the public. The forgotten sixth founding member of the seminal rap group N.W.A. The whirlwind lifestyle of California's busiest marijuana physician. The secret life of a clown—what happens when the people you're trying to please start hating you? The tiny island in the Pacific where dominating football players are made and exported in astounding numbers. The secret community of underground hash oil makers known as Wooks.

Plus: *Game of Thrones'* Peter Dinklage; Hollywood genius J.J. Abrams; TV pitchman Ron Popeil (Operators are standing by!); the male supermodel who spent twenty years as a member of a cult; The Most Interesting Man in the World, in retirement, and the former marketing man who is living off the grid on a small plot in suburbia.

As always, thank you for reading.

Mike Sager
La Jolla, CA

THE LONELY HEDONIST

THE FOUNDER OF BEVERLY HILLS' MOST ELITE SEX CLUB DIVORCED HIS WIFE, RENTED A MANSION AND FILLED IT WITH DEBAUCHERY. WHY IS HE STILL UNHAPPY?

In a leafy enclave near Beverly Hills, behind an aging Tudor mansion, Snctm is hosting a pool party. The sun is radiant overhead, the sky is cloudless and blue; the therapeutic aroma from the eucalyptus trees mixes in the air with the scents of expensive perfume and hydroponic weed. Couples lie here and there on chaise longues or large blankets on the grass. A trio of topless young women, members of Snctm's erotic-theater troupe, known as Devotees, float languorously on giant blow-up swans, sipping drinks through bent straws. Two more Devotees bounce on a trampoline. In a little while, the brunette will be tied up, the blonde will employ a suede flogger and other toys, dispensing pain and pleasure. A waitress circulates, delivering food prepared by the French chef—a choice today of sirloin sliders or fish tacos, with a side of crisp steak fries.

Sitting poolside in a wicker chair, presiding over all, is Damon Lawner. A handsome man of forty-five with a lean and chiseled physique, he wears gauzy, low-slung pants and a necklace of fragrant mala beads he picked up during a sojourn in Bali. With his longish tousled hair and high cheekbones, his inner glow and sober mien, he looks like a hunky Hollywood guru. Four years ago, he was a cash-strapped real estate agent with a beautiful wife and two young daughters, struggling with monogamy, facing with dread the prospects of his fifth decade. As many men do when they reach his age, he began to ask himself, "Is this all there is?"

Tattooed on Lawner's right shoulder is Snctm's official symbol, a teardrop shape containing a cross and an all-seeing eye. Lawner calls it the Oculus Dei. He drew it in a fit of inspired desperation one night in the living room of his small apartment after his family had gone to bed. The cross stands for faith. The eye stands for the Hindu chakra that leads to inner realms and higher consciousness. The tear was meant to stand for the earth's life-giving elements. But as Snctm has become more successful, as Lawner's life has been transformed, the tear has become instead a bittersweet reminder. In the quest to make your fantasies come true, he has discovered, you can sometimes lose as much as you gain.

One week from today, Snctm will hold its regular Masquerade, an exclusive monthly event with the guest list limited to ninety-nine people. As the name suggests, masks are required. The atmosphere is reminiscent of the erotic party scenes in Stanley Kubrick's *Eyes Wide Shut*, Lawner's initial inspiration. Among those already confirmed for next Saturday's soiree are a man who owns hotels in New York, a billionaire from Moscow, several wealthy couples who have each been married for more than twenty years, the producer of a number of well-known television shows, an actress with a respectable IMDb page, the twenty-one-year-old son of a movie producer, a number of international models, and a couple who are opening a big new store near Rodeo Drive.

When Lawner founded Snctm, he envisioned something more intimate than previous incarnations of swingers' clubs. From Plato's Retreat, the disco-era den of iniquity in New York, to Paris's thriving and swanky Les Chandelles, the more notable spots over the years have been known for unfettered debauchery. A child of hippies who spent his earliest years in a commune in upstate New York, Lawner has tried to create "a spiritual and erotic utopia" where people of like minds and desires can have as much sex and romance as humanly possible, in as many different ways as the imagination can invent, with the most beautiful and engaging people they can find. And no strings attached.

At the moment, Lawner is using a custom phone app to screen applications for this weekend's Masquerade. There are still a few more slots open for women, who can apply to attend for free. Sitting beside him, in a matching wicker chair, a dark beauty sips champagne. Call her Caroline. Tall and impossibly thin, with huge brown eyes, she has recently earned a degree from a college in Texas. She's visiting Lawner for a couple of weeks, seeing agencies, hoping to get into modeling.

Joining the couple is one of Lawner's most trusted collaborators, Phuong Tran, thirty-two, known to Snctm members as Bunnyman. By day he's a manager at a *Fortune* 500 company in LA. At Masquerades he wears a martial-arts outfit and the black leather rabbit mask that earned him his nickname; he's highly regarded for his expertise in the ancient Japanese rope-tying art of *shibari*. Tran was the very first to purchase a membership to Snctm. He joined, he says, "because some of my friends were in other private social clubs, like the Johnathan Club and the California Club, and I wanted to be able to reciprocate with something a little different."

"Check this one out," Lawner says, showing his phone to the others. "She works as a research chemist."

"She's that lovely librarian type," Tran says appreciatively. Today he's wearing Italian-made print pants rolled above the ankles and a short-brimmed straw chapeau.

Lawner reads aloud from the application: "I'm a hyperpolyglot and enjoy dirty talk so hopefully during a sexual escapade, other members will learn some kinky words."

"Hyperpolyglot," Tran repeats, sounding intrigued. "I believe that means somebody who has the ability to learn multiple languages really quickly."

"So," Lawner says, summing up: "She's totally hot, probably knows eight languages, likes to talk dirty—"

"And likes to get fucked really hard," Caroline interrupts. She's been reading over Lawner's shoulder.

"You think we should invite her?" Lawner asks.

Damon Emanuel Lawner never set out to be the founder of a sex club. His paternal grandfather was a wealthy sporting-goods manufacturer from Long Island. His father was a talented violinist who chucked it all in the early 1970s to join a commune upstate. Damon was given his name by the commune's leader, as was his sister, Hadria.

Lawner's parents split when he was three. Both moved across the country to the burgeoning hippie community of Fairfax, in Marin County, near San Francisco. Lawner's father, Loren, lived modestly off the proceeds of a trust. He once rented his house to Owsley Stanley, the famous LSD chef, and on a number of occasions he jammed with Phil Lesh and Mickey Hart, both members of the Grateful Dead. "There were late-night parties, lots of cocaine and acid, lots of booze," Lawner says. His mother, Melissa Rome Lawner, took up with a Jim Morrison look-alike who made leather clothes; to make ends meet, she received food stamps.

"We went back and forth between these two crazy households," Lawner recalls. "My sister and I were kind of ignored. We were like ghosts floating around. When we wanted breakfast, we'd go across to the neighbors'. They always had cereal and toast."

Every summer, Lawner says, he and his sister were packed off to the grandparents back east. "I'd go from food stamps and drug addicts and, like, dirty fucking clothes, wearing the same T-shirt every day to school, to this big house with a pool and ten bedrooms. It was paradise. Bagels and lox and French toast in the morning, bowling and movies and everything you could want. I don't know how that affected me. But I always knew that if I did what my grandpa did, I could have anything I wanted. And I knew if I lived like my parents lived, that's the life I'd have. Over the course of my lifetime, I guess, I've always gone back and forth."

When Lawner was nineteen, he says, he was skateboarding with some friends when he was approached by a scout for the photographer Bruce Weber. Soon he was signed by the Look Model Agency in San Francisco. He was featured in a Versace campaign, and in a Calvin

Klein jeans-and-coats campaign with supermodel Christy Turlington and the actor and heir Balthazar Getty.

After a brief stint at a junior college, Lawner supported himself through a combination of modeling jobs, photography, family money, and real estate investing. At twenty-five, he met and fell in love with Melissa Bernheim, an eighteen-year-old model and the daughter of a Stanford economics professor. In 2001, when Melissa was twenty-one, she was featured dancing with abandon in a popular commercial for the Gap. The ad drew the attention of David Letterman, who invited the lithe brown-haired beauty to re-create her happy dance on his show. Following her appearance—during which she proudly mentioned her engagement to a guy named Damon—Melissa signed with the powerful United Talent Agency and began going out for small acting jobs.

That year, after a half decade of dating, the couple eloped to Las Vegas. To benefit Melissa's career, they moved to Los Angeles, to a fixer-upper house just above the ritzy Chateau Marmont hotel in West Hollywood. Cameron Diaz, David LaChapelle, Sandra Bullock, and Lionsgate honcho Michael Burns, with whom the couple frequently partied, all lived nearby in the same neighborhood. Lawner says he became particularly friendly with Jared Leto, the actor/rocker/tech investor, who was dating Diaz at the time.

Through some of his connected friends, Lawner was offered a chance to invest in a Japanese restaurant called Koi. The place took off, became a chain. Meanwhile, Melissa modeled and found small acting parts on television shows like *CSI: Miami*. She was featured in a number of national commercials, including a Coors Light spot directed by Michael Bay that featured Kid Rock. The couple was flush.

"We'd stay up all night and party and have people over, or we'd walk down to the Chateau and meet people; they would always end up back at our house," Lawner says. "There were a lot of drugs and alcohol. A lot of fun, really. We were like this beautiful charismatic couple. It was always an adventure."

"Anyone who saw us together knew we are soul mates," Melissa Lawner says. "We were very, very connected and energetic with each other. We were inseparable. We were *that* couple; you called us *DamonandMelissa*."

When Lawner was thirty-five, Melissa announced she was pregnant. At first, he says, he felt "incredible joy."

Then the band he'd been playing with, called Fader, won a contest at the historic Whisky a Go Go on the Sunset Strip. A tour was discussed. Melissa made her feelings clear. "She was like, 'I'm going to be a mom now. All this crazy shit is over,'" Lawner says.

Lawner quit the band, sold the house in the hills, and moved his family to the flats of Hancock Park. With the profits from the sale, he concentrated on business, determined to feather his nest. He started a company that sold a high-end energy drink called Marquis Platinum and invested in another restaurant called Bridge. In short order, he and Melissa had a second daughter.

When the economy tanked in 2008, the Lawners lost everything. "By the time I saw what was coming," he says, "I was fucked. The cars were repossessed, the house was foreclosed on. We were $900,000 in debt."

Penniless and humiliated, Lawner packed up his family and flew to join his father in Bali, where he was living with his Balinese wife and two young sons.

In Bali, Lawner reinvented himself as a party impresario, using his nightlife experience to bring a little sizzle to the tourists visiting the Island of the Gods. With Melissa by his side, he put on functions four nights a week at high-end hotels and nightspots. By 2011 *Prestige Indonesia* magazine was calling the Lawners the "It couple behind Bali's most exclusive parties."

Though the Lawners were living comfortably—with an income of about $30,000 a year, they could afford a big house and servants—their lifestyle started to take a toll. There was a lot of drinking and partying, along with predictable marital discord. Lawner was the *man* on Bali; everything was available. "I was out every night. Things began to spiral a little bit. My breakfast of choice was a beer and a cigarette by the pool," he recalls.

After he was briefly kidnapped by local nightlife competitors and forced to pay ransom, Lawner says, Melissa put her foot down. "Our girls were growing up on an island in the middle of nowhere, without knowing any of my family," she says. In 2012 the Lawners returned to LA. They moved into a room off the kitchen in Melissa's mom's house, near UCLA. "We needed to go home," Melissa says. "I kind of forced him. He did not want to leave."

Bankrupt, with no car and no assets, Lawner began looking for a job. "I was applying all over the place. Waiter, cashier, valet parking. Anything. Whatever I applied for, there were twenty people in front of me who had more experience. They'd ask me, 'What have you done?' and I was like, 'Um, I owned the hottest restaurant in LA?' And they were like, 'Yeah, whatever.'"

Eventually, Lawner became a realtor. He went to work at Sotheby's in Beverly Hills and moved the family into a small apartment nearby to take advantage of the school district. He rotated two suits, rode a bicycle to work, told prospective clients his vehicle was in the shop. While he had some success, selling a few properties (and splitting the commissions with the agent who was training him), he was miserable. "The whole thing was ridiculous. I fucking hated it, I did not want to do it, it was not me on any level. I was at the point where I wasn't sure anymore what the fuck I was living for."

Around this time, Lawner rented *Eyes Wide Shut*. In the film, Tom Cruise and Nicole Kidman play a long-established couple facing middle age and disillusionment; both are secretly questioning their commitment to monogamy. When Cruise finds himself in a mysterious mansion, at a gathering of a members-only sex society, his life and the couple's relationship are inalterably changed.

The movie struck a chord. Lawner was forty-two. He'd been with Melissa for more than fifteen years—a third of his life. He still loved her deeply, still wanted her every single day, but things hadn't been good in their relationship for some time. The moves and the financial upheaval had worn on them. And even though he fell asleep every night beside a gorgeous wife, he and Melissa had all but stopped having sex. Every time he saw a happy couple in the street, he wondered how long it had been since they'd last slept together; he'd lost count himself. That he lived and worked in Beverly Hills—frequented by some of the planet's most beautiful women—only made him feel worse.

In time, an idea took hold. Wouldn't it be amazing if there were an answer for guys like him—for couples like them? Some kind of club, like in Kubrick's movie, that was secret and exclusive, where a couple like *DamonandMelissa* could go? A place where the fire could be rekindled.

As the days and weeks wore on, Lawner kept revisiting the notion—in fact, he could think of little else. Finally, one afternoon he went to a Paper Source store and bought an expensive notebook bound with silver cloth, and a fancy black pen. That night, after Melissa and the kids went to bed, he sat down at a makeshift office in the corner of his living room. The first thing he did was sketch the Oculus Dei. Then he wrote this: "The grand object of Snctm is the eroticism of the human race."

Lawner got the club rolling with a Facebook page and forty dollars' worth of promotional boosts. To his surprise, dozens of people started friending him. A ticket to the first Masquerade—held in a rented nightclub in Beverly Hills in March 2013—cost fifty dollars. Lifetime membership, which included admission to every Snctm event and discounts on dinners and table service, was $1,500.

For the first two years, the Masquerade was a movable party, held in a different mansion every month. Eventually, to cut down on problems with neighbors and the law, Lawner rented the Tudor. Today a table with liquor service at a Masquerade costs $2,500 a couple; lounge chairs at the pool parties are $950 a pair. An annual membership, which includes entry to all Snctm events and other perks, costs $10,000. Dominus membership lasts for a lifetime and costs up to $75,000. About a hundred people have signed up for membership, Lawner says, and "ten or so" have joined at the Dominus level.

One of Snctm's big draws is the promise of anonymity. A number of Hollywood celebrities, among them two Hall of Fame rockers and a talk-show host, have attended, and some have paid full price for a membership. An interview with Lawner ran on Gwyneth Paltrow's website, Goop, and her boyfriend, Brad Falchuk, the cocreator of the television shows *Glee* and *American Horror Story,* is producing a fictional series based on Lawner's life. A Showtime reality series will also be sold.

By late Saturday night, the Snctm Masquerade is reaching a crescendo. Hundreds of white candles flicker throughout the fifty-five-hundred-square-foot mansion; trance music issues from hidden speakers; red uplights lend a chthonian vibe. The men wear tuxedos, the women lingerie. Identities are hidden behind elaborate masks of lace, rhinestones, and feathers.

In the foyer, two topless Amazons, wearing pasties in the shape of the Oculus Dei, stand watch like queen's guards. Beneath a crystal chandelier, Tran is dressed now as his alter ego, Bunnyman, with his leather bunny mask, black Japanese *keikogi* top, and black *hakama* bottoms. His tuxedo slippers, one of twenty pairs in his collection, are embroidered in gold with a screw on the left foot, the letter U on the right.

His attention is directed toward a woman in a lace teddy. She is blindfolded and bound to a crushed-velvet chair with the traditional coils of jute rope used in *shibari*. A restless enthusiast who likes to "geek out" on a subject until he becomes an expert, Bunnyman's hobbies, besides the ancient bondage disciplines, include scotch, cigars, fine tobacco pipes, and post-WWII contemporary art. On a low table nearby, displayed on a silver tray, is his collection of sex toys—a flogger, a Lelo wand, a two-headed marital aid, and a retasked antique medical tool called a Wartenberg pinwheel, with radiating sharp pins. A circle of guests gathers around.

In the living room, a cocktail-party atmosphere prevails. People laugh and drink and flirt. Young Devotees from the erotic-theater troupe circulate through the crowd. One wears a piggy mask and a sign around her neck: *Touch me*. By day she is a digital research analyst. Snctm is her new hobby. Not even her boyfriend knows. The first time she worked a Masquerade, she spent two hours on her hands and knees serving as a human end table. This time she is being led through the proceedings on a golden chain by two of her fellows, one wearing a leather police hat, the other in an eye cage, garters, and stockings. The latter carries a crop. Like servers passing hors d'oeuvres, the trio circulates, encouraging members and guests to pet or whip the Devotee as they see fit. Later she will say she loved the way the guests looked at her with a mixture of shyness and desire, men and women alike.

Downstairs is an old wine cellar, empty of bottles. Two women and two men occupy a queen-sized bed. One man is an airline pilot, the other is a banker. They've both brought dates. They don't yet know each other's names—later they'll share a couple of beers at the bar. Close at hand is a considerable crowd, standing room only, unblinking. They keep a respectful distance, each person or couple occupying their own psychic space, as if they're watching a porno in unison at home on the big screen, only this one is in 3-D and surround sound and Smell-O-Vision. No one is fully undressed; shirts hang unbuttoned, bow ties and bras litter the floor, panties are pushed to the side, trousers sag around ankles. Sweat flows. Intimate noises. One of the spectators moves forward to join the proceedings, unzipping his fly as he goes. The new man has a small paunch. The woman who has been busy with the banker works for a casting agency. She takes the new man into her mouth. The woman with the pilot works for a television show. She reaches over with a free hand to help out with the new man. The red soles of her Louboutins rock back and forth, back and forth, like twin metronomes, keeping time.

Upstairs, a passageway leads to the attic playroom, available to members only. Two beds, a number of folding chairs for spectators. Diaphanous swaths of cloth hang from the rafters. One bed is occupied by a foursome of women. On the other are Alan and Janine. (The names of the guests, along with some identifying details, have been changed.) They live in Brentwood and have young children. They're both involved in entertainment. Alan is a little heavy but looks good in his tux. Janine looks like an active member of the PTA, which she is. Instead of lingerie, she wears a short frock. Before they found Snctm, they spiced up their marriage by going to high-end strip clubs. Tonight, for the sake of modesty, they keep their clothes on while they have sex. People sense their need for privacy and look away.

Kay and George are in the shadows in the corner, making out like teenagers. They have several kids, aged ten to twenty. He owns an ad agency; they fly in from the Midwest to attend. Some time ago, George says, "We started to think that it's not necessarily normal to be with one person your entire life." The first time they tried a swingers' club in Las

Vegas, Kay was overwhelmed. She remembers "strangers walking up with their penis in their hand." At Snctm's price, George says, "people have a lot in common. It's very sophisticated and private; you know there won't be any weirdos."

Sophia and Fernando are in the fashion business. The swaths of cloth hanging from the rafters were their idea. Something of a May-July couple, they don't come to Snctm to play, but they love to dress up in antique designer clothes and masks and watch others. Tonight they've both taken small hits of MDA. "It's incredibly sexy—the women are so beautiful," gushes Sophia. "You just can't believe the stuff you see," Fernando says. After a Masquerade, they suggest, things usually get pretty hot in their hotel room.

Harrison is twenty-one. He has a mop of silky hair and big brown eyes with long lashes. "You'd be surprised how many older women have a thing for young guys," he will later say, smiling like the Cheshire Cat. Earlier this week, his dad wrote a check for $50,000 to make him the youngest Dominus member of Snctm. At the moment he is sitting on a chair, watching the girl-on-girl action, a look of contented exhaustion on his face. A cute young Belgian woman is sitting on his knee. They bring to mind a couple resting between dances at the prom, except she is wearing only a bra and panties and has her hand down his pants.

At the back of the room, near the door, Damon Lawner surveys the scene in his Tom Ford tux. The top three buttons of his white shirt are open to reveal his tanned and well-muscled chest.

For the first two years of Snctm, as the club began to grow and flourish, as the money started flowing in, *DamonandMelissa* worked side by side to organize and run the parties. Once again, they were the It couple, though they never participated in the swinging.

"Yes, it was frustrating," Lawner recalls.

"I like to drink and have fun as much as the next girl," Melissa says. "But some of the sexual things that would go on in the club just turned me off. Damon really wanted to try all these things out. He wanted me to participate. And I was like, 'No. I'm not into it.'" At some point, Melissa says, "the parties just crossed the line for me." She quit attending. As time passed, she experimented with giving Lawner permission to experience nonsexual activities like flogging or bondage. But she could not envision a scenario where she'd be okay with him sleeping with other women, whether at a sex club or elsewhere.

"I tried to go along, but it became a place of discomfort for me," Melissa says. "We would have fights and I would cry and we would talk about it. It wasn't really working out for either of us."

In the fall of 2015, Melissa discovered that Lawner had spent time in a hotel with Caroline, the young woman from Texas. In the aftermath, Lawner confessed to a series of indiscretions. Furious and hurt, Melissa issued an ultimatum. Lawner could continue with Snctm, or he could act like a proper husband and father to Melissa and the girls.

"I don't really blame Snctm for our relationship ending, but it was a catalyst," Melissa says. "I had a certain vision of what our future looked like, and it was more domesticated and normal, kind of how I was raised, and he was raised very differently. But in a way I'm grateful for it, too. What I experienced in the Masquerade parties was positive for me, it opened me up to being more passionate, more exploratory— maybe not with pain or being tied up—but with other things.

"Damon's grown a lot from this, too," she adds. "He's gotten sober. But he still has those young girls over there and he's still a kind of playboy, tooling around in his new sports car, driving way too fast in residential areas. And you know what? That's how he is, that's just Damon. He's living his truth."

Meanwhile, in the attic, Lawner spots Caroline behind one of the diaphanous swaths, making out with a wealthy businessman.

Caroline is wearing a fishnet cover-up over a bra-and-panty set, and a pair of five-inch Manolo heels. Her mask is gone; she appears to be unsteady on her feet. At Lawner's insistence, she has agreed to an open relationship, but it doesn't take a genius to see what's happening. Throughout the night she has consumed a large quantity of alcohol and has flirted with multiple men. Lawner has kept an eye on her. You can tell he's torn. He's said as much: "I have feelings for her, sure. But I've come too far to tie myself down."

The businessman she's with is a handsome guy known among club members as an experienced swinger. Like Harrison, George, and Fernando, he paid Lawner a minimum of forty grand to join Snctm. He reaches down and begins to touch Caroline vigorously between her legs. In obvious distress, she does a half pivot and manages to slither free from his grasp.

She lurches across the attic and out the door, her face smudged with mascara and humiliation.

Lawner follows.

By 2 a.m. Sunday, the circular driveway behind the tall hedge is chockablock with high-end collectable cars. Inside, the Snctm Masquerade is peaking. Music swirls, laughter rises, bodies couple and writhe. Like a bar at last call, anonymous eyes search the crowd, looking to couple up.

In the living room, surrounded by guests on sofas and chairs, Bunnyman is at work on a somewhat established actress, her arms and legs akimbo, the knots and coils of rope at once strong and delicate, like macramé.

Bunnyman's parents are refugees from Vietnam—he hints that his family held high position in the old country. He doesn't mind using his name because "to Vietnamese people, Phoung Tran is like John Smith."

The actress on which he is working is blonde tonight; sometimes she's a redhead. She is more of a character actress than a leading lady— she'll play the friend of the lead or one of the teachers at the school. She's wearing an ivory-colored bra and booty panties from Victoria's Secret; a black suede mask covers her eyes. She has brought along four of her girlfriends. They are watching intently; she can feel their energy as Bunnyman deploys various toys, alternating between pleasure and pain.

A "control freak" who can be the bossy type, the actress will later say that being bound and dominated is like a form of meditation: "It's a way that I get to lose control, or give up control. For a little while I don't have to pay attention, I don't have to worry, I don't have to do anything. Someone else is looking out for me."

She met Bunnyman on a fetish website two years back, and she's been coming to Snctm ever since. In fact, she came tonight specially to see him. "He knew I hadn't played in a long time, ever since I left my dominant," she says. "I've been in a huge dry spell. It causes my ADD to go off, and I can't concentrate or handle things as well, because I don't have that outlet. It's like someone going without sex for a long time."

Bunnyman works through his toys, asking permission before each. At some point he selects a stainless steel number, two-headed in the shape of a lazy U, a prostate massager he finds useful for G spots. Before he came to Snctm, bondage wasn't a particular interest. He was always somewhat vanilla when it came to sex. At early gatherings, another man was hired to practice bondage on the guests. "What I was so captivated by was the fact that a lot of girls randomly volunteered themselves. I was like 'Shit, I need to learn rope.'" Since then, Bunnyman has found place and purpose, more than he ever imagined; his girlfriend is a former Devotee, part of the erotic troupe. The second time he met her, he tied her up —now they're facing parenthood together. "Everyone at Snctm has their different journey," he says.

Off the living room, in a bedroom with a mirrored wall, the Devotee in the piggy mask and garters and stockings, the research analyst by day, has been directed to a bed. She's on all fours; her two handlers have her arranged in such a way that her head is near the mirror; her bottom is facing a semi-circle of onlookers. She is naked except for the mask and collar. The Devotee in the eye cage begins whipping her with the riding crop; she alternates with a Devotee in a leather police hat, who kisses and strokes and gives oral.

Looking into the mirror, the Devotee in the piggy mask notices the crowd gathered behind her, around the bed, "not close enough to touch me but enough to have a full view of my asshole and pussy," she will later write in her diary. They keep their distance, "at once curious and intimidated." At last, she finds her own eyes in the mirror, "hooded and fierce with sensuality and lust, slightly lowered in obedience." *Holy fuck!* she thinks. *This is fucking beautiful.* "I knew I was accessing something deep within myself that I had always wanted to express," she says later.

Presently, the sounds of passionate release roll though the aging Tudor mansion. The people in the attic, in the living room, in the various private rooms available in the house, gather together their outfits and commence rebuttoning. In orderly fashion they file down the staircase and out the front door, like spectators at the conclusion of a sporting event. Black suited security guards, all of them handsome and muscular, pass through the house, moving along the stragglers.

Out back, by the pool, Bunnyman is smoking a tobacco pipe. It is a fine piece, a Peterson Spigot with a bulldog bowl, made of briarwood, with a green emerald finish and a sterling silver army mount.

The pipe extends from his mouth at a jaunty angle; with his left hand he kneads his right wrist. It's hard to say how many women he tied up and pleasured this evening. It might be a "labor of love," but it takes its toll.

"My arm is killing me," he says, exhaling a fragrant plume of his Hobbits Weed tobacco.

Late Sunday afternoon, post-Masquerade, the sun shines down on the Snctm mansion, exposing some of the cracks and flaws in the midcentury house. Lawner is in the living room, shirtless in the same gauzy cotton pants, strumming a rare 1963 Gibson Hummingbird guitar that Rolling Stone guitarist Keith Richards once played, a gift from a music producer as a thank-you for arranging to make a particular fantasy come true.

In the afterglow of last night's shindig, Lawner has grown reflective. From the tone of the text messages he's received, the Masquerade was a resounding success. The future looks bright. Masquerades have been planned for every month through the rest of the year. In September, in New York, during Fashion Week, he held a Masquerade on a hundred-foot yacht. Next month, in Miami, during Art Basel, Lawner is planning to hold a Masquerade at a private house. Falchuk's show is in development, and Lawner has hired a camera crew to follow him around to make a sizzle reel to pitch a series. Everything is going his way.

And yet he's feeling melancholy.

As the idea was originally hatched, Lawner was supposed to move into the Tudor with Melissa and the girls. Down the hall is the room where his daughters stay when they visit for occasional sleepovers. The girls are now eight and eleven. Melissa is dating a wealthy realtor, the kind of guy Lawner tried his best to become. In a few days she'll be leaving with her beau for a jaunt in the Mediterranean. Lawner will follow her posts on Facebook.

Since starting Snctm, Lawner has gotten everything he's ever wanted. There's a brand-new red-and-white Aston Martin Vantage GT in the garage; beside it is an identically painted Ducati motorcycle. A parade of beautiful young women share his four-poster bed. More and more people are hitting him up to join Snctm—it seems like he's found a nerve.

"I've had nights when I'm looking around the mansion and I can't believe what's really happening," Lawner says. "It's overwhelming. I've seen activities between guests that have been an incredible turn-on. I've sat down on the carpet in my room and listened to rock stars play my guitar. I've watched the most gorgeous women, everywhere you looked, just eating each other's pussies and fucking and I mean, God, on those nights I find myself really participating. I'm being pulled into stuff and I'm like, *Are you kidding me? No man should get to experience this. It's almost unfair.*"

And then there are the other times, Lawner says. The hollow feeling. The loneliness. He misses his daughters. He misses his wife. He misses having a place within the little family he created. Outside the box, it seems, you are completely on your own. Freedom can be daunting.

"If I had stayed in real estate, if I had put on the suit and tie, I would be coming home to this beautiful wife who loved me incredibly deeply and these two beautiful little daughters," he says. "I probably could have built a nice life. I could've done the picket fence. It probably would have been deeply fulfilling. I don't know. Instead I chose to absolutely follow my dreams. I knew I was going to lose my family. I made a conscious decision. I gave up the only thing I love and care about in this world."

He strums a sad chord on the rare and beautiful guitar. "The truth is I'm heartbroken," he says.

As if on cue, Caroline floats out of the master bedroom, into the living room. Freshly showered, dressed in short-shorts and a simple tee, she looks natural and gorgeous and smells of herbal shampoo. She straddles Lawner's lap, facing him.

"Remember last night in the members' lounge?" Lawner asks. "When that guy was kinda kissing you and touching you? Would you have wanted me to step in and stop that? Or was that something you wanted?"

She studies him for a moment—the square jaw and earnest blue eyes, the slight crinkles at the corners, the strands of gray sneaking out of the hedgerow of his center part, his Hindu mala beads, from which rises the scent of sandalwood. She kisses him deeply.

His eyes are wide open.

THE DAY PETER DINKLAGE WATCHED SOMEONE DIE

EVERYWHERE HE GOES, THE EMMY- AND GOLDEN GLOBE-WINNING STAR OF GAME OF THRONES CAUSES A STIR. OF COURSE, IT HAS BEEN THAT WAY HIS ENTIRE LIFE.

At Twilight on Tenth Avenue, the sidewalks of lower Chelsea, in the island kingdom of Manhattan, are thronged with creatures of every ilk—dewy working girls and snugly tailored metro boys, polyethnic couples and Euro-tourons; a burly man in a white apron splattered with blood; a fashionista pushing a rack of clothes; a bodybuilder leashed to a pug. Cars honk, buses whoosh, the sun setting over the Hudson River casts an energetic glow.

Peter Dinklage is sitting by a window in one of his favorite restaurants, facing northward, against the tide of the passing show. The overhead lights are bright; a jazzy soundtrack noodles through the inner atmosphere, which smells deliciously of baking bread. Few patrons are in evidence; the kitchen is shut down, retooling for dinner. He requested a seat in the back, but the staff is being fed. That he's lived in this neighborhood a while now makes him a regular. That he's the Emmy- and Golden Globe–winning star of HBO's popular *Game of Thrones* entitles him to this primo spot; it didn't seem right to turn it down.

Posted as we are, in a brightly lit room beside a large window, with darkness gathering outside on the busy street—and holiday lights all around, forming a kind of twinkling, flashing frame—I assume Dinklage is as visible to passersby as he would be inside one of the fabulous seasonal department-store displays uptown at Bergdorf's or Macy's. People stare, do double takes, snap cellies. Beyond the usual celebrity hubbub, there is something more: Looks of genuine wonderment. Spontaneous delighted laughter. *Oh my god, it's HIM.*

Dinklage's thick and longish hair is stuffed beneath a fuzz-balled knit cap. He sports his usual black jeans and T-shirt and James Perse hoodie, a brand he says is known for roomier hoods. Though at four feet six he is eleven inches shorter than me, he sits as if he were taller; I have to look up slightly to meet his blue-gray eyes, which seem more reflective of what's going on outside himself than of what's happening within. The drooping set of his eyes makes him look a bit sad, even when he's laughing. His heavy brow appears to be permanently furrowed in a state of wariness; he is indeed a veteran of life's odd possibilities, starting with the one-in-twenty-five-thousand chance that he'd be born with achondroplasia—a genetic disorder that causes abnormalities in bone formation. At one point, my shin makes contact beneath the table with the tip of his not-unlarge Chelsea boot, the style favored by the Beatles. I do not take the opportunity to observe the distance between the sole and the floor.

Since wrapping season four of *Thrones,* an eventful one for his much-beloved character, Tyrion Lannister, Dinklage has been home in New York for a month. Hitting the gym, working on a screenplay and producing a film, walking his hundred-pound lab-Great Dane-pointer mix, running a lot of errands, taking his turn as at-home parent to his two-year-old daughter while his wife, Erica Schmidt, directs a pair of plays back-to-back. After more than two decades and eight different apartments in Brooklyn and Manhattan, "I'm getting to that age where

I love New York City, but I don't call it a vacation anymore. It sort of drives me crazy." He's antsy to get back to their house north of the city. Hoofing it across the urban landscape, hailing cabs, just buying dog food—everywhere he goes he causes a bit of a stir. Of course, it's pretty much been that way his entire life. Celebrity has only multiplied the effect. Even when he's not recognized, he's noticed. One small consolation: After three decades of stage work and more than thirty movies—including a role *in X-Men: Days of Future Past,* coming in May—and a handful of awards, nobody confuses him anymore with Mini Me.

Now a woman is standing just outside the window, holding a toddler with a runny nose. She's speaking animatedly into the child's ear, kissing her rosy cheek, pointing at Dinklage rather like a mother at the zoo. *Look dear, it's Trumpkin from* Narnia*!*

This he can't ignore.

He smiles overlarge and issues a spoofy royal wave.

"Hellooo," he calls, at once sardonic and resigned. His voice is a beautiful deep baritone, a woodwind sound that resonates in the airspace around our two-top. *"Helloo. Hellooo-oooo."*

You must have some interesting encounters on the street, I say, attempting to commiserate.

He rests his cheeks in his not-unlarge hands and shakes his head. "Sometimes the encounters can be meaningful," he offers satirically.

Which reminds him of something.

"One morning," after his breakout role in *The Station Agent* (2003), "I was walking down Melrose Avenue in Los Angeles. There was this guy on a motorcycle right in front of me—about as far away as that plant, maybe six feet? And he looked at me. He didn't wave, but he looked at me, and then he pulled out into traffic and this car, like, *boom—killed* him instantly."

Holy Shit. And you were the last person he saw?

"Yes. I was the last person he saw on earth."

And you connected with him.

"And I connected with him. And then he pulled out into traffic and *boom.* There was an old guy driving the car. I ran into this coffee shop that I'd been on my way to. They had somebody call an ambulance. And then I ran back outside to be with the guy, but he was already dead. I didn't want to get too near him. The old guy had stopped and he was slowly getting out of his car. It was in the morning, so there was no one around, you know? This was in LA, where nobody walks. It was empty. So there was this quiet moment where it was like I was the only person in the world who knew this guy was dead. And I was there looking at him, you know, in those moments of calm after something horrible happens, the calm before the melee starts, before the ambulances and the cops arrive and it becomes a scene. There was that moment when I was with him."

He raises his photogenic chin, contemplating the immediate heavens, the vicissitudes of fate, his face turned away from the window. I can't help but think of Tyrion Lannister delivering one of his rich monologues, a conflicted modern thinker among the primitives, a pragmatist with a deep well of melancholy.

"There's such a difference with dying," Dinklage says. "You can have somebody who is really sick for a long time. Like, my father had cancer for many years and he passed away. He was too young. He was in his seventies, which is too young. But there's something different between an older person dying and this guy. He was probably about twenty-five. He'd probably just had breakfast at the same place I was headed. And then he died. It's like, he was *robbed*."

We sit it for a few moments, sipping our coffees. He eats some cheese and apple off the plate but skips the bread.

Then it pops into my head, so I ask: Do you think you might have distracted him?

Dinklage's eyes saucer. His face contorts into a hideous mask.

"No, no, no, no!" he cries, raising his hands defensively, as if to fend off the notion. "No! I *never felt* like that! *NOT AT ALL.*"

Just wondered, you know, given the—

"Oh, my God! *Fuck you.* How dare—Oh, *Mike.* I never thought of that before. This was supposed to be a story about how I actually *connected* with a stranger. Oh, fuck. Oh, man. *Dude!*"

I'm so sorry. It just seemed—

"It's over. This is over! I'm gonna have nightmares tonight. I'm Catholic, remember?"

Four guys hunkered in a half-round leather banquette on a Friday night in Greenwich Village. "You wanna talk about the Womfy?" Dinklage asks.

He grabs the business end of a small microphone plugged into my recorder. "This is my friend Brendon Blake," he intones, playing reporter. "He's an entrepreneur and inventor. That's B-R-E-N-D-O-N," spelling it out.

"Everybody always wants to say *Brandon*."

"He's also a lacrosse player, bartender, and copywriter," adds Jonathan Marc Sherman, known as Sherm.

We are gathered in a well-worn and cozy booth in the back corner of the Knickerbocker Bar & Grill. Outside, a cold rain is falling. The front windows are fogged. A jazz trio swings oblivious in the center of the room. The crowd has thinned, a cast heavy with blue hairs who remembers a time when the Knick functioned as a downtown alternative to Elaine's uptown, attracting writers and actors and other swells.

Dinklage and I have been here since seven. Around ten, his pals rolled in. A splinter cell of a larger group of Bennington College grads known as the Burger Boys, these three natives of northern New Jersey long ago dubbed themselves the Tofutti Cuties, in deference to Dinklage's vegetarian diet. For the last seven or eight years, whenever possible, they've met here about once a month. Now it's nearly midnight. There is a yet-unused Scrabble board on the table along with the carcass of a cheesecake slice and a number of sullied forks. Several rounds of drinks have already been consumed. Dinklage, Bennington class of '91, is known to his friends as Dink. He prefers bourbon with one cube. He's nursing number three.

"Explain to the people what a Womfy is," Dink prompts.

"It's a disruptive technology in the pillow space," says Brendon, class of '92. A lit major turned adman, he sees the Womfy as his chance to build a brand on his own from the ground up, he explains. He even designed it himself. "There's an ear hole for when you sleep on your side, so you don't smoosh your face."

"And was the mold taken from a sex doll?" Dink asks. "Or is that just a rumor?" Sherm asks.

The eldest of the three, class of '90, Sherm met Dink when the latter visited Bennington as a prospective student his senior year of high school. A midnight production of *Orphans,* in which one of the student actors shaved his head, sealed the deal for Dink. His first term, he and Sherm acted together in *The Cherry Orchard.* Sherm was a big man on a small campus known for its distinctive student body (and lopsided female-to-male ratio). He'd suffered a tragic childhood and at eighteen had written a play that was produced as part of the Young Playwrights Festival in New York. Later it was adapted for television. In *Orchard,* Sherm was cast as Trofimov, the revolutionary. Dink played the eighty-seven-year-old butler, Firs. "Certainly the best teenage Firs in the history of the state of Vermont," Sherm says.

Sherm's semiautobiographical play, *Knickerbocker,* premiered at the Williamstown, Massachusetts, Theatre Festival several years ago, with Dink handling a role inspired by... Brendon. Later the play ran at the Public Theater in New York. Come to think of it, Sherm says, many of his plays have a role inspired by Brendon, the youngest of the Cuties and the only one still single.

"It was just developed for sleeping," says Brendon. He has spent an inheritance from his grandma to make this happen. The tone in his voice says he's not screwing around.

"It's a sleep aid," confirms Dink, sensing the stakes. He's been gone the last several months filming in Europe and may be a bit behind the curve.

"A side-sleeper pillow," corrects Brendon.

"The Womfy dot com," declares Sherm. "You'll love it."

"And now I get 10 percent of all sales!" Dink enthuses. "How many have you sold so far?"

Brendon shrugs. He thinks for a beat. "Ten?"

Dink's path to Bennington and the Tofutti Cuties began in the suburbs outside Morristown, New Jersey. As he tells it, despite being born with an obvious physical difference to deal with, his was an uneventful childhood. His father was an insurance man who found solace in fly-fishing and other hobbies. His mother was a music teacher who would often lug home the school's large video recorder for her sons to fiddle with. Beyond a painful surgery at age five to straighten his leg bones, Dinklage says his parents did nothing out of the ordinary to prepare him for life. "They never acted like I was special. It was just who you are. You're just a little bit more unique because you're not like, you know, everyone else."

Sent to an all-boys Catholic high school, Dink learned his love of acting and the cinema from an eccentric priest whose vow of poverty apparently didn't extend to his huge TV and extensive VHS collection of movies. "He showed me Fellini for the first time and all of Cassavetes. It sounds pretty pretentious to say you found, like, Antonioni at such an early age. But there you have it."

In college, Dink had "long flowing hair. The hair was unbelievable, like total hippie hair," Brendon says later. There were only six hundred students at Bennington; Dink thrived in an atmosphere of studied otherness. "At first, he seemed like one of those people who was just a little coldish or, like, shy or something. A little sort of standoffish. But when you got to know him, he's like the funniest motherfucker ever."

"One of the sort of things that just blows my mind is I remember just years of where we'd be walking down the street and I would be so aware of people, you know, looking at him because of his size," says Sherm, recalling later their postcollege days together in the city. Dink worked full time for nearly seven years at a company called Professional Examination Service.

"I still don't know what the company did," Dink says. "But I just, like, plugged information into a computer. I stuck it out because they let me—it was goofy, I had a little cubicle, I made people laugh, I smoked cigs with the guys from the mail room. They didn't seem to mind that I called in sick every Friday because I would go out Thursday night with my friends and get drunk."

"Pete would get twice as wasted as we would because he's, like, half as big," Brendon says. "He'd fall asleep in my apartment with his boots on. We called it his 'boots phase.'"

Dink also performed in a punk-funk-rap band called Whizzy. One night, he has said, playing at CBGB, he was "jumping around onstage and got accidentally kneed in the temple. I was like Sid Vicious, just bleeding all over the stage. Blood was going everywhere. I just grabbed a dirty bar napkin and dabbed my head and went on with the show."

Meanwhile, Dink continued to seek a career in writing and acting, though his early plans for a Steppenwolf-inspired theater company in Williamsburg, called Giant, came to naught. Refusing to attend lucrative seasonal commercial calls for leprechauns and elves, he struggled to distinguish himself as an actor who happened to be a dwarf. Over time, he would fall in with a crowd of actors and indie filmmakers who included Steve Buscemi *(Living in Oblivion),* director Alexandre Rockwell *(13 Moons),* and Tom McCarthy, whose script about a man seeking solitude in an abandoned train station in New Jersey, *The Station Agent,* was written with Dink in mind. The part became his breakout role.

After Sherm married, he was at his apartment one day, discussing a future playwriting project with director Erica Schmidt. At some point, Schmidt bemoaned her social life. Sherm brought out his cell phone and started scrolling through his friends.

"I said, 'Let's see if there's anyone who'd be right for you; we'll invite him over and play Trivial Pursuit or something,'" Sherm recalls. "When we got to Pete, I hesitated. And she was like, 'Why are you hesitating?'

"And see, the thing is, like, in college, Pete would have his walls up with someone he was interested in romantically. They'd become, you know, great friends. Incredible friends. And then one night down the line, he'd blurt it out at a party, you know, the fact that he had feelings. It didn't always work out well.

"So I told Erica, I said, 'I'm hesitating because this is my best friend for ten years. He's amazing. But if you fuck this up, you and I can't be friends anymore.'"

That night, Dink won Trivial Pursuit. The couple have been together ever since.

"When I think back on it now," Sherm says, "it was amazing how, even back in the day, at such a young age, Dink had already worked out his stare, his blinders, his whole coping mechanism—his way of dealing with the world. It's not like stuff didn't piss him off. Of course it did. But he was like, 'Okay, if you're going to look at me because of this thing I have no control over, then I'm going to give you something to look at, and I'm going to be as in control of it as I can be.' Now people see him and they're looking at him because of the work he's done. Without getting too cheesy, it's a pretty beautiful thing."

Back at the table, there is a lull in the banter.

"Are we gonna play Scrabble or what?" Brendon asks.

"Yeah," says Sherm. "Are we playing here or just screwing around?" Dinklage holds out a cloth bag. "Pick a tile, bitch."

At 2:00 a.m., the Cuties straggle out of the Knickerbocker. Standing in the portico, zipping up against the rain, we fend off a thick-tongued rummy from the bar—"You're not as clever as you think!"—and a hot brunette—"You're my favorite celebrity crush!"

Walking westward on Ninth Street, we soon reach Sherm's apartment building. There is a bird in a cage visible through a well-lit second-floor window; we bid Sherm goodnight. Brendon lives a little farther west on Ninth; he pleads with Dink to come upstairs to meet his new cat, which turns out to be the size of a fat pit bull and involves a noirish journey to the seventh floor in an antique birdcage elevator manned by a talkative night-shift operator who excitedly recognizes Dink from what he calls "Game of Thorns."

After petting the cat and viewing an actual Womfy, we head back down the weird and creaky elevator. In the interim, the operator seems to have Googled Dink. "I meant to say *Game of Thrones*," he says with an embarrassed face.

"Think nothing of it, my good man," Dink says theatrically.

We hoof it along the wet and glistening street, awash with the festive multicolor glow cast by headlights and traffic signals, forsaking the sidewalk as one does on a rainy night in Manhattan—taking turns walking forward and then pivoting around backward, like hitchhikers, trying to hail a taxi for the long trip back to the far western shores of the island.

There are cabs aplenty; none are unoccupied. They splash past, their dark roof lights mocking us. Though he sits taller than me at the table, Dink is considerably shorter when he stands up, perhaps even quite a bit shorter than the official "four and a half feet," which a little subsequent research shows to be kind of tall for an achon. As we trudge along the empty, puddled, and potholed thoroughfare, I fight a fatherly instinct to reach down and take his hand.

It is Dink who breaks the silence. "That first night? After I left you? I meant to tell you what happened."

I'm all ears.

"I was walking back to my apartment and this woman, a very pretty woman, probably about my age, maybe a little older, saw me and stopped and broke into tears.

"She didn't seem crazy or anything, so I asked what was the matter. And she was like, 'I just wanted to tell you, my boyfriend died today. And *The Station Agent* was his favorite movie. This is like a sign that I saw you. I can't believe this. May I please have a hug because I'm dying right now?'

"And, of course, I gave her a hug," Dink continues, "and she said, 'This is amazing,' and then she thanked me and she walked away. It's like, there are the idiots with cell phones taking your picture all the time, and then there's something like that woman. And it really moved me, because it was honest and so pure and so sad. I'm assuming her boyfriend wasn't very old—of course, I didn't ask what the circumstances of his death were. But I just thought I'd mention that because it was, you know . . . " his voice trails away.

More cabs splash past. We give up trying and retake the sidewalk. Sinking down a little further into our respective knit caps and hoodies, we pick up our speed a notch, our expectations reset for a longer trek. Dink's Chelsea boots thunk purposefully along the concrete.

Suddenly a police car appears. It pulls to an abrupt stop beside us. The back door flies open, a uniform jumps out.

"Man! I can't believe it!" exclaims the cop, a huge African American who dwarfs us both. There's another cop, with her head stuck out the window on the passenger side of the vehicle, smiling ear to ear. "I just had to shake your hand!" the big cop says, shoving his mitt toward Dink.

Making noises of appreciation, Dink responds with his own hand. He waves royally toward the car. *Hellooo. Helloo-ooo.*

The transaction completed, we stand in the awkward afterglow of the moment. It is late and cold, the rain continues to fall.

"Can we give you guys a lift somewhere?" the cop asks.

THE LIFE OF A CLOWN

SPARKY HAS A WHITE FACE, A RED NOSE, AND A DEEP-SEATED NEED TO PLEASE. YEARS AGO, CLOWNS WERE COOL. NOW EVERYONE RUNS THE OTHER WAY. DON'T HATE HIM BECAUSE HE'S CLOWNISH.

A clown wearing whiteface, a psychedelic jumper, and a pair of rainbow-colored Crocs knockoffs has gathered his youthful charges beneath the shade of a spreading tree. The birthday girl is seven years old. There is hardly a front tooth in evidence among the dozen kiddies sitting in an eager semicircle around her, their parents arrayed behind in a wider semicircle of lawn chairs, sipping beer and Chablis. "Can you say Sparky?" the clown exhorts.

"Sparky," the kids bleat, not quite sold.

"I can't hear you!"

His stentorian voice, cultivated on stages as large as Carnegie Hall, where he once sold out two straight performances, carries through the swirling smoke from the barbecue and across the carefully manicured terrain of Marina Park in San Leandro, California, just south of Oakland. Beyond his little audience of kids and parents, groups of friends and families of every hue and ethnicity pursue the traditional American pleasures of a weekend visit to the public green. An Asian family gathers around an elder; a bouquet of Mylar balloons tied to his wheelchair bobbles in the breeze. A pretty brunette in a princess costume applies makeup to the first little girl in a line of excited princesses. A squadron of women on motorcycles, throaty engines revving, back into parking spots. A dozen compact Hispanic men play short-field soccer; a boom box on the sidelines blares mariachi. A trio of young girls in Muslim head scarves climbs on the jungle gym.

"SPARRRRRKYYYYYY!" the kids yell, rising to the challenge.

Sparky the Clown has blue circles of makeup on either cheek; on his nose is a red circle dusted with pink and silver glitter, which takes a bit of effort to make circular owing to the cleft at the tip, which he ascribes, along with his sturdy build, to his Lithuanian ancestry. Purple lips offset his trademark dyed-black "Village People–inspired" handlebar mustache, a remnant of his days as a trumpeter in a Grammy-nominated klezmer band that appeared with Neil Diamond in the 1980 remake *The Jazz Singer.* His green beret is made of Astroturf, crowned with a golf ball and a flag from the nineteenth hole.

"Do you want to see me ride my tiny clown bike?"

"Yes!"

"Who likes candy? Say 'I do.'"

"I do!"

"Who likes prizes?"

"I do!"

"Who likes balloons?"

"I do!"

"Do you want to see some magic?"

"Yes!"

"I can't hear you!"

"YESSSSSSSSSS!" they cheer.

Sparky's wheezy baritone voice is loud and grating. He is at once funny and annoying, ingenious and stupid, insightful and insipid, friendly and backstabbing, attractive and repulsive. During his more introspective moments, when his face is cleansed of makeup (he often misses a patch, usually on the inside of an ear or nostril), he will speak eloquently about the yin and yang of clowning, about the light and the dark of comedy, about the clown as the personification of the human id. Pranks, pratfalls, slapstick, stories of outrageous misfortune, a video of a father being whacked in the balls by his toddler son—somehow these odd and negative twists of fate make us laugh. "It's like those 1940s movies where the guy and the girl hate each other—until suddenly they kiss. That's the essence of clowning," he will later say, sitting around in his cluttered apartment.

Right now, however, Sparky has no time for deep reflection. Right now he's walking the party-clown tightrope. He's got thirty people, aged two through seventy-five, sitting and standing in front of him, needing to be entertained. Their faces are expectant. There are distractions all around—the thrum of the motorcycles, the mix of different music from the different encampments, the screech of the seagulls that keep swooping down, trying to steal the party food... in a few minutes the soccer ball from the nearby game will hit Sparky square in the back, surprising the bejesus out of him; for *that* he'll get a huge laugh. Not only is there $275 on the line, there is pride at stake. Reputation. Tradition.

And a deep-seated need to please.

Sparky settles the kids into their seats with a motion of his hands. The call-and-response has bought him momentary control. Later the kids will follow him around and around in a circle as he plays beautifully on his pocket trumpet in a game of musical chairs without the chairs. His canny starts and stops will make fools of all—to the delight of the adult crowd—revealing in the process much about the characters of the child participants. By the end of the game, it will be clear that the birthday girl is a type who needs to win at all costs. Sparky will make sure she does.

Now Sparky spreads his arms wide. "Nothing up my sleeves, right?"

Awkward silence: A handkerchief hangs obviously from the left sleeve of his custom-made polyester clown suit.

Sparky presses. *"Nothing up my sleeves, RIGHT?"*

A four-year-old speaks out, innocently indignant. "There's something right *there,*" she insists, one index finger pointing to the suspect handkerchief, the other at rest inside her mouth.

One of the boys is selected to pull the handkerchief out of Sparky's sleeve—on the condition that he face away from Sparky, toward the audience. His name is Nicky. He says he is six and one half years old. He pulls and pulls and pulls over his shoulder, one handkerchief after another. Everyone laughs and laughs.

"Keep going, Nicky," his dad encourages.

Finally the end is reached—though of course Nicky can't see what's there—*a huge pair of clown boxer shorts, red-and-white polka dot!*

Everyone laughs.

Sparky covers Nicky's head with the boxer shorts.

Everyone groans. *"Gross!" "Ewwww."*

"Don't worry," Sparky assures the audience. "It's just a *briefing.*"

The parents laugh.

"Lately I've kind of hit the *skids.*"

Groans.

"Of course I washed them," he tells Nicky, removing the polka-dot hood. *"Six months ago!"*

Groans, laughter, applause.

"What's my name?"

"SPARKY!"

The Wacky World of Brian Wishnefsky is headquartered in a rent-controlled apartment in San Francisco, in a foggy neighborhood called Inner Sunset. The place is stuffed beyond capacity with props and outfits and trinkets to give out as prizes—because a party is nothing without prizes and Wishnefsky wants, almost more than anything else, to please people, to make them happy, to give them the gift of FUN.

"Come on *dowwwwn,*" he says, ushering me up several steps to his first-floor apartment. From the moment we meet, he's on antic overdrive—punning, mugging, cracking wise. In company, at least, he is always on—he likens his internal monologue to a large box of Super Balls he bought on closeout to use for prizes. "I'm like a meth-addict without the meth," he says.

Since the mid-1980s, Wishnefsky has supported himself as a free-lance clown, most often playing Sparky. He can be found on the Internet through one of his many URLs—including Worlds Greatest Clown, Worlds Greatest Pirate, Best Clown in Town. (There are other sites and a long story about a rival clown being angry about Wishnefsky buying up all the domain names; unlike most circus performers, clowns tend to be loners.) No matter which one you search, you'll be diverted to his main site, "Pranks for the Memories," where he promises "unique entertainment, from the ridiculous to the sublime."

Wishnefsky does singing telegrams, parties, appearances, musical gigs. In the flower of his youth, he did comedy strip-o-grams; he recently drove his 2007 Yaris three hours through a nasty storm to deliver a one-minute gag rendition of the Barney song "I love you / You love me." Have a prank you want to pull? Call Wishnefsky. He'll throw a pie, engineer a deception, deliver an hour-long fake lecture on Soviet history or ethnomusicology (which he studied at the California Institute of the Arts). For ten years he worked as Dracula at Six Flags. He'd get some guy up on the stage, strap him into a prop guillotine, and start in with the puns: *You're gonna get ahead in life. Don't stick your neck out for me.* "I just keep going and going and going. That's what I do," Wishnefsky explains.

He owns a frog costume, a turkey costume, and a *Star Trek* costume, complete with a tricorder and a blow-up model of the starship *Enterprise* attached to a Trek-brand bicycle helmet. You can hire Wishnefsky to be a teddy bear, a biker dude, a professor, an English barrister, a trumpet-playing gorilla, a kung fu master, a safari leader, a purple dinosaur character called Blarney. Or he can play Santa Claus, Hanukkah Harry, a baby in diapers, a cow, an elf, the Grim Reaper, Bacchus, a pirate named Captain Schnook. If those don't work for you, he'll come up with something else.

Three years ago he auditioned on the air for *America's Got Talent*. He played a supernerdy character named Mr. Special. Wearing his turkey costume and oversized glasses, he rode out onstage on his pocket bicycle while playing "Anchors Aweigh" on his pocket trumpet. That he was fifty-seven years old and not so svelte anymore added difficulty points. He wanted to play "I Believe I Can Fly" because he thought it made a good statement with his turkey costume, but the producers asked him to play something else. Wishnefsky believes this was because they didn't want to pay the fees to use the song; obviously, that layer of meaning was lost from his performance.

The judges on the show—Howard Stern, Sharon Osbourne, and Howie Mandel—were particularly vitriolic. They seemed insulted that Wishnefsky had the audacity to try to pass himself off as being talented. Mandel strongly discouraged Wishnefsky from *ever* performing again and suggested he "should get help." Mr. Special whined back in a put-on nasal voice, managing a few zingers in defense of downtrodden nerds everywhere, inciting cheers from the studio audience.

According to some Internet comments, Wishnefsky's performance was a brilliant display of disruptive art, something Andy Kaufman might have done.

Others seemed more in agreement with the judges. *This idiot needs to be locked away.*

Wishnefsky plans to try out for the show again, this time playing his theremin. He's been practicing the *Star Trek* theme. He thinks the loopy electronic sound of the instrument is well suited to the song.

Wishnefsky was born in Long Beach, California, and moved to Brighton Beach, near Coney Island, when he was one year old to live with his grandparents after his mother had a stroke. Paralyzed and brain damaged, she became the subject of late-1950s-style experimental treatments, Wishnefsky says. She lived until ten years ago in a nursing facility with minimal memory and function. "She was sorta like, 'You're not my son,' because her mind was back there, not here, that kinda stuff," he says.

His father, who went by the name of Weber, was a printer and later a bartender and later a maintenance man for a ritzy apartment building. Eventually, Brian and his two older brothers went to a foster family in Encino, California. Dad saw the boys once a week; often they went to Disneyland or Knott's Berry Farm. The foster family had two daughters; money was tight but the boys were well cared for.

As the youngest, Wishnefsky was often the object of his brothers' torment, especially the eldest, Mark, who would tease him about his crew cut, do this thing where he'd grab the underneath part of Brian's collarbone through the skin.

One day their father took his unfortunate boys to Corriganville Movie Ranch, a theme park named for the once-famous cowboy actor and stuntman Ray "Crash" Corrigan. Wishnefsky was three or four; his middle brother was about five; the eldest, his tormentor, was probably nine. At the park, there was a clown. Wishnefsky remembers him as being a Bozo. Created in the 1940s for a children's record album and read-along book set, Bozo the Clown became an icon as a mascot for Capitol Records. (Whiteface makeup was pioneered by the English actor Joseph Grimaldi in the early 1800s. Grimaldi is credited with expanding the role of the clown in British theater's harlequinade. He became so popular that whiteface clowns became known as Joeys.) In the 1950s, Bozo was franchised to local television stations across the country; every big city had a *Bozo the Clown* show.

At Corriganville, Mark went to get an autograph from Bozo.

"There are all these kids around Bozo, he's up on this little hill," Wishnefsky remembers. "And my brother goes up to him, and the next thing I know, I see Bozo take my brother and push him to the ground. And I was like, 'Bozo pushed Mark on the ground!' I was in shock."

The next Halloween he can remember, Wishnefsky dressed as a clown.

After leaving CalArts in 1976, Wishnefsky moved to San Francisco. Walking along Fisherman's Wharf one day, he encountered a man in a gorilla suit playing a classic Yiddish song on an accordion. In college, Wishnefsky had specialized in Eastern European and Middle Eastern music. He noticed the guy was playing a passage of the song incorrectly. As musicians do, he stuck around and struck up a conversation.

The gorilla invited Wishnefsky to join him in a duet; together they played for tips from the passing throng. Soon he acquired his own gorilla suit. And soon after that, he met a one-man band named Rick "Professor Gizmo" Elmore.

One day over pizza, Wishnefsky and Gizmo realized they'd sat next to each other in the junior high school orchestra. Gizmo told Wishnefsky about this klezmer band in Berkeley in which he was playing. It was a perfect fit.

Over the next seven years, as a member of the Klezmorim, Wishnefsky toured the country and the world, performing infectious Jewish dance tunes and irreverent, agitprop, vaudevillesque humor. In 1980 the six members of the Klezmorim were featured in the Neil Diamond movie *The Jazz Singer.* In 1982 the Klezmorim was nominated for a Grammy for Best Ethnic or Traditional Folk Recording for its third album; they lost to Queen Ida. In 1983, the Klezmorim sold out two shows at Carnegie Hall and was featured in a glowing review in the *New York Times.* First among equals was Wishnefsky, who was known for his comic bits... in a gorilla suit. His alter ego was called Hairy James.

Citing creative and marketing differences, Wishnefsky left the band in 1984 and went to work for a company that, among other things, delivered singing telegrams in a teddy-bear suit. It wasn't long before someone requested a clown.

And so it was that Sparky the Clown was born. Wishnefsky began buying and making more prizes and props, assembling more costumes. He learned magic. He learned balloon twisting. He learned hypnotism, part of the reason he began purchasing entertainment insurance from the National Association of Mobile Entertainers. He learned how to command an audience no matter what their age, which he believes is his greatest talent. In time, Sparky became Wishnefsky's most steady source of income, up to five gigs a weekend.

Clowning goes back to the Fifth Dynasty of Egypt, roughly 2500 BC. Unlike the jester, who has always been designated to play the fool, the clown in some societies served a socioreligious function; the roles of shaman and clown were often played by the same person. Over the last century, clowns in their several forms became symbolic of the human condition—the sophisticated and sly whiteface clown, the clumsy auguste clown (with white muzzle and eyes), and the character clowns like Emmett Kelly, Buster Keaton, and Charlie Chaplin.

Then along came Stephen King's 1986 horror novel, *It,* featuring Pennywise the Dancing Clown. Sadistic and wisecracking, Pennywise turns out to be an interdimensional predatory life-form *masquerading* as a clown. The bestselling book was made into a TV miniseries.

By the mid-1990s the notion of the scary clown was burned into our national psyche. There was *The Simpsons'* degenerate Krusty the Clown, and Heath Ledger's manic Joker in *The Dark Knight.* Last year the nation was gripped by Twisty, the murderous clown on *American Horror Story.* Then there's the upcoming *Clown,* about an insidious clown suit that possesses its wearer. It is a cultural given now that clowns make a lot of people uncomfortable. There's even a word for it, *coulrophobia* (roughly fear of stilt-walkers). We'd always known the clown would tease us, but there was usually a reward at the end—laughter or maybe a prize. Pennywise broke our trust, woke our deep-seated suspicions. *Who's supposed to be laughing at whom?*

In the late 1990s, Wishnefsky says, his clowning fortunes began to turn. The 2008 financial crash didn't help, either. Today, the Ringling Bros. and Barnum & Bailey Clown College in Sarasota, Florida, is closed. Even in our web-friendly era, finding a traditional whiteface clown in southern California who regularly performs at parties was itself an odd and comic odyssey that took several weeks—and landed me in northern California.

"There are a lot of clowns in this business these days who aren't really clowns," Wishnefsky laments. "I call them *clones.* They're daycare workers who dress up in a clown suit. They've been taught four tricks. They're supposed to bolster self-esteem and all this crap. They give everybody hugs, like *Oh, you're so special. I love you!* The fake clowns are driving the real clowns out of business."

His voice takes a serious tone: "The kind of thing that makes a person a clown—that's who I am. Growing up, I never really fit in anywhere. Everyone would ask, 'Where's your mom and dad?' Having foster parents made you feel like a freak, basically. I used to have to fight every day in high school. People thought I was a wimp or a nerd. I guess you could say my whole life has been about *otherness.* That's why I'm the clown."

Sparky the Clown is visiting Fisherman's Wharf, a trip down memory lane. The sun is warm. The air is scented with fish and brine, diesel fuel and deep-frying oil, duty-free perfume and the loud-smelling deodorants popular with younger men. Tourists overflow the sidewalks and the trinket shops.

Late in the afternoon, Sparky has just finished another party; he was cruising past the neighborhood and thought he'd stop for a quick visit to the scene of past glories (the tourist who liked his act so much he flew Wishnefsky to his hometown in Illinois, put him up in his guest room, and paid him to work for a week in his furniture store in the gorilla suit) and past indignities (the ruffians who kicked his trumpet case with his earnings inside, and he was forced to give chase... in the gorilla suit). I am accompanying Sparky today as his clown assistant, wearing my own whiteface and jumper, holding a prop plunger for occasional placement on Sparky's head—a zany tug-of-war bit ensues.

Sparky laughs and waves and mugs, wishes the tourists well. That he has no reason to be here in a clown suit and full makeup doesn't seem to matter. He comes off as just another habitué of the Wharf, like the World Famous Bushman, who has assumed the role that was once shared with his former partner, hiding motionless behind some eucalyptus branches. Every so often he'll pick an unsuspecting passerby, part the branches, and holler. "*Oogah–boogah!*" Most people jump a foot into the air. For that, they give Bushman a tip. Walking past, Sparky gives him a high five.

Cell phones and long lenses come out. Sparky mugs and waves some more; he plays his trumpet. A dozen German tourists ask him to pose; they are charmed when he begins singing a German folk song.

A little boy walking hand in hand with his parents: "*Payaso!*" he exclaims delightedly, Spanish for clown.

The sight of a pair of clowns coming down the street makes some laugh and wave, as if they've seen someone they know, fun and familiar. Others make exaggerated scary faces or cover their eyes.

"Yikes, clowns!" someone exclaims with mock fear.

"Look at those *clowns,*" someone says derisively.

Later, at the end of a long day, we are walking to his apartment. Never one to attract attention to himself, Sparky comes to a full stop in the middle of the sidewalk. Bipedal commuters, homeward bound, pass us on both sides.

"When people come up to me and say, 'I'm really freaked out by clowns,' you know what I do?" Sparky asks. "Stand here in front of me and tell me you're really freaked out by clowns."

I stand there in front of him and tell him: "I'm really freaked out by clowns."

Sparky leans down and puts his face an inch away from mine. He smiles sweetly. And then he yells at the top of his lungs:

"REALLY? YOU'RE SCARED OF CLOWNS? HAHAHAHA! I AM, TOO!"

A small drop of vehement spittle plants itself on one lens of my sunglasses.

"People try to make clowns into this evil, sinister thing," Sparky says, gesturing with the case of his pocket trumpet. His puffy yellow collar makes me think of a dancer's tutu, or Queen Elizabeth. "Part of me likes the scary-clown stuff. I think it's funny, tee-hee, whatever, it's fine. And then the other part of me REALLY HATES IT. It's bad for business! Very few people want clowns anymore. The Grim Reaper they want. But a clown? No! Because CLOWNS ARE TOO CREEPY.

"The other night I was watching this movie, *Silent Night, Deadly Night*—you ever heard of it? Santa Claus is a serial killer. Then there's this movie with a leprechaun, and he's deranged. It's like they've taken everything that's innocent and cute and demonized it. It really gets on my nerves. Can you tell? I have these deranged clown stickers I bought, a big box of them. Whenever people tell me they're scared of clowns, I don't argue with them, I just mock them and give them some stickers, because that's what clowns do."

With that, he proceeds up the block to his apartment. Reaching the front door, he fishes into the deep pocket of his psychedelic jumper and pulls out a handful of clown detritus—Super Balls, balloons, confetti, fake dollar bills with his picture and phone number on the front. Then he tries the other pocket. Finally he locates his keys.

"I think the party went well, don't you?" His eyes bore through me, searching for a review.

He was flawless, I assure him. Even Grandma was in stitches.

THE SAMOAN PIPELINE

HOW DOES A TINY ISLAND, FIVE THOUSAND MILES FROM THE US MAINLAND, PRODUCE SO MANY PROFESSIONAL FOOTBALL PLAYERS?

O n a rain-soaked field of artificial turf, the Washington State University Cougars, a team inscribed in the annals of college-sports infamy for suffering one of the worst four-year records in the history of NCAA Division I football—with only nine wins between 2008 and 2011—are lined up against the reigning Rose Bowl champions, the University of Oregon Ducks.

It is a nasty day in early October, the fourth game on the schedule. The air inside Autzen Stadium, located in Eugene, Oregon, is thick with humidity. The roar of fifty-seven thousand fans is cacophonous; on the sidelines you can feel the rumble underfoot.

Last year the Ducks were led by Marcus Mariota, a Hawaii-raised Samoan quarterback who won the Heisman Trophy and went second in the National Football League draft. This year the Ducks are still on a roll: They've already put up 163 points in their first three victories.

A few minutes earlier, with the clock running out, the game all but over, many of the Ducks' fans — some with their faces painted yellow and green, none seemingly aware of the prohibition against mobbing the field — rushed the stadium aisles, ready to celebrate.

Then a first-down call went the other way.

With one second remaining in regulation, the Cougars scored a touchdown to tie the game.

Now it is fourth down, nine yards to go, in the second overtime period.

The Ducks have the ball.

Improbably, the Cougars are ahead 45–38.

In the stands, the Duck faithful mill around the exits, alternately cheering and wringing their hands. A field goal won't do; they need a first down or a touchdown. In the militarized vernacular of football, it's a do-or-die situation. The last time the Cougars defeated the Ducks at home was 2003. Over on the Cougar sideline, an island of crimson and gray in a sea of green, the coaches yell adjustments and issue hand signals.

At the timeout, the defensive staff made it simple. All they need is a stop. Standing in the middle, Joe Salave'a was a giant among a tribe of giants. Six foot four, 325 pounds, the forty-year-old defensive-line coach played nine years in the NFL. The third youngest of eight children from a small village in American Samoa—an unincorporated US territory in the South Pacific—he first came to Southern California during the summer before ninth grade. When he got on the plane, he thought he was making the trip to participate in an all-star baseball game; nobody told him he'd be staying permanently with relatives to attend school and play football. A scholarship to the University of Arizona followed, and after a solid career as an NFL defensive lineman—with Tennessee, San Diego, and Washington, DC—he went into coaching. For the past four years, he's been with the Cougars.

"You've got to make something happen. You've got to put this game on your shoulders," Salave'a told the squad. Among them were seven Samoan players he had recruited from high schools on his home island.

At the opening of the 2015 football season, there were more than two hundred American Samoans on rosters of Division I college football teams. Twenty-eight were slated to play in the NFL. If you begin to count other Polynesians—Pacific Islanders from Hawaii, Tonga, Easter Island, and New Zealand—the impact is even greater: Five of the first sixty-six players selected in the NFL's 2015 draft were Polynesian.

On the Cougar roster, there are a total of thirteen players of Samoan descent, counting those raised in the United States. Since Joe Salave'a arrived with the coaching regime of Mike Leach in 2011, the Cougars' record has improved to 17–28. In 2013, they played in their first postseason bowl in ten years. In no small measure, the Cougars' turnaround can be attributed to Salave'a and his Samoan pipeline.

The ball is placed at the center of the field on the twenty-four-yard line—near the Pac-12 logo, the symbol of the "Conference of Champions," whose members (including USC, Stanford, and UCLA) have won more national team championships than any other college conference. The Cougars have consistently dwelled in the cellar.

On offense the Ducks have three wide receivers arranged on the left side of the field, a trips formation. The tight end is on the right side; the running back is offset and behind the tight end. The quarterback is in the shotgun position, his hands extended prayerfully, awaiting the snap. Everyone in the stadium is expecting a pass.

On defense the Cougars go with three down linemen. Destiny Vaeao is playing tackle. A 6-foot-4, 298-pound senior, Vaeao was coached at Tafuna High School in Samoa by Salave'a's older brother, himself a former pro player. At nose guard is Daniel Ekuale, a sophomore. Six three, 288 pounds, he is a graduate of Nu'uuli Vocational-Technical, another Samoan high school. At the other tackle is Darryl Paulo. Raised in Sacramento, he has relatives in Samoa. The majority of ethnic Samoans—a diaspora of traditionally large families numbering some five hundred thousand worldwide—live somewhere other than Samoa, primarily in the United States, New Zealand, and Australia.

In the backfield, at the strong-safety spot, is Taylor Taliulu, 6 feet, 205 pounds, a Samoan raised in Hawaii. Next to him, at free safety, is Shalom Luani, a 6-foot, 200-pound transfer student from a junior college in San Francisco who also attended high school in Samoa. Luani shares the title of all-time leading goal scorer for the Samoan national soccer team, which has the distinction of being one of the worst in the world. The team went 0–30 over nearly two decades of international play before claiming its first victory in 2011, against Tonga, on a squad led by Luani and Jaiyah "Johnny" Saelua, a transgender player known for being the heart of the team.

At last the ball is hiked.

The all-Samoan Cougar defensive line puts on a spirited rush. The Ducks' quarterback, Jeff Lockie, bounces back a few feet, looking downfield for a target, then steps up into the pocket to buy more time. Cougar nose guard Ekuale charges past his man, taking the long route around the outside on Lockie's left. Lunging for the quarterback, Ekuale catches him glancingly around the midsection and slides down to the ground at his feet. As Lockie releases the ball, Ekuale flails his arms and grabs hold of Lockie's front leg, a second effort that disrupts the thrower's motion and causes his pass to fall short... into the hands of free safety Luani, the former soccer player, who does a baseball slide at the two-yard line to secure the upset.

As the sun sets over their practice field, a patchwork of dirt and forlorn grass strewn with rocks and coral, the Warriors of Tafuna High School sit cross-legged in tidy rows. It is Friday evening in Samoa. The third game of the season is scheduled for ten tomorrow morning. The boys are sweaty and bloodied, their helmets placed on the ground uniformly before them like battered war drums. Forty sets of eyes shine attentively. Some wear maroon-and-white jerseys, the school's colors. Others wear blue-and-white jerseys. Much of the equipment has been donated by local boosters and former NFL players and coaches. A number wear white Nike cleats given out for free this past summer at the annual football and volleyball clinic put on by former Pittsburgh Steelers great Troy Polamalu, an ethnic Samoan with strong ties to the island, who was raised in Southern California.

Standing before the group is their coach, Okland Salave'a, the brother of the Cougars' Joe Salave'a. Coach Oak, a physical education teacher, has been the head football coach at Tafuna for seven years. The team has played in the island championships for each of the past three years, ending with two victories and a one-point loss. Tafuna's junior varsity has claimed league titles five years in a row. With only four starters returning to varsity this year, however, the season has gotten off to a shaky start. The Warriors are 1–1. Now they face archrival Samoana High School, another perennial contender, coached by a man named Pati Pati, who played football at Iowa Wesleyan College. After Pati graduated in 1996, he came back home to be a music teacher—coaches on the island are paid only a small stipend.

For reasons of team building, Coach Oak has called a night practice—in Samoan a moetasi, or sleepover. For the past hour, the team has practiced plays and execution and run wind sprints. Next will be showers, a spaghetti dinner cooked by some of the moms, team meetings by position. Then lights out; they will sleep on pallets and traditional woven mats on the floor of one of the classrooms.

Coach Oak is six foot five, longer and leaner than his brother but still a mountain on a hike. His voice is soft and lilting, a little hoarse. The other volunteer coaches stand and sit nearby with their arms gravely folded. For the benefit of his guests, Coach Oak speaks English. Talking about the game film from the previous week, he sounds like a typical stateside high school coach, annoyed and a little befuddled.

"I can't see any reason why we shouldn't win that game," he says, scanning the faces before him. "Offensive line, it starts with you."

Off in the distance, beyond the rooftops of the low-slung classrooms that form a quadrangle around the field, the lush and jagged mountains of Tutuila are shadowed against the darkening sky. Tutuila is the largest of the five volcanic islands that make up American Samoa, known to residents collectively as "The Rock."

Pronounced Saa-moa, the territory, which is five thousand miles from the mainland United States, was annexed at the turn of the twentieth century for its strategic, deep-water harbor. Today it has a population of about fifty-five thousand, nearly all of whom live on the fifty-two square miles of Tutuila, a land mass that is substantially smaller than Washington, DC. In many ways, the culture on The Rock still hews to the ethos documented in Margaret Mead's landmark but controversial work of anthropology, *Coming of Age in Samoa*, published in 1928. There may be cell phones and Internet and plenty of pickup trucks and consumer goods, but the kids still go home after football practice and do their chores, which typically involve feeding pigs, harvesting taro root and bananas, gathering coconuts, building a fire, cooking dinner, and serving the adults, whose word is paramount.

There is one main road on Tutuila, about thirty-five miles long. There are no stoplights. The speed limit is twenty-five miles per hour. Two tuna canneries are the largest employers; workers make less than $10,000 a year. The island has two McDonald's, one movie theater, several new Chinese restaurants, and a T-shirt shop called Pacific Roots. With job opportunities limited and an unemployment rate between 10 and 20 percent—a main reason for the diaspora—it is not surprising to learn that American Samoa has the highest rate of military enlistment of any US state or territory.

"The biggest dream of everyone in Samoa is to leave the island and look for a better future," says Peter Gurr, the deputy director of the American Samoa Department of Agriculture. "Right now, if you don't get a college scholarship, the only thing to do is join the military. And then there's football. Our largest exports are the tuna and football." Even though school is conducted in both Samoan and English—often mixed into the same paragraph or sentence—the largest obstacle for football hopefuls is college standardized tests.

Samoans have been playing rugby since the 1920s, when it was introduced by Marist missionaries. American football didn't come to the island until the 1960s, after an article in *Reader's Digest*, headlined "America's Shame in the Pacific," brought attention to the deplorable conditions of the tropical-island-cum-American-military-base: "Amid enchanting scenery and smiling Polynesians—praised by Robert Louis Stevenson as 'God's best, at least God's sweetest, works'—the visitor is shocked to encounter government buildings peeling and rotting on their foundations, beautiful Pago Pago Bay marred and befouled by hideous over-water outhouses, rutty and teeth-jarring roads unrepaired for years."

Responding to the outrage that followed, the Kennedy administration provided a makeover that pushed the culture into modernity. Along with plumbing, electricity, roads, schools, and a high school football program, the Samoans received cable TV. Watching football became a favorite pastime.

The first Samoan to play in the NFL was Al Lolotai. After starring at Mormon-affiliated Weber State University in Utah, he played for the Washington Redskins in 1945 and then five more years in the now-defunct All-America Football Conference. It wasn't long before the island was discovered as a wellspring of football talent. Leading the way were coaches at universities with strong Mormon ties. The Church of Jesus Christ of Latter-day Saints, which believes that Polynesians are heirs to the blessings promised to Abraham's descendants, has been sending missionaries to the region since the mid-1800s.

Over the years football coaches have found on the island a ready inventory of large, big-boned, and nimble Samoans, with the kind of solid base that football coaches love: massive from the waist down but still able to move their feet. Samoans' facility with footwork is often attributed to tribal dances and the common practice of going barefoot. Their love of combat is derived from a fierce warrior culture that goes back hundreds of years. With an upbringing that stresses hard work, discipline, and devotion to authority, both heavenly and earthbound, Polynesians have come to be considered the ultimate clay from which to mold a football player. It is as if a childhood of gentle obedience translates into a passion for ferocious violent contact, the kind of collisions that resonate through a stadium and electrify the crowd.

By the 1970s, coaches from Hawaii and Utah began to recruit heavily from Polynesia; in time, the practice spread. More than one hundred Polynesians have since played in the NFL. By now the names are well-known. Troy Polamalu, Junior Seau, Jesse Sapolu — and last year's Heisman winner, Mariota. Hundreds more, like Coach Oak and Pati Pati, have benefited from scholarships.

Today five high schools on Tutuila have football programs; they play their games Thursday through Saturday on the island's one football field, Veterans Memorial Stadium. Night games on the dusty grass field, with concrete bleachers on both sides, have been outlawed due to frequent fighting and episodes of rock throwing among rival fans. Through a government program, all students receive two hot meals each day; there is no budget for football. Much of the equipment consists of hand-me-downs shipped from the States. A pair of shoulder pads repaired with fishing line is not unusual.

"I know it's very hard to play football," Coach Oak is telling his team. A lot of the kids have indigenous tattoos; Coach Oak himself has a traditional tattoo that stretches from just above his knees to his mid-section. Some of the kids wear their hair close-cropped; others have more elaborate cuts, with shaved sides and a streak of color. A few have the long, flowing style that has become the trademark of Polynesian players in the NFL; here and there can be seen a man-bun.

"After school you practice," Coach Oak continues. "Then you go home for chores. You're tired; all you wanna do is eat and then to sleep. But you gotta stay up and finish those homework. Don't fall behind in your schoolwork! If you need help, there is tutoring."

Okland Salave'a was sent to the States when he was a junior in high school—unlike his younger brother, he understood why he was going. He lived with relatives in the heavily Samoan enclave of Oceanside, California, north of San Diego.

"The transition was tough for me because of the language barrier," he says later, sitting in the bleachers of the outdoor gymnasium. "When I left Samoa, I didn't speak much English. We had it in school, but we didn't try to speak it when we were hanging around with our friends. If one of us was trying to speak English we were like, 'What you trying to do?' And we would start laughing and teasing each other. The thought behind it was that we didn't want to try to be something that we weren't. So it kind of hurt my learning process, not only inside the classroom but on the field. I didn't really understand exactly what the coaches were saying."

As a senior, Salave'a was selected first-team all-county as a defensive end and was signed to a scholarship by the University of Colorado. Coach Oak smiles wanly, shaking his head. "First of all, it was cold. I'd never seen snow. And I still wasn't really out of the woods with the language, not only speaking it but understanding the words and stuff." Switching to linebacker proved an additional challenge. Later he would be switched back to defensive end. It was as if he was always a step behind, hustling to catch up.

Oak graduated with a degree in sociology but went undrafted. Eventually he signed as a free agent with the San Diego Chargers; the next season he joined the Birmingham Fire of the World League of

American Football. Then he tore the anterior cruciate ligament in his knee.

"In college, whenever I called home and talked to my dad, he always said, 'I don't care about football. The only thing I care about is you graduating and getting your degree, because that's what's gonna carry you after your football.' At the time I didn't really think about it because the dream of a football player is to make it to the NFL. But when I came back home, I realized, more than anything else, I wanted to coach football. I figured I could give these kids the kind of help I didn't have. I could make it a little easier."

As of this season, Coach Oak has one former player at Ohio University, two at the University of Arizona, one at Boise State, one at Oregon State, and three at Washington State with his brother. A few others are in Division II colleges and junior colleges. Three of his current seniors already have scholarship offers.

Standing in front of his team, the light quickly fading, Coach Oak winds up his talk. "We have a big day tomorrow," he says. "I want everyone to get a good sleep tonight. If you don't go to sleep, I'm not afraid to make you come out here and do the worm all the way down the field and back. OK?"

"Coach!" the team calls in unison.

After collecting all the cell phones in a bucket, Coach Oak dismisses the kids for showers. Stepping away, he checks his watch. To supplement his income, he works for Hawaiian Airlines, handling baggage and assisting wheelchair passengers to their seats. There are four flights a week. On Monday and Friday nights, the inbound from Honolulu lands at 9:30. The outbound leaves at 11:20. As soon as the kids get fed and settled down, he'll head over. Conveniently, the airport is across the street.

In the shade of a rough-hewn shelter built around his family's permanent umu—a stone-lined pit with a corrugated tin cover that serves as a traditional oven—Tutuila Manase, who is forty-five and named after the island, takes a pull on an icy can of light beer, supervising the afternoon's chores. It is Saturday. The punishing sun is still high overhead; the temperature and the humidity are in the nineties.

Eddie Manase, one of Tutuila's nine children, is a seventeen-year-old senior at Tafuna High. Shirtless and wearing the maroon lava-lava skirt that is part of his school uniform, the 6-foot-2-1/2, 290-pounder is hosing out a concrete pigpen recently built with the help of the US Department of Agriculture and the Environmental Protection Agency after the family's traditional pigsty was found to be unsanitary.

Eddie's younger cousin, Manase Manase, also a varsity player for Tafuna High, is out for a stretch after nearly losing a finger when it became caught in a rival's facemask. He is well enough today to use a weed whacker—for centuries Samoan children have engaged in a constant battle to keep back the jungle.

Inside the cooking hut is senior Frederick Mauigoa, Eddie's best friend since first grade. At 6 foot 4, 290 pounds, the seventeen-year-old lives in a village nearby; he is the only person Eddie knows, besides Coach Oak, who makes him feel small. Freddy busies himself husking and slicing open coconuts with a machete, then shredding the white meat into a bowl.

Despite a sleepy start to the morning's football game—causing Coach Oak to question the efficacy of future moetasis—the Tafuna Warriors beat the Samoana Sharks 33–29. The normally rainy island has lately suffered a drought, leaving the field mostly dirt; clouds of dust swirled with the trade winds. Animated fans and drum sections on both sides lent a big-time atmosphere, as did the booming PA announcer, whose calls could be heard for miles across Tutuila. Beyond the end zones, booster clubs raised money by selling snacks and drinks.

With his team down at halftime, the normally soft-spoken Coach Oak rained down a torrent of agitated Samoan on his players. "This is not the football we have taught you," he said, switching to English. "You boys need to get your freakin' heads out of your asses." Tafuna High found its footing and went to work.

Now, two hours after the game, we are in the village of Futiga, about seven miles inland from the school, an ancient community made up of three family groups. The houses in Futiga are arranged haphazardly across the green and gently rolling landscape, ranging in size and condition from large and nearly suburban to small and primitive.

In most front yards are well-maintained burial plots. There are three churches of different denominations. Each village has a chief and a long list of lesser officials as well as its own fono, or legislature, which meets in a thatched building with open sides. There is also a fono that represents the entire nation; it meets in the capital, Pago Pago, where the governor is housed.

Despite playing nearly every down of this morning's game, anchoring both the offensive and defensive lines, Eddie and Freddy make no noise about doing their chores, giggling between themselves as they work. Next year they will both be playing college football. Scholarships have already been offered. The question remaining is which letter to sign.

In the 1980s, Tutuila Manase played high school football himself, offensive line and defensive line. He had scholarship offers from schools in California, Arizona, and Montana, he says. The only problem: His family wouldn't let him go.

"I was trying to explain it to our parents, especially my mom. I tried to convince her that I could get a future out of football," Tutuila says. He went instead to Samoa's community college and joined the Army. Eventually he finished his four-year degree and became a vice principal at an elementary school on the island. Along the way he served two tours in Iraq. He is now retired from both the military and the school system.

Beyond the clearing where Manase whacks weeds are family plots of banana, taro, breadfruit, and coconut. "Some of the families on the island are considered poor because we don't have a lot of paper money, we don't have the income," Tutuila says. "But we're not worry of that. We can make the living out of the surroundings that we have. Our parents passed it on to us, and now we're passing over to our children. My belief is, families who have very strong ties with the culture are the ones who are still continuing with this process."

Still, Tutuila is excited for the opportunities the boys have. Even his mother—who is enjoying a sweet tea with his father on the shady porch of the large house in which they all live—is excited for Eddie. "Now my parents understand better that if you get a full ride you don't have to spend any money on anything," Tutuila says.

Youth football only started in Samoa in 2009. Eddie and Freddy belong to the third set of seniors to graduate as products of a feeder system that has raised the quality of the game in Samoa. College coaches routinely struggled to raise Samoan players' football IQ to match the levels of their attitudes and athletic talents. Tutuila has helped coach the core of the Tafuna team since the boys were peewees; he has followed them upward through the years and now serves as an assistant coach for the varsity.

Eddie finishes cleaning the pigpen and moves over to the shade of the cooking shelter, joining Freddy and his dad. He kneels to build a fire, sweat streaming. Soon he will have to decide which school to attend. Like most high school seniors, he's a bit clueless — he has no way of imagining the life that awaits him.

"I'm excited to play college ball," he says in a deep but bashful voice. There is a hint of a mustache growing on his upper lip. "That's one of my goals: I want to continue on with my career in college and make it to the NFL. It's my favorite sport."

Freddy agrees, saying that his favorite position is tackle, but he would "play any position they ask if it means winning the game and making it to the championship."

As the boys busy themselves with their tasks, I wonder out loud if Tutuila ever thinks about the football scholarships he turned down. If he had gone off-island, his story might have turned out differently.

Tutuila finishes off his beer, taking time to consider a response. "I was born in this life," he says. "When I was just a little boy we feed the pigs and we make the plantation and we cook the food. And we do all different kind of stuff, Samoan traditional chores. Maybe it would have been fun for me to try a different life for a while."

Eddie places a pot of green bananas over the grill, then moves to another bench to begin pressing milk from the shredded coconut. As a strainer he uses a tangle of strong, fibrous, straw-colored strands called tauaga, taken from the laufao plant. Placing the tauaga into the bowl of coconut meat, Eddie uses the same twisting motion one would use when wringing out a dishrag. The pressure brings milk from the meat. The muscles in Eddie's thick wrists and forearms ripple with effort. He will simmer the milk with salt and onions for a sauce.

"See there?" asks Tutuila, pointing toward his son's big hands. "We don't need a fancy gym here. These kids have been working out their whole lives."

On a cool Monday in Pullman, Washington, six Samoan members of the Washington State Cougars are sprawled around a conference room in a brand-new football complex set on hilly farmland east of the Cascade mountains.

The seventh Samoan Cougar, senior Destiny Vaeao, is still in class. A graduate of Tafuna High who played under Coach Oak, Vaeao was the first to be recruited to the Cougars by Coach Joe, whose regular trips to the island have made him a celebrity—a man who arrives each year to bring scholarships for the kids. "He's more famous than I am, to be sure," says Samoa's governor, Lolo Matalasi Moliga, who last year appointed former Cincinnati Bengals defensive end Jonathan Fanene as director of American Samoa's Department of Youth and Women's Affairs.

It has been two days since the double-overtime upset of the Oregon Ducks. Today there is no practice. The guys have just finished class. Most are criminal justice majors; several want to be law-enforcement officers if they don't make it to the NFL. One wants to enter the military. The two freshmen are still undecided. Without helmets, the group looks unimposing—all sweet smiles and dimples, with an endearing eagerness to please. All of them say their first goal is to bring home a college diploma for their parents to frame and hang on the wall.

Robert Barber, a junior, starts on the defensive front line alongside Vaeao. He went to Faga'itua High School, which beat Tafuna High last year for the championship.

Daniel Ekuale, one of the heroes of the victory over the Ducks, is a sophomore. A backup on defensive line, he attended Nu'uuli Vocational-Technical on the island. Sophomore Frankie Luvu from Tafuna High and freshman Logan Tago from Samoana High are second-string linebackers. Amosa Sakaria, a freshman lineman, is redshirting this season after knee surgery. He also played for Coach Oak at Tafuna High.

Shalom Luani, who graduated from Faga'itua High, plays free safety; he is the junior transfer student and former soccer player who pulled down the winning interception against the Ducks. (Next week, against Oregon State, Luani will come up with 11 tackles and two more interceptions, returning one for an 84-yard touchdown; for this he'll be named the Pac-12's defensive player of the week. He will also be central to the following week's upset victory over the Arizona Wildcats.)

Vaeao has his own apartment; the other four upperclassmen live together in a rented house seven minutes' walk from campus. The two freshmen live together in the dorm, but they rarely go there, preferring instead to crash at the house.

"When you first come here it's not scary, but you're feeling homesick," Barber says. He is the eldest present and takes the lead.

"Nervous," adds Ekuale. Even though Ekuale is only a sophomore, Coach Joe has asked him to step up and be prepared to fill Vaeao's leadership role after the senior graduates.

"I been to the States a lot of times to visit my family, but coming here by myself was way different," Barber says.

"That's another reason I came here, because I know that Robert, Daniel, and Destiny and them were going to be here," Luvu says.

"Because it's pretty different from home," Tago says.

"When you got off the plane here it was hot," Ekuale says. "It's humid back home, but here they have dry heat."

"And there are a lot of crazy people," Luani says, laughing.

"And things like time management," says Tago. "You look at the time and you have to be somewhere, and then the next thing you know you get the text, like, 'Why weren't you here?'"

"And they have a lot of traffic lights here," Luvu says.

"And here the streets have names, like Duncan Street," Barber says.

"In the village back home you just point to the place," Luani says, pointing to demonstrate.

"You don't have to know any directions," Ekuale agrees.

Down the hall, Coach Joe is in his office, running through game footage. When he brought Vaeao and Barber to the Cougars, they were the first Samoans to be recruited by the school since 1988. (The Cougars' first Samoan player was the "Throwin' Samoan," Jack Thompson, who played in the mid-1970s.) Vaeao was also recruited by Alabama and other big football programs; what sold him on the Cougars was Coach Joe.

More than just a coach, Coach Joe plays the role of village chief. He regularly talks to the boys' counselors and hangs out with the group. He is mindful of the promises he made in all of those large and crowded living rooms across Tutuila. A few other college coaches might come and go to the island—it takes two different planes and nearly 24 hours to reach Samoa from the West Coast—but Coach Joe is the one the islanders trust. He is one of them. "If something would happen to one of these kids, I gotta answer to their families," he says. Last year, after the Cougars' first postseason bowl appearance in ten years, Pac-12 rival USC offered Coach Joe a job at a substantial raise. After some thought, and a counteroffer from Washington State, he turned them down.

Back in the conference room, the boys are talking about college life. "Mostly, we just like to chill when we get our free time," Luani says.

"Sometimes we like to play uke and sing and joke around," Barber adds.

"Or play video games," Ekuale says.

"And order pizza," Barber says.

"Especially Amosa," Ekuale says, indicating the freshman from Tafuna. "He always be hungry at midnight."

"When he came over here he was not that big," Luvu says.

"He was 290," says Ekuale. "Now he's 340."

The freshman raises both hands in the air, a helpless gesture. "I had surgery on my knee, so... " he explains sheepishly, his voice trailing away.

"It's hard when you get hurt," Ekuale says empathetically, changing his tune. He leans forward playfully and punches his teammate on the shoulder.

The massive Sakaria turns his head to Ekuale, his expression blank. Then he wipes off the surface of his sleeve, as if to remove a spot of dust.

Everybody cracks up.

THE GOLDEN CHILD

J. J. ABRAMS IS THE MOST INFLUENTIAL FILM AND TV MAKER IN HOLLYWOOD. HE'S NOT JUST REANIMATING STAR WARS. HE IS WHAT STAR WARS BEGOT.

A long time ago, in the tony suburb of Brentwood, California, a chubby, bespectacled kid of middle-school age busied himself in his bedroom.

It was a large space by any standard, with big windows and exposed beams, packed to the high ceiling with the matériel of his many complementary interests, everything in its designated place. There were orderly shelves of books about magic and movie makeup, a collection of soundtrack albums, stacks of magazines with titles like *Famous Monsters*, *Super-8 Filmmaker*, and *Cinemagic*. Figurines, board games, Aurora models, *Star Wars* paraphernalia. One side of his closet was his magic zone; there he kept all of his tricks—his favorites were Zombieball, Strat-O-Sphere, and Spooky the Spirit Silk, any kind of sleight of hand. The other side of the closet was his special effects zone—makeup and homemade prosthetics and other instruments of cinematic illusion. (He had an ongoing correspondence with the legendary make-up special-effects wizard Dick Smith, known for his work on *Altered States* and *Scanners*. At one point, Smith gifted him one of the long prop tongues used for Linda Blair in *The Exorcist*.) On a crowded table were the props for whatever he was currently building, in various stages of completion, some of them jerry-rigged with ingenious mechanical parts for use in the Super 8 movies he was constantly filming. Another zone in the room served as his editing bay, usually the floor.

His sister remembers friends coming and going, working on various projects, sleeping overnight. She was four years younger and watched his every move. She, in turn, was his favorite subject. In countless gory films and shorts she was strangled, shot, pushed off a roof, attacked by zombies, taken away by aliens. Often, he would wake her up in the middle of the night. You've got to hear this... you've got to watch this... you've got to see what I just did. And she was always like, Oh my God! Once, he made a six-foot-long pencil and took it to school. It looked exactly like a yellow Ticonderoga Number 2. When she asked him why he went to such lengths, he looked at her. "I don't know," he said. "I just thought it would be funny."

He was never a great student. He didn't play sports. At recess he was sometimes seen looking through his fingers as if they were a camera lens and observing other kids. When he was in kindergarten or first grade, his teacher called his mom, concerned that he was refusing to participate in games of dodgeball with the rest of the class.

Are you aware, the teacher asked, that your son is bringing a red cape to school? He runs around the playground pretending to fly like Superman and making up stories.

Not so long ago, on the far edge of Santa Monica, Jeffrey Jacob Abrams, known since birth as J.J., bounds down a floating staircase into the waiting area of the National Typewriter Company, the fanciful name on the redbrick building that houses his movie and TV empire, Bad Robot.

Outside, a glowing sign over the doorbell *asks are you ready?* Inside, the reception desk showcases a vintage collection of toy robots. Carved out of the foyer space, with its high ceiling and exposed beams, its big windows in place of walls, is a waiting area surrounded on three sides by shelves loaded to capacity with toys, magic tricks, antique movie cameras. There are *Star Trek*, *Star Wars*, and *Spy vs. Spy* figurines, all carefully posed. Plastic Aurora models of the Hunchback of Notre Dame and Godzilla; an original *Planet of the Apes* ape-head prosthesis in a plastic case; collector's-edition dolls of the pig-faced doctor and nurse from "Eye of the Beholder," a classic episode of *The Twilight Zone*. A stack of board games from Parker Brothers and Ideal, including Close Encounters of the Third Kind, The Six Million Dollar Man, and Mission: Impossible. On a coffee table are bins of pens, markers, colored pencils, and drawing paper. A sign suggests: please create.

Abrams is wearing his customary sneakers, blue jeans, and plaid shirt. At forty-nine, he is a father of three and no longer chubby; he has the paleo-diet, high-thread-count veneer of the Hollywood affluent. His dark shock of wavy hair has been likened to that of Zeppo Marx. Geeky black-framed glasses rest on a bulb of a nose that shadows a delighted smile. Like a character in one of his time-bending plots, he seems perpetually in awe of his surroundings. *How did I end up here?*

Leading a tour, Abrams points out the various zones in his work space—the editing bays, a recording studio, a prop workshop, a screening room, a new kitchen under construction. His sister, Tracy Rosen, now a screenwriter, calls the offices of Bad Robot "a glorified version of his bedroom." Bryan Burke, a producer with Bad Robot who has been his friend and collaborator since high school, says it's "evidence that we're all embarrassingly trapped in our youth." Damon Lindelof, showrunner of *Lost*—one of a slew of beloved TV series Abrams has produced—has called the refurbished building "a self-contained Death Star." From here Abrams has seemingly conquered the entertainment galaxy.

As a writer, composer, director, and producer, Abrams may well be the most hyphenated mogul the film industry has ever seen; he is certainly among the most influential of his time. Abrams's particular storytelling sensibilities have become the prevailing recipe for popular entertainment. Tangled, deceptive serial plots that jump back and forth in time; a liberal pinch of magical realism; rich, stylish, and playful cinematography; eerie music that evokes early horror films (the one-note theme he composed for *Lost* on a Spectrasonics synthesizer won an ASCAP award)—all of it liberally buttered and salted with the kind of romance, mystery, swelling strings, and schmaltz that is the stuff of classic Hollywood, of classic drama. And the special effects are totally awesome.

"He's a seriously empathic storyteller, which means that he does not selfishly put stories out there that only mean a lot to him and may not mean much to anyone else," says Steven Spielberg, who has worked with Abrams since Abrams was a teenager. "He puts stories out there from a very large heart that are simpatico with a lot of other people's needs and desires. J.J. is the kind of director who can make an audience's dreams come true."

Over the past three decades, Abrams has had a hand in more than thirty movies and television series, the most significant of which has been *Lost*, the supernatural network megahit that helped turn the direction of small-screen programming away from the formulaic one-offs of the Dick Wolf/*Law & Order* era and toward the addictive serials we binge-watch today.

Perhaps even more significant has been Abrams's longtime collaboration with a group of close friends and mentors, all of whom he met by the time he was a freshman in high school. Including actor Greg Grunberg (*Alias, Heroes, Heroes Reborn*), cinematographer Larry Fong (*Lost* and the movies *300* and *Watchmen*), writer-director-producer Matt Reeves (*Felicity, Dawn of the Planet of the Apes*), Bad Robot's Burke (a player in most of Abrams' projects), Kathleen Kennedy (the president of Lucasfilm), and Spielberg, the group forms a sort of Algonquin Round Table of the postmodern movie era. Instead of drinking heavily, this crowd favors magic and monsters. Many a blockbuster idea has been hatched on weekends, at family dinners, in the parking lots of the various Westside schools their children attended together.

More recently, Abrams has been handed the reins to a number of flagging big-screen franchises. He breathed life into Tom Cruise's tired *Mission: Impossible* series (directing *M:I:III* and producing its sequels, *Ghost Protocol* and this year's *Rogue Nation*) and overhauled *Star Trek* (directing the *Star Trek* relaunch in 2009 and *Star Trek into Darkness* in 2013), bringing a more human element to the Vulcan-dry techno-gasmic scripts of the past.

Now comes *Star Wars: The Force Awakens*, among the most widely anticipated movies in history, which Abrams has directed and produced. The spawn of a $4 billion megadeal in which the Walt Disney Company acquired the rights to the *Star Wars* juggernaut from George Lucas, the movie is the first of a new trilogy Abrams is slated to produce. The second is already in production.

We walk around the first floor; Abrams points out some of his trophies. Side by side on a wall are the shooting slates from the last scene of *The Force Awakens* and the last scene *of High Voltage*, a film he made when he was fifteen that eventually brought him to the attention of Spielberg's then-assistant, Kennedy. It was she, as head of Lucasfilm under the Disney umbrella, who hired him for the *Star Wars* gig.

Abrams pauses in front of an antique machine that looks like a huge glass jukebox with no records inside. A vintage Mold-A-Rama, like the ones first manufactured for the 1964 New York World's Fair, it offers visitors the opportunity to make their own plastic replica of the Bad Robot logo, which appears at the beginning or end of all his movies and TV shows and which Abrams created at home one weekend with Adobe After Effects. (His two eldest kids supplied the voices that chirp "Bad Robot.")

"They used to have one of these at Universal Studios," he says, patting the antique machine fondly, as if it were a loyal old dog. "I remember the first time I went on the tour, I got the Frankenstein head. Now you can get a Bad Robot. You wanna try?"

Upstairs in his office, Abrams takes a seat on the sofa. Two plastic cups of raw nuts have been arranged before us, a small plastic spoon in each. To his immediate left is a life-sized rubber head in a glass case, a likeness of Douglas Fairbanks Jr. crafted by Abrams's childhood idol Dick Smith for the movie *Ghost Story*.

"I was always a little bit of the outsider," Abrams is saying of his caped youth. "I wasn't athletic. And I was never a particularly great student. You find yourself somewhere in between the schoolyard and the library. That's the gray area of no-man's-land. You have to find something that interests you, something to focus on."

Abrams was born on Long Island; his family moved to Los

Angeles when he was five. The firstborn grandchild and only son in a Jewish family, Abrams was always the "nexus of the house," according to his sister. Their father is Gerald W. Abrams, a *Mad Men*–era ad salesman for CBS who quit his high-paying job in the early seventies to take a shot at movie producing. Over the past four decades, he has produced something like seventy films for television, many of them Movies of the Week. Still active in Hollywood, he recently produced *Houdini*, with Adrien Brody, for the History Channel. It was television's top-rated miniseries of 2014.

Abrams's mother, the former Carol Kelvin, was herself a dynamo. When the kids were young, she sold real estate. At age thirty-nine, she enrolled at Whittier College School of Law and graduated first in her class. Eventually she became a professor at Whittier, teaching for five years before embarking on her own career as a movie producer. Later she would coauthor two books. She died of cancer in 2012 at sixty-nine.

By far Abrams's biggest influence as a child was his maternal grandfather—Abrams fans can find references to Harry Kelvin buried in much of his work. There is a U.S.S. *Kelvin* in the *Star Trek* reboot. On *Lost*, Kelvin is the guy who occupied the Swan Hatch before Desmond. In *M:I:III* there's a postcard addressed to H. Kelvin; on the series *Fringe*, a character works on a project called "Kelvin Genetics"; in *Super 8*, the service station where the alien first appears sells Kelvin brand gas—the large sign from the movie is sitting against a wall downstairs at Bad Robot, waiting to be hung.

Harry Kelvin owned an electronics business, first in TriBeCa in Lower Manhattan, later in Farmingdale on Long Island. Starting when Abrams was very young, the pair would frequently visit Tannen's Magic Shop, the oldest operating magic store in Manhattan. To get to the bathroom in Abrams's private office at Bad Robot, you go to the bookshelf beside his desk and tug on a copy of a book titled *Louis Tannen's Catalog of Magic*. The wall opens; the privy is revealed.

At his electronics shop, Abrams remembers, his grandfather "would take apart radios and telephones, all kinds of electronics, and explain why and how they worked. In a way, when I was a little kid, he was more of a father figure than my father; like most dads of that era, mine was always busy working."

"J.J. was the son Grandpa never had," says Tracy. "They would go on adventure walks together, just walk around the neighborhood and make up stories. My grandfather was really influential for J.J. When you think about it, storytelling is a lot like electronics—it's all about how you take things apart and why each piece is necessary and where it fits in. The same is true of magic and illusion. That's what filmmaking is all about."

Kelvin also took Abrams on the Universal Studios tour. Abrams was seven or eight years old. "It was this *aha* moment for me," he says. "I saw how movies used illusion in this grand way. They talked about technology in a way that was fascinating. The use of cameras and special effects and different techniques—it just felt like the answer to a question I didn't even know I was asking. Suddenly I realized: *This is the thing I want to do.*"

Abrams borrowed his dad's Super 8 camera and began to experiment. Ten years earlier, Kodak's introduction of the Super 8 format had revolutionized the consumer film industry. Unlike in the past, when movie equipment was large, complicated, and expensive, the Super 8 line of cameras, projectors, and editing machines were small and affordable. The film came preloaded into cartridges, making the process virtually foolproof, opening up the opportunity for home movies.

Actor Greg Grunberg met Abrams "in the sandbox" when they were both about five. (Abrams jokes that the age Grunberg claims becomes younger each year.) The boys were in the same troop of Indian Guides and went to the same elementary school. "I was into sports, but there was a side of me that wanted to be creative, and J.J. was incredibly creative," Grunberg says. "We'd walk to his house from school and J.J. would be splicing film or we'd shoot stuff. He'd be like, 'We've gotta get that shot of you driving your bike down the street.' There were always all kinds of things we had to shoot. I was the actor. It was more like I was helping him out."

One movie they made together was called *The Attic*, in which two kids find a hatch in the ceiling and unleash a monster—and then they have to hide it from the mom when she gets home. Grunberg's mom played the mom. Later, in postproduction, Abrams would add the monster to the movie by scratching its image on the film itself, one frame at a time.

By then, Abrams's father was producing movies. Grunberg remembers Abrams bringing him along to the Paramount Studios lot, where the boys got to go on the sets of the television shows *Mork & Mindy* and *Happy Days*. Perhaps making up for lost time together, Gerald Abrams sometimes brought along his son on trips to film sets around the world—together they went to Budapest, to Rome, to Germany for the filming of *Berlin Tunnel 21*. In London, Abrams met Michael Caine on the set of *Jekyll & Hyde*.

"I think he was fascinated that you could get to work with famous writers, producers, directors, actors, and actresses," Gerald Abrams says. "They fly you first class, put you up in first-class accommodations. And then the most unbelievable part was that after you did all this, they actually *paid you*. So he understood that concept from me. He saw that I was looking forward to getting up in the morning because work was exciting for me."

When Abrams was twelve or thirteen, he went outside one day to find two older kids making a movie of their own. Larry Fong was already in high school. He lived some distance away in Rolling Hills Estates; as it happened, he was visiting a friend whose parents were divorced—the dad lived across the street from the Abrams family.

Fong was another self-professed "nerd" and "*Star Wars* fanboy" who had also appropriated his family's Super 8 camera. Back then, in the early 1980s, before the Internet, a kid had to work much harder to pursue interests that were off the beaten path. There was a lot of looking in the phone book, making calls, searching out the right specialty bookstores and magazines. "I had a lot of reference books for someone my age," Fong says. "Mostly about monsters and magic and film. When I went over to J.J.'s house the first time, I couldn't believe it. He had all the same books and magazines as I did. It was totally weird."

In those dying days of the analog world, Abrams says, the young filmmakers were left to wing it. "Nothing was ever easy. If you wanted to do a visual effect where you split the screen, for example, and wanted to have two versions of your sister at the same time, you would have to film something, then rewind the film, then figure out where you were, then block out the lens with a piece of tape and film it again. We made up the tricks and techniques as we went along—like if you wanted to manually backwind the film, you could put a piece of Scotch tape over the capstan on the cartridge. It was almost like what hacking became, like an analog version of hacking. You'd go see something in the movies, some effect, and it would have an impact on people. You'd want to know how they did it. Invariably, six months later in *Super-8 Filmmaker* magazine, they'd have an article. That was our YouTube."

Though Fong would go on to become a cinematographer (including on the upcoming *Batman v Superman: Dawn of Justice*), his area of interest at the time was special effects. When Abrams was fifteen, he started working on *High Voltage*. He enlisted Fong's help. "J.J. wanted to do this effect like in *Altered States* where the skin rippled," Fong says on the phone from Hawaii, where he is scouting locations for the *King Kong* reboot *Kong: Skull Island*. "I'd read about Dick Smith doing air bladders and whatnot to create his effects, so I got balloons and put them under a stocking and put them on the actor's arm. And then a bunch of us had tubes and were blowing air into these balloons that were wrapped around his arm, and it made this kind of weird ripple effect."

About this time, Abrams learned of a public-access show called *Word of Mouth*, hosted by a thirty-five-year-old named Gerard Ravel, who would interview musicians, actors, filmmakers—anyone interesting he could get. At the end of each show, Ravel would solicit calls from future prospective guests.

Abrams called. Inexplicably, Ravel humored him and drove out to Brentwood to see his stuff. "He put the films on his Super 8 projector, and I knew this kid was going to make it," Ravel told *Filmmaker* magazine a few years ago. He ended up doing two shows with Abrams. A week later Ravel got a call from another fifteen-year-old, Matt Reeves. He put the two kids in touch.

"I actually remember the first night I was talking to Matt on the phone. We talked for like four hours because it was literally like we had both found a twin," Abrams says. "We were both working on movies that were about—without any shock or surprise at all—losers in high school. His was a much more sophisticated, dark comedy that was a better story and a better movie. Mine was a special effects-filled ridiculous comedy." Eventually their friendship and collaboration would lead to Abrams's first television show, *Felicity*.

Meeting all these film-mad teenagers, Ravel had an idea. What resulted was "The Best Teen Super 8mm Films of '81," held at LA's Nuart Theater in March 1982. Abrams submitted *High Voltage*, his special-effects loser comedy. Reeves screened a Hitchcockian thriller called *Stiletto*. Fong's film was a spoof called *Toast Encounters of the Burnt Kind*. Future producer Lawrence Trilling (*Parenthood*) and screenwriter Mark Sanderson (*I'll Remember April*) also had films in the lineup.

The *Los Angeles Times* published a story about the festival, "Beardless Wonders of Film Making," so titled because their film-making idols—Spielberg, Lucas, Francis Ford Coppola, and Martin Scorsese—all had beards at the time… and these kids weren't even old enough to drive. Much of the piece was given over to Abrams, who told of making his first film, a work of claymation, at age seven. "I see stuff by Steven Spielberg and John Carpenter and I want to do it, too," he was quoted as saying.

Spielberg's then-assistant, Kathleen Kennedy, read the article in the *Times*. As it happened, sitting near her desk was a dusty cardboard box full of 8mm movies (the predecessor to Super 8) that Spielberg had made, starting when he was a middle-school kid. They'd only recently been retrieved from the basement of a house on the top of Lookout Mountain in the Hollywood Hills.

"A man called me saying, 'Hey, I found this box of movies and I think they belong to Steven Spielberg,'" Kennedy remembers. "At first I thought, 'Okay, there is *no way*, this is just some crackpot.' But it turned out to be absolutely true. The man lived in a house that Steven had lived in years ago. He'd left behind this box."

Kennedy laughs at the memory. "I have no idea why, but I read that article and I suddenly had this idea to say to Steven, 'Hey, why don't we hire these two young kids to clean up the film?'"

For Abrams, it was like receiving a call from on high. The films of Lucas and Spielberg had been "transformative and incredibly exciting," he recalls. "*Star Wars* and *Close Encounters* came out the same year. It was hard not to be a fanatic about those stories."

The Spielberg archive was in rough condition. Over the years, the tape or glue used for editing had broken down. Every single edit on every film needed to be re-spliced.

Spielberg says he took a hands-on role. "I was entrusting my entire collection of 8mm movies that I had made as a kid to these two up-and-coming Hollywood hopefuls. And they were fifteen years old. Absolutely I was very concerned. I wanted to make sure that they weren't going to try to reinvent the wheel."

For their work, the boys were paid $150 each.

Sometime around 2010, as *Lost* was coming to the thunderous, befuddling conclusion of its award-winning six-year run, Larry Fong got a call from Abrams. "There's a movie you *have* to do," Abrams said.

After graduating from high school, Abrams had gone off to Sarah Lawrence College in New York. During Christmas break in his senior year he ran into his friend Jill Mazursky, the daughter of Paul Mazursky (*Bob & Carol & Ted & Alice, Down and Out in Beverly Hills*). The two became writing partners; upon graduation they sold their first screenplay, *Taking Care of Business*, a 1990 comedy starring Jim Belushi. Next Abrams wrote *Regarding Henry*, starring Harrison Ford. A number of other films followed, including the 1998 megahit *Armageddon*. That same year, Abrams and Reeves created *Felicity*, a fan favorite that introduced Keri Russell and followed her adorably confused character through her four years at the fictional University of New York.

In 2004, following the success of *Alias*, featuring Jennifer Garner as a college-student super undercover double agent, ABC tapped Abrams to produce a prime-time drama that would capitalize on the success of the tropical reality show Survivor, something like Robinson Crusoe meets *Lord of the Flies*. Abrams came up with *Lost*.

To shoot the supernatural prime-time soap—about the survivors of a plane crash who find themselves on a magical, mystical, metaphysical island—Abrams tapped his old friend Fong. Of course, *Lost* became the most-talked-about show in television history. Meanwhile, Abrams and Bad Robot began churning out television series (*What About Brian, Fringe, Undercovers, Person of Interest*) and his big-screen action blockbusters.

One day, while working on *Star Trek*, Abrams says, he got the idea to do a movie called *Super 8*, about a group of film-mad middle-school-age kids. Abrams called up Spielberg and asked him to produce. He signed on immediately. Next Abrams called Fong.

"J.J. wanted me to read this script," Fong says. "He had me come to the set of one of his TV shows—they were shooting on location. And he said, 'You can't take the script, you have to read it right here'—you know how top secret he always is. And I'm like, 'Right here? Standing in a park?'

"So I'm starting to read and it's all about these kids. And slowly I find out the kids are making a movie to put in a film festival, and then all these fantastical things happen to them. Talk about personal. That was us. I don't know how much more personal a movie could get, although we never saw an alien or had a military conspiracy in our lives. When we were decorating the kid's bedroom for the film, J.J. was like, 'We gotta put magic tricks in his room and *Famous Monsters* comics.' We had all of our old magic books in the shot. It's those little things that no one else cares about that were huge for us, you know?"

The idea of *Super 8*, Abrams says, was to make a movie like the ones he'd grown up with, "sort of a lost Amblin movie," he says, referring to Spielberg's early production company, Amblin Entertainment, which produced *E.T.* and *Gremlins*. "There's something about that era that I have a fondness for. There's a sweetness and an innocence to that time and those characters. What's interesting is when I was writing the movie, my mom was diagnosed with brain cancer. In the script, one of the kids has just lost his mom. So it ended up I was writing a movie about losing your mom while I was losing my mom."

Abrams says he and Spielberg labored over the film cut by cut. As Spielberg sees it, "We consciously were trying to recapture the spirit of the Amblin films, not necessarily trying to pay homage."

"It was an homage with a capital *H*," Abrams says. "It was like going back to my childhood with the person who helped narrate my childhood."

In his office, Abrams is talking about an homage of a different sort—his work on *The Force Awakens*. The challenge, he says, is to find the right balance, borrowing some from the classics while moving the story along. In that way, he says, the undertaking is not unlike a television series. "It just happens to be a series that George Lucas created that ended up being one of the most culturally impactful things of all time."

Abrams insists the decision to take on the *Star Wars* franchise—as director of *The Force Awakens* and executive producer of two sequels—was not easy. He knew that one reason Lucas had decided to sell were the personal attacks he'd suffered over the years from overzealous fans who had their own ideas on how to run a movie dynasty; it just wasn't fun anymore. Kennedy says she had to do a lot of convincing to bring Abrams aboard. "The interesting thing is that our kids—Steven's kids, J.J.'s kids, and mine—all went to the same school. We used to all see one another as we would drop off and pick up the kids or go to school events and things like that. There was a very short list of potential candidates to step into *Star Wars*, and J.J. was way at the top of the list. It's already been talked about that he at first turned it down. I remember having endless conversations with J.J. when he was trying to make the decision. A lot of it happened while we were standing around at school."

When he committed, Abrams went in deep. He persuaded Harrison Ford, Carrie Fisher, and Mark Hamill to reprise their original roles as Han Solo, Princess Leia, and Luke Skywalker for the first time in thirty years. (He's also added fresh faces like Adam Driver and Lupita Nyong'o to the mix.) Details about plot and characters have been kept obsessively secret, of course—according to many accounts, the screenplay was still being reworked as shooting began in the spring of 2014—but Abrams has frequently said, as he repeats now, that he's made only sparing use of computer-generated effects. It is as analog as he can make it, shooting on 35mm film (rather than digitally, as almost all movies are shot now) and indulging his longtime fascination with monster makeup and model building.

"When I first saw *Star Wars*, I remember being touched by the tangibility of it. The actuality of it. It just felt real," Abrams says. "I didn't know that the Tatooine shots were done in Tunisia—I just knew I was in a real fucking place, on an actual desert planet. There was an actual sunbaked sandscape, and it was great because it was 100 percent real.

It helped me believe that these two droids were really in the middle of the desert arguing and separating, or that this kid from a moisture farm would happen upon this droid in the sandcrawler."

Abrams says his quest for a more tactile, analog film has been well served by the technological advances that have been made with small servos and motors and skin materials. "When you look at creatures on the set—I have scenes where we might have used a little bit of CG, but it was more likely to *remove* something, not to *add* something, like to remove the puppeteer. There are a couple scenes in this movie where you might think, 'Oh, I bet that's CG,' which is fine, but you're never gonna look at it and go, 'That doesn't look real.'"

It may be a unique feature of our feedback culture that a chubby middle-school *Star Wars* nerd grows up to become the instrument of *Star Wars'* rebirth. It feels freaky even to him.

"I would be disingenuous if I didn't say there weren't hundreds of times during this process of working on this movie where I didn't have a kind of *Oh my God, I'm meeting the Beatles* feeling. It's like, suddenly you're here, finding yourself on the set of the *Millennium Falcon*. It's hard not to feel a reverence toward that, a sense of awe. Every day there would be a moment or two or three where I would find myself stunned by what was actually happening."

He shakes his head. "It makes no sense that Kathy Kennedy would see an article and that she and Steven Spielberg would decide to trust these priceless original copies of his childhood films, the only copies, to a couple of kids. That makes no sense. Trusting a fifteen-year-old with that stuff? You don't do that. And then the idea that Kathy would become a friend, that Steven would become so close to me. None of it really makes any sense. It doesn't quite feel real. It's like something you make up. I don't know how it ever happened."

Twenty years or so after J.J. Abrams' teacher called his mom to make her aware that he was spending his recess periods flying around the playground in a Superman cape, Carol Abrams ran into the teacher.

"Carol is in a supermarket here in Brentwood and she feels a tap on her shoulder," recalls Gerald Abrams. "She turns around and it's Mrs. Newman. They talk awhile about this and that, and finally Mrs.

Newman says, 'Tell me, what ever happened with J.J.?'
    "Carol looks at her. 'You're not going to believe it,' she says."

DAB ARTISTS

THE CRAFTSMEN ON THE OUTLAW EDGE OF THE HASH OIL BOOM CALL THEMSELVES WOOKS. ONCE A YEAR THEY CONVERGE ON THE SECRET CUP FINALS IN LAS VEGAS.

We were somewhere around Barstow, on the edge of the desert in a driving rain, when my passenger, James "Skywalker" Johnson, began to fidget with the well-traveled, antiballistic, Pelican-brand polypropylene case resting on the floor mat between his feet. Hazard yellow and covered with stickers, equipped with double-throw latches and a heavy-duty handle, it resembled something the modern army might carry into battle, a safe box for a delicate gun sight or high-end piece of electronics.

Skywalker is a chunky man of thirty-two with a burner cell phone, an exceptionally well-developed palate, and a bit of an asthmatic wheeze. A former intern for a Republican US senator—his season in Washington politics left him sprinting for the exit—he has worked as a bartender, a chef, a computer programmer, and a marijuana grower. Now, he says, he's "an ambassador for a California-based lifestyle brand inspired by the culture of hash oil." As such, he buys and sells marijuana buds and trim, hash oil and edibles, T-shirts and hats. He'd tell you more, but many of his activities are illegal, even though his products are not. His and the names of many other individuals and companies in this story have been changed.

On a stormy December afternoon, we were headed to Las Vegas for the fourth annual Secret Cup Finals, the culmination of a yearlong series of regional judged events that bring together the best artisanal hash-oil makers in the country. The festivities were to be held in a rented mansion off the Strip. Skywalker had paid dearly for a room in a guesthouse by the pool. His fledgling concern, Jedi Extracts, was one of the sponsors. Besides looking forward to representing his brand, making new contacts, and sampling all the entries—some of which for sure would be "fire," meaning the best of the best—Skywalker was stoked to meet up again with his friends in the elite community that has grown up over the past half-decade around the business and craft of making hash oil, called extraction.

Cool but nerdy, deliberately unkempt, more comfortable alone or in small groups, these self-taught Heisenbergs of hash oil call themselves Wooks, after the fierce but cuddly Star Wars creatures many of them resemble. Mostly men in their twenties and thirties, they favor beards and tats, blown-glass pendants, food-stained hoodies, and flat-brimmed ball caps with collectible pins decorating the crowns. Known by their colorful handles—Big D, Brutal Bee, Task Rok, Witsofire, the Medi Brothers, Hector from SmellslikeOG—the Wooks devote their lives to producing and smoking the very finest hash oil, a form of concentrated marijuana that can be extracted from the leaves and flowers of the pot plant by a variety of chemical processes, the most common of which employs ordinary cans of highly volatile butane lighter fluid as a chemical solvent.

Hash oil (the formal name is butane hash oil, known as BHO) is a modern version of hashish. The butane gas and lab equipment replace the intensive labor of patting, sifting, and compressing marijuana flowers that go into the traditional method of creating hash. Since the 1960s, devotees have been making a sludgy form of hash oil, usually on the stove in a pot using a variety of toxic solvents including naphtha, hexane, or isopropyl alcohol. A precursor to BHO began to appear around 2000 in Los Angeles's San Fernando Valley. The first recognized iteration was called Juice. It was smoked primarily on top of a green screen—a pipe bowl full of pot or pot ash. Some preferred to chase the dragon, using a straw and a hot knife or a piece of foil and a flame.

Almost from the beginning, enthusiasts started making their own pipes. Soon the glass blowers became involved; today you can buy elaborate blown-glass pipes that cost tens of thousands. When smoked, hash oil produces a more substantial rush than marijuana flowers, but the overall high doesn't last as long. A heavy smoke session often leads to a spontaneous nap. The Wooks call this condition DTFO, Dabbed The Fuck Out. They take great sport in posting DTFO photos of one another on social media.

BHO was first widely publicized in 2009, when it won "best product" at the *High Times* Cannabis Cup in Amsterdam. The founders of the Secret Cup, Jeremy Norrie and Daniel de Sailles, were part of the team that first brought hash oil to the Amsterdam competition. According to many but not all, they helped popularize the term dab, which was coined to describe the approximate dosage. ("Dabbing" means smoking hash oil.)

Like pot, hash oil can be purchased legally in a dispensary or illegally from an extractor or a dealer. The categories of hash oil vividly denote the different textures of the stuff, which originates as a liquid but eventually hardens into a solid state unless otherwise prepared. There is wax, shatter (as in broken glass), budda (butter), honeycomb, live resin (sticky), crumble (like crack), and honey oil. Hash oil of a lesser grade and potency is also used for edibles, tinctures, lotions, drinks, and e-vape cartridges.

The colors range from vivid greens to golden yellows to burnt-sugar browns. A translucent golden amber is considered the connoisseur's choice. As a rule, Skywalker will not smoke anything that's not clear, even some of the Secret Cup entries. "I'm not putting that shit in my lungs," he often says, implying that he doesn't know who'd extracted it or how.

Because of the stigma against smoking, the medical marijuana statutes recently passed in New York allow only the use of hash oils, edible or vaporized. Smoking pot remains illegal. If New York is a predictor, hash oil may well be the future of the marijuana industry—a national market expected to reach $47 billion in total revenue by 2016.

Twenty-three states and the District of Columbia allow some form of legal marijuana use, medical or recreational. Twelve states explicitly allow for the use of marijuana extracts, which lack the telltale skunky smell of marijuana—the buzzword in the industry is *discreet*. However, only two states permit extraction, Colorado and Washington, where rigorous laboratory specifications must be met. "In the other ten states," says Paul Armentano of the National Organization for the Reform of Marijuana Laws, "arguably the extracts are legal when they fall from the sky."

Today, as large companies and venture capitalists rush into the rapidly expanding hash-oil arena, Skywalker and his fellow Wooks are fighting for their piece of the future. Echoing the sentiments of artisanal craftsmen in other fields, they are hoping that quality and discriminating palates win the day—or at least keep them in business as the giants grab bigger shares of the market.

For the Wooks, attending the Secret Cup is like attending a high-level trade show. (For legal reasons, the finals are considered a private party.) It's sort of a March Madness for extractors—not the only such contest in the world, but maybe the most exclusive. The regional winners were going to be present at the finals as well as some of the winners from the previous year. In all there would be twenty entrants. Bragging rights and future contracts were at stake. If Skywalker and the others want to compete in their rapidly growing field, they need to be known, to be intimate with the doings and players in their industry, to cultivate an aura of insider success.

But it won't be just work. It is, after all, Las Vegas. These Secret Cup gatherings have become somewhat dear to Skywalker. Wooks are loners. Their lives are furtive and solitary. Most reside in rural areas in states where they could easily be busted. If they are busted—as was a friend of Skywalker's who blew up a house when the butane exploded—none of the other Wooks will dare to call, fearing their friend's communications are being monitored by police. As it is, their community exists mostly on social media. Attending the Secret Cup would be some of Skywalker's best friends, the people with whom he Facebooks and Instagrams regularly. Hanging out for five days in Vegas with his fellow Wooks, eating, smoking, wreaking a little havoc on the Strip— "What's not to like?" Skywalker said in his gruff East Coast manner.

By three in the afternoon the storm was still raging, and we had two hours left to drive. The desert sky was black. Gusting winds buffeted the car. As we made our way toward Las Vegas, the red lights in front of me were a watery mirage. Skywalker was biting his pinkie fingernail, a nervous tell I'd begun to notice during our time together. At some point, I heard a deep sigh emanating from his vicinity, followed by a rattling cough. Out of the corner of my eye I noticed him reach down between his feet, throw the double latches of his Pelican case.

From the custom foam padding arranged inside, he withdrew his Mini Sundae Cup rig. Five inches tall, made of clear glass by a company called Hitman, the pipe retails for $500 and uses a small amount of water as a filter. The bowl on top, called a nail, is an after-market add-on, fabricated of the finest quartz. (Some enthusiasts prefer nails made of Grade 2 titanium, a type used in missiles.) Placing the rig in the cup holder, Skywalker reached into his backpack and removed a bottle of water, a small paper bindle of hash oil, and a butane torch.

The torch was bigger than a cigar lighter but smaller than a Bunsen burner. He pulled the trigger, a loud click like a gun dry-firing. A four-inch cone of orange-blue flame burned briefly, illuminating the inside of my car.

"Mind if I do a dab?"

Two months earlier. October in central Phoenix.

A couple dozen white canopy tents, arranged roughly in a circle, baked in the sun like so many covered wagons on an asphalt prairie. Plumes of light smoke rose here and there, mixing in the enervated air with the smell of hot dogs from the vendors by the gate.

The Secret Cup Desert Regional was the sixth stop on the 2014 Secret Cup circuit. Like all the others except the final, it featured a weekend expo open to the public. The Secret Cup could be called a smaller, more specialized version of the huge gatherings made popular over the years by *High Times's* Cannabis Cups. A cross between a farmer's market and a renaissance fair, the expo is a pop-up festival for connoisseurs of artisanal hash oil, edibles, and other concentrates. Available for sale alongside various marijuana products were paraphernalia, art, and clothing. In one area, glass blowers demonstrated their skills. For the price of admission—$20 per day—anyone who presented a medical marijuana license could smoke as many dabs as they were able. There were also deals to be had: A gram of top-shelf hash oil was selling for as little as $50, about half the going rate in dispensaries.

Beneath one of the white tents, in a booth rented by Jedi Extracts, Skywalker and his right-hand man, a guy called the Captain, were working the crowd with the zeal of boardwalk hucksters, pushing a drinkable hash-oil extract. Suspended in cherry syrup, it is sold in a small red pharmaceutical bottle to resemble the narcotic cough medicine known in hip-hop circles as Purple Drank, a combination of promethazine and codeine. You might call it a novelty item, but it has a pleasing taste and a copacetic effect, especially over ice in the heat. Sales were brisk.

Seated alongside Skywalker and the Captain at a folding table was an extractor named Sloth Bear, one of several with whom Skywalker works. By necessity there's a lot of collaboration in the hash-oil trade. Skywalker neither grows pot nor extracts oil, though he has done both. These days, he finds the weed. He finds the extractors. He finds the producers of hash-oil capsules or gummy bears or syrup. He finds the dispensaries to take these items off his hands. Each deal is different, but the best scenario for Skywalker is when dispensaries provide all the marijuana and Skywalker takes it to someone like Sloth Bear, who extracts the oil. Skywalker and his extractor usually take a 50 percent cut; often they consign their product back to the dispensaries for sale. Skywalker is essentially a middleman. His talent is knowing the right people and finding the right pot, making deals happen, opening territories.

Sloth Bear, who is twenty-nine, has an entry in the Desert Regional this weekend. He's well-known in Wook circles; in the past, he placed in the top four in the hash-oil division of a *High Times* Cannabis Cup. On the table in front of Sloth Bear was a large slab of fresh oil, gold tinged with green, a pungent form called live resin that's made with fresh frozen buds. Also on the table, along with the bottles of syrup and cans of soda mixer, were a couple of dab rigs and a butane torch.

Like many of the booths at the Desert Cup expo, Jedi Extracts was giving away free dabs. A double line of customers trailed ten deep into the brutal sun, waiting to taste and buy. They reflected a cross-section of who is interested in dabbing erl, Wook slang for hash oil. A father and son looking like they made a wrong turn on the way to a Lions Club picnic. A graying hippie with a pendant pipe around his neck. A withered man in an electric wheelchair. A fiftyish woman wrapped head to toe in diaphanous scarves. A pair of Suicide Girls with extensive facial piercings. A pair of high school boys trying to look like they belonged.

"Step right up," called Skywalker, pocketing the proceeds of another sale. "Who needs a free dab? Who wants a pour?"

Born in Queens, Skywalker moved to rural Pennsylvania at an early age. His father was a service manager for a car dealership, his mother worked for a logistics firm. High school in the middle of nowhere was an invitation for hijinks. "Because we were so bored, whenever some little thing popped off," Skywalker said, "we would go hard at it and just be assholes." He and his friends would drive down roads taking out mailboxes with baseball bats, hang out at the houses of people who weren't home, heckle the police, smoke as much weed as they could find.

Skywalker dropped out of tenth grade and went to work for a local newspaper, where his facility with computers and message boards became prized. After getting his GED, he paid his own way through college. From there he drifted around the country, trying various trades. Then he fell into the medical marijuana business and things just clicked. He ran a grow in the Northeast for four years; later he taught himself extraction. In 2011, seeing an opportunity to expand, he moved to California and started Jedi Extracts.

As the day wore on, the temperature continued to rise. Heat eddied off the pavement but the customers kept coming; Skywalker and the Captain kept pouring Styrofoam cups, $10 for a one-ounce drank with soda, $35 for a four-ounce bottle. Meanwhile Sloth Bear had brought out another slab. Under arrangement with Skywalker, he was selling (and giving away) his own stuff. Already he'd made back his expenses. Sloth Bear and Skywalker agree it's cool to travel around the country meeting up with your fellow Wooks and furthering your craft and your business. But it's quite another thing to pay for all that travel and feed yourself. Accordingly, spirits inside the booth this afternoon were high, despite the wilting temperatures.

"I wish I'd brought another case of syrup," Skywalker said, looking through the empty boxes at his feet. He would not reveal the source of the syrup or the arrangements under which he was selling it. Like any entrepreneur, however, he basically has three goals at the various Secret Cup expos and gatherings: To make his brand ever more prominent. To continue to make new friends and visit with established ones, opening up lines of commerce and goodwill. To make enough money to continue to operate.

"Gimme two more bottles," said a returning customer, a tall black man with dreads.

"That's what's *up*," enthused the Captain, taking four twenties and making change. The Captain brings to mind Turtle from *Entourage*. A couple of years ago, when he met Skywalker, he was working as a janitor in a fast-food restaurant. Now they're roommates.

"Mind mixing me a drank?" Sloth Bear asked, weighing out another gram of his live resin on a small electronic scale. A bead of sweat broke free from his thick hairline and slid down his temple.

"Only if you give me a dab," the Captain said.

"All you need do is ask, my good man," said Sloth Bear.

Born and raised in Southern California, Sloth Bear is the son of a contractor and a chiropractor. In high school, he was busted with two pounds of weed. Three months before his probation was to end, he rear-ended an elderly lady and was charged with DUI. He turned twenty-four in jail. "It was the worst birthday ever," he said.

After working in a movie theater and then in construction with his dad, Sloth Bear was hired at a hydroponics store. Over four years, Sloth Bear—who is large and furry but not slothful—worked as a manager. Meanwhile, he learned hydroponic growing from his boss, a farmer of legal crops, and from his customers, many of whom cultivated pot. Sloth Bear started growing for others and eventually discovered his aptitude for extracting. At one of the competitions, he met Skywalker and the Captain. They became fast friends and co-conspirators in criminal enterprise that somehow never feels criminal to them. It might be hard and stressful, but at the end of the day, over a number of dabs, each of them will tell you, as Sloth Bear said: "It's what I was born to do."

Now, under the white canopy tent, Skywalker grabbed one of the rigs from the folding table and pointed to a dab that Sloth Bear had just prepared for the frat boy standing in front of the folding table. "I'm ready for another dab."

"*That's* what's up," said Sloth Bear.

Everybody laughed.

Early November in the California high desert. Harvest season at Merlin's MediFarm.

According to the ten-day forecast, a storm was headed toward us. Rain on the plants at this point could wreck the buds. All around the farm, everyone worked with a sense of urgency. A pair of men used a pulley to haul pot from the lower terraces. Inside the curing shed, three laborers hung buds on hundreds of lines to dry. On the porch of the house a woman sorted seeds. Sloth Bear was beneath a shade tent, preparing to blast his next batch.

Making hash oil is an ever-evolving art. Every extractor working today learned his or her craft largely from YouTube, chat rooms, social media, and trial and error. Some extractors choose to leave the buds on the plant longer, some want an earlier harvest. Some prefer the buds, called nugs, to be dried for up to ten days. Some deep-freeze immediately. There is no particular consensus on which method is best. Each strain produces a different result, which is the essence of artisanal erl. As with wine or cheese or beer, there is creative variance between products, a diverse palette of smells and tastes and effects.

Marijuana has two major active ingredients. Tetrahydrocannabinol (THC) causes people to feel energetically inspired. Cannabidiol (CBD) relieves pain and a number of medical conditions, from glaucoma and seizures to arthritis and anxiety. Pot is also rich in terpenes and terpinoids, aromatic hydrocarbons produced by plants to deter herbivores. Hash oil can smell like tangerine, lemon, grapey purple perfume, pine, earth, or cherry candy.

Merlin's MediFarm grows sixty-three different strains, among them standards like Chemdawg, Girl Scout Cookies, and Sour Diesel. Sloth Bear has a contract this year to convert about three-fourths of the farm's two hundred to four hundred pounds of crop into hash oil. Sloth Bear supplies the butane and the equipment; in return he receives 50 percent of the oil produced, with an option to sell it back to the grower.

Depending upon the strain and the method of growing—and the techniques, tools, and prowess of the extractor—a pound of marijuana will yield anywhere from 30 to 120 grams of oil. The oil will sell wholesale to dispensaries from $20 to $40 a gram and to buyers for between $80 and $100. (For comparison, flower marijuana sells retail from $10 to $20 a gram in dispensaries.)

BHO extractors use one of two types of equipment to make hash oil, either an open-loop or a closed-loop system. For this batch, Sloth Bear employed a SubZero Scientific brand open-loop extractor with tripod legs that he bought used for $400. It fits easily into his vehicle along with the rest of his equipment: a couple of medium-size plastic propagation trays (usually for growing seeds or clones); two Pyrex baking dishes; a supply of parchment paper; a two-inch hose clamp; and a couple of round filters (one paper, one silk) to place at the bottom of the cylinder.

Now, under the shade tent—which allowed for plenty of ventilation—Sloth Bear introduced the nozzle of a large can of refrigerated butane into a receptacle at the top of the SubZero Scientific extractor, which at the moment contained a quarter pound of a strain called Sour Maui Dawg.

As we sat on beach chairs behind a folding table, the liquid butane passed under pressure through the bud-packed metal cylinder, dissolving the crystallized resins in the marijuana flowers, including the THC, CBD, terpenes, flavonoids, and also something called myrcene, one of the primary components of hops, which is partly responsible for the sedative effects of beer. In a few moments, a viscous stream of clear amber oil began to flow. The oil landed atop the organic parchment paper, which was folded to form its own tray within the Pyrex dish, which itself sat in a warm bath of one hundred–degree water in the propagation tray.

Pleased with himself, Sloth Bear gestured toward the healthy flow of golden oil. "I always wanted to make a million before I was thirty," he said.

By the time this harvest was through, he said, he'd be halfway there.

December again. The Secret Cup Finals in Las Vegas.

By late Saturday afternoon a cloud of smoke, cookout grease, and man funk hung over all the rooms of the rented mansion. Beneath the thunder of the DJ's rap music could be heard the soundtrack of serious dabbing—the mini-jet-engine whoosh of butane torches, the gurgle of percolating bubbles, the continuous series of barking coughs emanating from here and there like the croaking calls of frogs in a wetland.

The venue, as advertised, was enormous. To one side of the foyer, with its winding staircase and crowning chandelier, was a grand dining room. Under a hand-painted ceiling, the chairs were filled with Wooks. Everyone had a Pelican case. The long table was littered with pipes and bindles and dead cans of 'tane. Many had brought their electric nail, a bowl wired to a heating element to maintain a constant temperature, keeping the pipe ever ready to melt the next hit. Thinking ahead, some even brought extension cords.

On the other side of the foyer was a sitting room. Like much of the house, it was decorated with faux-gold Versace furniture. A faux-gold-plated custom motorcycle occupied a velvet-covered platform in the bay window.

Skywalker was arranged on a gold fainting couch, his eyes at half-mast. The room he'd anted up for had turned out to be a tiny converted cabana. During the storm, which lasted several days, there was a nasty leak. He hadn't gotten much sleep.

Sitting opposite Skywalker in a Louis XIV knockoff was a Wook named Gerald, from Boston. The two first met at the Secret Cup's Beast Coast Regional in Providence, Rhode Island. Since then, they've collaborated on some deals. They were supposed to be sharing the full-size bed in the wet cabana; mostly they had powered through the gathering without sleep. Their rigs and torches were arranged haphazardly on a coffee table between them. Nearby, on another gold chair, was a VIP guest—one of one hundred people who'd paid $300 to $500 (depending upon the quality of the gift package included) to be allowed to attend the mansion between 3 and 11 p.m., smoke free samples of the entries, and rub elbows with the finalists. The VIP's glass pipe was also on the table. A pricey piece, it was artfully blown to resemble a dead infant with a bloody amputated leg.

Gerald is twenty-one. He calls his company Southie Extracts. Like many of the other Wooks, he started extracting because he liked erl but couldn't find any. Last April, at the Beast Coast Regional, he was one of the finalists. "I never really thought I'd win," he said. "I just did it for fun."

"Did you try number seventeen? That's the winner right there," Skywalker said with his usual confidence. "It's the Samurai Bros entry."

"How do you know it's the Samurai Bros?" Gerald challenged. The entries wouldn't be unmasked until the scores were tabulated Sunday afternoon.

"I've bought three or four grams of that shit," Skywalker said dismissively. With a lot of the West Coast guys, he's found, you can't do much arguing; they're too mellow. But guys from the East Coast like him and Gerald see arguing as sport. Sometimes he misses that. "Don't you smell that fuckin' tang?"

Gerald dipped into his judge's pack, a leather-covered jeweler's box with foam spaces for twenty small glass jars, each one numbered. As a Secret Cup finalist he was charged with tasting and grading his competitors. He selected number seventeen.

Twisting open the top of the jar, Gerald retrieved a small folded-up square of nonstick parchment paper, the same as Sloth Bear uses. (Having failed to make the top four at the Desert Regional, Sloth Bear was off in Hawaii with his girlfriend, following the proceedings online.)

Gerald unfolded the bindle once and then again. Between his fingers was something that appeared to be a small, thin, translucent piece of used chewing gum pressed between the sheets of the paper. Gerald pulled apart the halves with a precise movement, bringing to mind Velcro and causing a similar sound. What confronted him at last was a half-gram of shatter —think of a small piece of amber glass you might find on a beach.

Gerald brought the sample to his nose with the practiced air of an oenophile or foodie. "This smells like tangie," he said, meaning tangerine.

"It's grapefruity," Skywalker corrected. "I definitely get more of a grapefruit."

"It looks flame," said Gerald.

"It *is* flame," assured Skywalker, folding his arms like, *Told you so, dude.*

Gerald triggered a large butane torch and proceeded to heat the Halen Honey Hole of Skywalker's Mini Sundae Cup rig.

As he aimed the orange-and-blue cone of fire toward the bowl, I asked if they ever worried about going to jail. After all, their passion and livelihood is illegal in all but two states, and neither lives in one.

"I do think about the legal aspects, but you can't really worry about it," Gerald said. Heating a nail can take up to thirty seconds, depending how much fun the user is having, or how mesmerized he gets, or how much residual oil needs to be cooked off. "I am a big believer in karma," he said, "so I feel like if you live a good life and you're a good person then bad things don't happen to you."

"Extraction is going to be legal eventually," Skywalker said. "More sooner than later. To be involved in the community now means we'll have that first jump in our own states when big business comes in with their millions and millions of dollars. That's why I feel good to be at the Secret Cup. It makes you feel like you've made it a little bit. The people here are the major players."

Gerald continued to heat the nail until the quartz glowed red, then removed the flame and set the torch on the table. He tested the temperature of the nail by holding it near the underside of his wrist, the place where a father might test a few drops of baby formula.

At last he applied the four-inch titanium dabber to the inside of the heated bowl. At the end of the dabber was a glob of the entry in question. Immediately upon contact with the hot quartz, the dab liquefied, then bubbled, then vaporized. A light white smoke traveled through the chambers, spinning a tiny glass propeller. At the other end of the dabber was a cup called a carburetor cap. Gerald placed the cap over the nail to trap the smoke as he continued to inhale. When he finished the hit, Gerald put down the rig, inclined his chin, and exhaled a thick stream of smoke toward the chandelier.

He noted an immediate increase in his energy level, a cerebral sensation of floating, a tingle at the top of his head. His eyes felt recessed, his point of view at once more internalized and more externalized, everything more vivid and intense. The music washed pleasantly into his ears, into his brain, something hypnotic by Kendrick Lamar: *Bitch, don't kill my vibe. Bitch, don't kill my vibe.*

"That *is* flame," Gerald said at last, eyes wide. He looked over to Skywalker for concurrence.

Homie was DTFO.

January in downtown Denver.

I followed Ralph Morgan, the chief executive officer of two related but independent companies, Organa Labs and O.penVAPE, through the front door of a nondescript brick industrial building. Morgan, who is forty-two, was dressed in Rocky Mountain casual. We'd just finished lunch at his favorite sushi place. Before he got into the pot business, he sold replacement joints, primarily knees and hips. His wife, Heidi, sold pharmaceuticals. "We were totally naïve to cannabis," he said. "We saw the push for legalization in Colorado on the news and were intrigued. As soon as we started doing our due diligence, we fell in love with the idea. I used to tell people, 'Hey, we've been selling joints and drugs for years, so we're qualified!'"

The Morgans opened Evergreen Apothecary in 2009. It is located on South Broadway, in an area called the Green Mile, an up-and-coming neighborhood with one of the highest concentrations of dispensaries in the world. The business took off. But Morgan was unhappy with the inconsistency of his products. "We were telling patients, 'Hey, eat this brownie, but just a quarter of it—hopefully that's the same strength as the last time.'" Morgan said. "If this is medicine, shouldn't a doctor be able to prescribe a specific type and dosage? We were looking for something that could be reliable and reproducible."

The Morgans opened Organa Labs in 2010 and O.penVAPE in 2012, the latter in partnership with a chain of dispensaries. For tax reasons, the two companies are separate. O.penVAPE, which makes several different models of battery-powered portable vaporizers, or e-vapes, does not touch marijuana, so it is not subject to the higher taxes on pot-related industry. Organa does all of the extracting. Financial analysts say it is conceivable the combined companies will be worth a billion dollars in two years.

Morgan led me into a laboratory full of gleaming stainless-steel machines and tanks. Dials, hoses, knobs, and wires were everywhere. From floor to ceiling, everything looked spotless. In front of me stood three Supercritical Fluid Extraction Systems manufactured by the Waters Corporation. Equipped with a computer interface and CO2 recycle options, capable of extracting at pressures of 5,000 psi, the machines cost about $165,000 each.

Organa makes hash oil using a process called supercritical CO2 extraction, the same technique for decaffeinating coffee and drawing essential oils from rose petals for perfume. Supercritical CO2 is an organic compound that exhibits properties of a gas as well as a liquid. Because of this, the CO2 is able to flow through the chopped marijuana as a gas would, but it also acts like a solvent, as a liquid would, pulling out the desired molecules of THC and the rest. To achieve this supercritical state, great amounts of pressure are needed, one reason the machines are so expensive.

By growing its own pot, Organa can make hash-oil products with consistent standards and strengths. Its hash-oil cartridges are designed to be used with O.penVAPE's electronic vaporizers but can be used with others as well. According to the company, it is selling cartridges at a rate of one every ten seconds, more than 250,000 per month. To keep up with demand, Organa has about ninety thousand square feet of indoor grow space in Colorado. It has recently bought a three hundred-acre ranch in Pueblo; city and banking officials are working with the company, because they believe it will bring jobs and commerce.

Among Organa Labs' most intriguing products are CannaTabs, small tablets designed to dissolve under the tongue. The tabs are sold in pill bottles, twenty-five milligrams per tab, and are available in several forms, including sativa, indica, and a hybrid. Sativa has a lot of THC, for an "up" feeling. Indica has a lot of CBD for sleep aid and pain relief. Patients can feel effects in as little as ten minutes, as opposed to thirty to forty-five for edibles.

"Our target market is a lot of people who haven't tried marijuana in twenty years, and now that it's in this really convenient dosage, they're willing to try it," Morgan said, leading me through the facility. In one area sat large industrial vacuum ovens. In another, women with surgical masks and gloves used syringes to fill cartridges with hash oil.

Going through Organa's extensively inspected, medical-grade lab—where, according to law, every batch of pot gets tested for strength and is given a bar code that follows it from field to dispensary—I couldn't help but think about all the Wooks I'd met over the preceding six months. Working as fast as possible, Sloth Bear can blast three pounds a day with his single-loop extractor. Organa's three CO_2 extractors can blast between sixty and 100 pounds a day; the company has recently purchased an extractor that can process ten times faster. As more and more states pass their own medical or recreational marijuana laws, companies like Organa—with millions in capital at their disposal—are poised to move into the market and dominate.

Skywalker and his fellows will likely never become giant players like Morgan. But it's also hard to envision a world where creativity, enthusiasm, and refined craft are trampled into dust. We live in an age of multiple choices. We can choose processed cheese or something funky from France. Wine in a box or wine from Italy. Hash-oil tablets from Organa or shatter from Jedi Extracts. As long as there are people like Skywalker and Sloth Bear, there will be makers of erl. For these guys, hash oil is about much more than money. To them, dabs are art, dabs are lifestyle.

The last time I saw Skywalker in person, I was dropping him off at his house after the Secret Cup Finals. He was exhausted from lack of sleep but happy. He had made a new connection with a respected grower who had asked Skywalker to shepherd him through the complexities of the hash-oil marke—and to split the profits.

As he gathered his stuff, I told Skywalker I was on my way to Denver because I wanted to see how a government-regulated lab operated with clean CO_2. After all the sneaking around, all the paranoia and janky connections, I was jazzed about witnessing an operation that was legal and safe.

Standing outside the car on the passenger side, James "Skywalker" Johnson leaned into the open window.

"That CO2 shit tastes like ass breath," he said.

THE POT DOCTOR WILL SEE YOU NOW

A LONG AND JANGLED DAY WITH ONE OF THE COUNTRY'S BUSIEST (AND MOST CHARISMATIC) CANNABIS MEDICAL PROFESSIONALS.

In a renovated building on the hipster fringes of LA's Skid Row, the pot doctor is open for consultation.

At ten in the morning an alarm is *chime chime chiming* from a laptop in one of two soundproofed cubicles built into the center section of this rectangular thousand-square-foot loft, which also includes a kitchen, a living room area and the curtained-off bedroom where the pot doctor sleeps. The queue of patients is already full, a virtual line running out the door, into the distressed white marble hallway—a forty-three-year-old mom with panic disorder; a fifty-nine-year-old man with back pain; a thirty-three-year-old clerk with chronic knee pain; a college kid who has trouble getting to sleep at night.

Most of the patients are referrals from an online marijuana delivery service, Eaze, that operates in ninety-some locations around the Golden State. Check the website, order up. Your weed, hash oil or edibles will be delivered to your door, usually within a half-hour.

But first—at least until pot is legalized in California for recreational use—you need a Medical Marijuana Identification card (MMID).

That's where the pot doc comes in.

Chime chime chime

Don Davidson flicks a key on his laptop and the face of his first patient appears large on his screen.

"Nice to meet you!" he says into built-in microphone, upbeat and professional, a little bit amped, moving through his practiced patter at a fair clip.

A graduate of the Virginia Commonwealth University School of Medicine in Richmon, Davidson is thirty-one. He would rather be known by something more dignified than pot doc, something like cannabis doctor, or marijuana MD, but generally, that's what people say: *I need to see the pot doc.* Someday, he hopes, he'll be serving people's medi-card needs in every state in the nation—and selling him his complete line of Dr. D. Products.

At the moment, Davidson is the lead physician for EazeMD, a California-based on-demand telemedicine service that pairs licensed physicians with California patients seeking access to medical marijuana. Eaze makes no money from the referral, but approved patients gain immediate access to delivery. By the end of the usual twelve-hour workday, the pot doc and his rotating crew of part-time MDs—working from their own private offices across the state—have recommended cannabis to dozens of patients, who pay the doctors $40 each for their one-year certification, recognized at all dispensaries across the state ($30 for the consultation, $10 for the actual certificate, which is mailed to the patient's home).

As recently as three years ago, a California MMID required a visit to a brick-and-mortar doctor's office. The settings tended to be a bit tawdry; you got the feeling the physicians were on their last hurrah. In some offices, there wasn't even an actual doctor. You sat down at a computer screen in an empty room and waited for one to appear. A medi-card was likely to cost $150 or more. And of course you had to go in person.

EazeMD is now in its second year; it is reportedly the largest telemedicine service for pot referrals operating at the moment in California. The queue is busy seven days a week, 10 a.m until 10 p.m. Sixty patients by 3 p.m. is standard, Davidson says. After 4 p.m., happy hour begins and the number of patients ramps up; it usually stays busy until closing time.

At six foot two and two hundred pounds, the young doctor more than fills his cubicle, which feels a little more expansive thanks to the wall of grimy windows that looks out into the windows of the other lofts around the center courtyard.

A former Division I college tennis player, Davidson is dressed in a skinny Hugo Boss tie and a Hugo Boss dress shirt that shows off a CrossFit-carved physique. His paleo breakfast—hard-boiled egg and avocado—is half-eaten on a paper plate atop the glass desk. Once in a great while, if he's running late, he will forgo the dress pants and Varvatos lace-ups and work in boxer shorts and flip-flops. To his patients he's just a smiling image on a computer screen or smartphone, on a secure version of Skype—a friendly thumbnail with blue eyes and a blondish faux-hawk.

"My name is Dr. Davidson," he says, "and this is a laidback visit, nothing to worry about. Let me run through your chart."

Don Davidson, MD, is one of a new generation of physicians who see therapeutic value in pot. He is equally an entrepreneur who sees the economic muscle his medical license brings to the biggest growth industry in the nation—valued in 2016, according to an article in *Forbes*, at $7.1 billion, a 26 percent rise over the previous year. Davidson, who declined to reveal his current income, has recently struck a deal with a group of investors that will bring him closer to one of his future goals—a brand of marijuana products of his own.

The son of an orthopedist and a successful catalog model named Kathy Loghry, Davidson grew up on the west side of Richmond, Virginia. While attending James Madison University in Harrisonburg, Virginia—a pre-med student with a modest record of victories as a member of the varsity tennis team—he got his first taste of business success when he helped his older brother start a fresh-baked cookie company on campus. It has since grown into a franchise.

Like many of the munched-out students who were ordering up Campus Cookies, Davidson did, indeed, inhale during his college years and beyond. "I didn't go out and party that much," he says. "I had a 3.9. I studied, worked hard, played sports. And then I smoked some pot on the side. A little cannabis didn't hurt. And it didn't turn me into a leprechaun. It was healthier than drinking, that's for sure."

The summer after his first year of medical school, Davidson started an outfit that led kayaking trips on the Chesapeake Bay. Later, while doing research at the University of Arizona, he opened a web-based date-coaching and lifestyle design service, Dr. D Lifestyle.

"It was just like *Hitch*," he says, referencing the Will Smith movie about a professional date doctor. "We did everything from self-confidence building to fashion help to programs for working out—all men's lifestyle stuff. How to cook better, what to wear, what to say, where to go. I even had one client fly me to Malaysia. It was going really well."

Meanwhile, Davidson says, while studying ventilator-associated pneumonia prevention in the emergency room, he began reading with interest about the sweeping changes that have been remaking the medical and recreational marijuana industries.

"I just saw the writing on the wall, dude," Davidson says with a sly laugh.

"The peer-reviewed papers are fascinating. The science behind this stuff is crazy exciting in a lot of different ways. You've got people using pot instead of taking ibuprofen every day. Or instead of using sleeping pills. Some people are using a high-dose regimen of CBD-rich oils (also called cannabidiol, the pain-relieving ingredient in marijuana) as an adjuvant when battling cancer (as an agent that helps to make their primary treatment work better). Or they're using high CBD oil for seizures. Or they're using it to help suppress Crohn's disease.

"What it comes down to is this: Would you rather have them try a cannabis tincture, three or four drops under their tongue every few hours for pain, appetite or sleep? Or would you rather give them Celebrex, Wellbutrin or Xanax—which all have side effects or are addicting?"

At ten in the evening Davidson closes his laptop; the *chime chime chiming* comes to an end. While his tie is still straight, his dress shirt has wilted in the late September heat; his faux-hawk has devolved into a more wind-tossed look. On his desk there is an empty yogurt container, a healthy energy drink and a few last uneaten chicken nuggets he'd baked for himself in between calls—he hasn't been outside his loft since last night.

All of the consultations with patients are protected by the usual doctor/patient privilege—Davidson can tell me only in general terms who he treated for what. Typically, he spends five to ten minutes with each, discussing general health, specific symptoms and the advantages of one type of marijuana-based therapy over another. In some cases, Davidson will follow up with links or informational PDFs. Often, he encourages a patient to contact him at a later date with further questions or results.

Over the course of the day, some patients logged in from laptops in dorms, or from desktops in kitchens or offices. Others were on smartphones—one was even driving his car; Davidson insisted he pulled over before continuing. Among the patients, who ranged in age from about nineteen to seventy-eight on this day, a majority complained of migraines, anxiety, pain, inability to sleep. There was a cancer patient; the marijuana helped with her appetite. Complaints of body dysmorphia, lower back pain and post-traumatic stress were also listed.

In his time in front of the laptop camera, Davidson says, what has struck him most about his patients is their general "distrust of Western medicine, of Big Pharma. They will do anything they can first before they take any sorts of pills. It's not just the people who believe in the healing powers of crystals. These are people who have seen what medicinal drugs can do. They've seen friends get addicted to opiates after a surgery. They've seen people like Prince, like Rush Limbaugh—there's an opioid epidemic ripping through America. If we could have a little cannabis in everyone's cabinet instead of a bunch of pills, I think we would be better off."

When he first dipped into cannabis, Davidson says, he didn't anticipate running an entire operation, or working twelve hours a day. For the last year, since he took over, he's been going seven days a week.

The track lights shining down from the high ceiling make deep hollows of his eyes. He hasn't been exercising enough lately. He doesn't get out as much as he should.

But he knows a bonanza when he sees it. He's willing to put in the time.

"After doing a surgical residency, I know how to sleep on the floor, eat shit, and get yelled at," he muses. "At least now I'm working for myself."

Drifting away from his cubicle, Davidson heads toward the living room side of the space, two big sofas and a TV. His part-time admin staff—a USC-trained registered nurse with experience running dispensaries, and an IT guy who sometimes sleeps on the couch after a long day—have left for the evening.

The loft is quiet and still. The sounds of weeknight domesticity swirl around the courtyard and drift in through the open windows—music and laughter, the clatter of plates, the yapping of a small dog. On one shelf is a display of pot paraphernalia used for instructional video posts—a large vaporizer, a bong, an assortment of vape pens for hash oil. On another is a collection of health supplements—vitamins and protein powders and energy boosts.

Everywhere around the room are partially packed boxes. Things have been going well. The lease on the loft expires soon. He's planning to move his operation to a house in Malibu with a view of the ocean. Like he said: If he's going to spend all day, every day in a cubicle seeing patients via the Internet, "it might as well be one at the beach with a big window."

Davidson lowers himself onto the sofa and uncoils, loosens his tie. He looks at his watch and sighs.

In barely twelve hours, it will begin again.

Chime. Chime. Chime.

He reaches for the bong.

THE MOST INTERESTING MAN IN THE WORLD, IN RETIREMENT

A CROSS BETWEEN JAMES BOND AND DON JUAN (WITH A DASH OF DON QUIXOTE), HE WAS INTERNATIONALLY KNOWN AND LOVED—UNTIL DOS EQUIS DECIDED TO SEND HIM TO MARS.

In retirement, The Most Interesting Man in the World is still pretty interesting.

He is lounging on a stack of throw pillows, on a bench overlooking a hillside terraced with grapevines, set among the lush green hills of LA's Topanga Canyon, smoking a fat Cuban cigar.

A pair of hawks circle overhead, riding the updrafts; in the distance, the blue sky meets the blue Pacific Ocean. The sun warms his face, deeply tanned with bronzer by a makeup artist, framed within the razor-sculpted lines of his familiar salt-and-pepper beard, which has been darkened here and there with a product called Liquid Hair. A small patch of lightly forested belly lies exposed by an errant flap of his untucked shirttail. The little hillock of pale skin rises and falls, rises and falls, measuring his even breaths.

The lookout spot is part of an estate that's been rented by an ad agency for a series of commercials about Luma, a new kind of wireless router system that provides network security for the home. Goldsmith is here to play himself—wise and wisecracking, the ultimate help-desk authority. *The web is a cesspool of digital sickness, and you're swimming in nothing but goggles.* A catered lunch for the fifty-person crew has just concluded. With another half hour to go before his next shot, Goldsmith has climbed the fifty or so steep stone steps that wind up the hill. Because he's wearing a brand-new pair of blue suede shoes—an inside joke among the wardrobers?—the soles are unscuffed and slippery. Faltering a bit along the trail, he rested his hand upon his son's forearm for balance.

His name is Jonathan Goldsmith. He is seventy-eight years old. Since 2006, when he first showed up in regional commercials as the brand spokesman for Dos Equis, a formerly obscure Mexican brewer owned by Heineken, Goldsmith has been known across the planet as the Most Interesting Man in the World. An ageless, debonair adventurer with a suave Latin delivery and big brass balls who has lived life to the fullest, his only regret was not knowing what regret feels like. A cross between James Bond and Don Juan (with a dash of Don Quixote), he became internationally known for his aristocratic bearing, his incredible feats of daring, his kindness to children, his addictive charm.

Over time, a series of clever ads painted a pointillist portrait: His shirts never wrinkled. He could parallel-park a train. His mother had a tattoo that says S-O-N. One time he went to a psychic—to warn her. Sharks had a week dedicated to *him*. His business card read, "I'll Call You." He was allowed to discuss *Fight Club*. His beard alone had experienced more than a lesser man's entire body. He lived vicariously through himself.

He was... the Most Interesting Man in the World.

Until last year, anyway.

"It was the company's decision," Goldsmith says. He shrugs his shoulders, blows a gray cloud of smoke into the air. His accent is classic New York City, where he was born. "They decided to go in another direction. They thought I was too old. They wanted to bring in a younger guy. They'd made a deal to sponsor the college football playoffs, I guess. They thought the demographics would be more favorable to connect with their audience."

For its part, Dos Equis played the exit to the hilt. They used the hashtag #adiosamigo and distributed life-size cardboard cutouts to grocery stores and bars around the world so fans could take selfies. They ran a sweepstakes, giving customers the chance to win some of the Most Interesting Man in the World's possessions, including his mariachi suit. His concluding commercial appearance, which aired in March 2016, was reminiscent of a state funeral, attended by fictional representatives from across the fictional globe.

After shaking hands all around and giving a set of keys to a Buddhist monk, the brand representative who saw Dos Equis sales rise more than 34 percent during his stewardship—taking the product from an unknown regional brand to one of America's most popular—boarded a rocket for a one-way trip to Mars.

He was replaced by a forty-one-year-old Frenchman. Initial response on the company's website wasn't good, as reported by TMZ:

Susan Brahm Czysz: I so miss the original guy. He was 10 times better. They really messed up those commercials.

Shelia Duncan: There is only 1 most interesting man in the world. And this guy is not it!!! Bring back the real Most Interesting Man... Please.

Saralea: They did that switch all wrong there. They should have said the most interesting man in the world is so interesting that he has a son! The most interesting DUDE in the world. Duhhh... can't be on board with this NEW interesting man. I don't buy it.

According to a poll by the research firm YouGov BrandIndex, the numbers agreed. Early numbers showed that brand consideration in the target age group dropped by more than half. "Millennials aren't finding the new Most Interesting Man in the World all that interesting," wrote Advertising Age.

"Of course, it turned out they were wrong," says the former Most Interesting Man in the World, tilting his head imperceptibly and raising an eyebrow. You can almost hear the strains of Flamenco guitar.

"You can't just act interesting, my friend. You have to be interesting."

At the time he landed the Dos Equis gig, Goldsmith had been knocking around New York and Hollywood for nearly half a century, scoring small parts in some 350 theater, TV, and film productions by his count. His specialty as an actor, he likes to say, was "falling off horses and getting killed in a variety of ways."

During the course of his career, he worked with Burt Lancaster and John Wayne, Shelley Winters and Joan Fontaine; caroused with playwrights Tennessee Williams and Arthur Miller; crossed egos with Dustin Hoffman; painted houses with Nicholas Colasanto (the guy who played Coach on Cheers); slept with a bevy of starlets, including Tina Louise, who played the hot marooned actress on Gilligan's Island, and "six vegetarians, nine Buddhists, eighteen nurses, six teachers, countless receptionists and one runner-up to Miss Florida."

Later, he started a production company with his great friend, the Argentine actor and bon vivant Fernando Lamas, who was married to Hollywood's favorite aquatic nymph, Esther Williams. At age sixty-seven, facing a roomful of much younger Latino actors who were auditioning to become the face of a new Mexican beer, Goldsmith would channel the accent and mannerisms of the departed Lamas, whose ashes Goldsmith had some years earlier sprinkled into the ocean from his sailboat. (Billy Crystal's archetypal playboy character, Fernando—"You look maaaaarvelous"—was another borrow from Lamas.)

The friend, lover, and colleague of stars—but never star himself—Goldsmith had long ago given up his Hollywood hopes by 2006, when he auditioned for the part of the Most Interesting Man in the World. At the time, he says, he was a desperate man, broke and broken, living in the bed of his 1965 Ford Diesel pickup truck in a cold-shower campground in Malibu.

As he tells me over the course of two days and writes in his forth-coming autobiography, *Stay Interesting*, Goldsmith's life story—to the extent it can be verified—seems every bit worthy of the persona he would later wear in public, albeit without the accent. Unlike his TV persona, there is a mix of heartbreak and tragedy with the adventure and triumph. As it turns out, the Most Interesting Man in the World was not always so cool.

Goldsmith was born in 1939 in New York City. His mother was Greta Roth, one of Harry Conover's Cover Girls. In the years follow-ing World War II, Conover was known for having the first ultra-elite modeling agency; the term "cover girl" was derived from Conover's early concepts. Looking back, Goldsmith says his mother might have lacked a certain innate ability to nurture. Case in point: When he was six months old, he says, she left him in a grocery store in Riverdale. ("Though she did remember to take her groceries," he adds.)

Roth had tragically lost her own mother when she was young, leaving her father to raise her and an older brother, which he did mostly by farming out the children to different relatives. Despite a "debili-tating deformity of his legs that made it difficult to walk," Goldsmith writes, his grandfather was "a radical eccentric, an intellectual and a drifter" who wandered the country for a time in a camper, lived on a pirate boat off Costa Rica, and helped start Muscle Beach. Emotionally, his mother and her brother were left to fend for each other.

Goldsmith's father was Milton Goldsmith. He too was an eclec-tic sort. Briefly a semipro basketball player, he later trained boxers. According to family lore, he'd beaten the New York City quarter-mile champion in a foot race while wearing street shoes. Later Milton settled down and became a PE teacher. A devoted outdoorsman, he taught his son to fly fish and shoot a Winchester .22 rifle. Jonathan's uncle once said to him: "Your father is the most successful man I know because he has no ambition at all."

After a short marriage, Goldsmith's mother divorced Milton and married Jerome S. Lippe, the owner of Leipzig and Lippe, which man-ufactured housewares, baskets, barbecues, and other home products. After a lavish ceremony in Havana, they took an apartment in a Park

Avenue hotel. There were servants and silver trays and a Haitian maid Goldsmith recalls as One-Eyed Betty, who believed in voodoo and went fishing with him in the reservoir. Lippe adopted the boy, and his last name was changed. In fact, even early in his acting career, Goldsmith went by the name Jonathan Lippe.

At age five, Goldsmith was packed off for a place he remembers as Mrs. Hunt's Boarding School in Cedarhurst, Long Island. His mother told the headmistress he was a "difficult child at home—a naughty, unloving, unmanageable boy." When he saw "the taillights of her taxi disappear," he writes in *Stay Interesting*, he ran as fast as he could, trying to catch her. Unsuccessful, he "hid under the yellow flowers of a forsythia bush," but was soon found and remanded.

In the coming years, Goldsmith would frequently go AWOL from the school and take a series of trains to his father's humble apartment in Harlem. Among his favorite memories of childhood were mornings when he'd "wake up on the couch under the sheets he kept for me in the closet," sleeping in one of his oversized T-shirts. "I've had trouble sleeping all my life, but never in those shirts. It was like a shield, and my father was my protector."

After a series of misadventures, disciplinary problems, and matriculations to different boarding schools, Goldsmith ended up back in public high school in Westchester County, where he played on the basketball team and met a friend (the only other Jew in the rural school) named Anthony Hatzenberg, who wore his hair slicked back and went by the nickname of Tony Mambo. It was Tony who took him into New York City and introduced him to his first hooker, who was "pretty enough" and wearing a long, oversized T-shirt. "Edie Matthews, bless her, made me a man," he writes in his book.

Always eager to earn money since it represented independence to him, Goldsmith worked throughout high school at a variety of jobs. He delivered newspapers, was a stock boy at a liquor store, and worked on a Christmas tree farm near the Sing Sing Prison. "Whenever they would execute somebody, the lights on our Christmas trees would grow dim," he recalls. He also worked at a number of Catskills resorts as a busboy, salad man, and waiter. One memorable afternoon he stuffed two thousand prunes with peanut butter. He was fired at every stop for one reason or another—side hustles, charging extra food to guests (which he'd eat himself), placing bets at the Saratoga racetrack for guests.

After two years at a Boston junior college, where he "majored in gin rummy and minored in dog handicapping" at the Wonderland Greyhound Park, Goldsmith returned to New York. Since he was small, Goldsmith says, he'd suffered from anxiety and night terrors; for his whole life, he says, he felt unwanted and insecure. He saw his first psychiatrist at age five or six and continued going to therapists on and off throughout his childhood, mostly to please the adults. After college, concerned about his son's future, his father sent him to meet a friend of his—Fredric Wertham, a well-known German-American psychiatrist and author most remembered for his crusade against violent imagery in mass media and comic books. This time, something clicked.

At the conclusion of their session, Goldsmith remembers vividly, Wertham told him: "Your mother, I feel sorry for her." For the first time in his life, Goldsmith says, he felt like someone truly understood him. Then the doctor told him he was going to arrange an introduction to Broadway director Philip Deacon, who was teaching acting classes on the Lower East Side.

Attending his first class, Goldsmith was asked to do an improv—a man carrying a heavy suitcase full of cash across a desert. "When I had finished, I looked around," Goldsmith recalls. "The entire class was standing and clapping. I had done something extraordinary, and it felt so natural. The applause alone was intoxicating. I knew from that moment my life would never be the same. I'd found my calling."

Goldsmith spent the next several years taking more acting classes, living in cold-water walk-ups, and playing small roles off Broadway and at regional theaters around the country. In 1961, he got his first big break in an early run of *Natural Affection* by William Inge (who would later invite him to his house in LA and propose taking a shower together). The play was directed by Harold Clurman, founder of the Group Theater in New York and the husband of legendary acting coach Stella Adler. The female lead in the play was Shelley Winters. After Goldsmith appeared again with Winters in a 1962 Broadway production of Tennessee Williams' *Night of the Iguana*, Winters urged him to come to Hollywood to meet her agent.

Goldsmith can't quite remember the exact year, but sometime around 1963 or 1964, he bought a used VW Bug and drove across the country to LA. He crashed with a friend from the Neighborhood Playhouse in New York, Walter Koenig, who would later become well-known for playing Chekov in *Star Trek*. On his first night in Hollywood, he saw The Doors at the Whisky a Go Go.

Over the next thirty years, Goldsmith would pursue the rocky life known to generations of Hollywood's Almost Famous—living in odd places (an abandoned frog farm), doing odd jobs (driving a garbage truck), and having odd experiences (locked out of a woman's house naked, his car broke down on the drive home; the responding officers thought he was insane). In time, he began to land roles, most of them small parts. He did a lot of Westerns: *Gunsmoke, Bonanza, High Chaparral, The Virginian* and *Hang 'Em High*. But there were also roles on *The Doctors, My Three Sons, Dynasty, Charlie's Angels* and *Knight Rider*.

Regardless: "Usually I was cast as a guy who was about to be killed," he says.

He was pushed off roofs in *T. J. Hooker, Dallas*, and *Streets of San Francisco* (in another episode he drowned in a bathtub). In other shows, he was mowed down by a machine gun, electrocuted, blown up by dynamite, run over by a car, pushed off a boat into a mucky swamp, and hanged from a gallows.

In *The Shootist*, the last film starring John Wayne, Goldsmith was killed by the Duke himself, shot in the forehead. The scene took nine takes. Wayne's gun had blanks, but off-camera, there was a prop man with an air gun who fired pellets filled with fake blood at Goldsmith's forehead, "leaving a nasty welt." The director of the film was Don Siegel, famous for *Invasion of the Body Snatchers*. After the scene was over, Siegel told him: "If it makes you feel any better, most of the people the Duke shoots turn out to be stars." It would take thirty-five years, but it turned out to be true.

On the other hand, Goldsmith had no trouble with social life. In the pages of *Stay Interesting*, he tells how he pissed off Clint Eastwood after "a dalliance" with his girlfriend during filming of *Hang 'Em High*. There was an affair with studio mogul Jack Warner's young girlfriend, with one of Groucho Marx's wives, with two congressmen's wives (both Republican), with a psychologist who liked to reverse roles, with a beautiful French model and her girlfriend, and Henry Fonda's mistress—the lovemaking was so boisterous, he writes, they broke the bed.

In time, Goldsmith says, the acting parts began to dry up. Facing sixty and still struggling, married, trying to raise and educate a family, he decided to end his acting career. "There was no doubt I worked hard to make it," he says. "I put in my best efforts. I was friends with a lot of stars. I knew plenty of people around town. I owned a production company with Fernando. But I just couldn't seem to get over the last hump. Finally, I decided, *Screw it. I'm done.*"

Instead, Goldsmith started a company that marketed waterless car-wash products. At one point, he says, he employed more than one hundred people and "was netting more than $150 million a year in profits," according to his book. He was married with children, lived in a custom-built house on 120 acres in the High Sierras and owned a sixty-foot sailboat. But after nearly a decade, for reasons he declines to discuss, the company disintegrated, Goldsmith says. His marriage soon followed.

By 2006, when the call came for the Dos Equis audition, Goldsmith was at his wits' end. "I had no income and lots of bills—attorneys, mortgage and more. I was looking at bankruptcy," he says. His sailboat, the one from which he'd sprinkled the ashes of his old friend Fernando, was on the auction block. With nowhere else to turn, he decided to give acting another shot.

After shaving in the sideview mirror of his truck, Goldsmith drove to the audition in Hollywood. The line of actors disappeared around the block, all of them younger and Latino. According to his agent, the Dos Equis people were looking for "a Hemingway kind of guy." For the audition, all the candidates would be asked to do an improv, ending with the line, "…And that's how I came to arm-wrestle Fidel Castro."

As he had in that first acting class so many decades ago on the Lower East Side, Goldsmith killed it. There was applause in the audition room. They called his agent that afternoon with the news.

Over the next decade, the Most Interesting Man in the World became part of the zeitgeist, a universally beloved figure, the ultimate personification of cool. Michael Jordan asked for a selfie with him. Leonardo DiCaprio crossed a restaurant to shake his hand. President Barack Obama invited him as the guest of honor to his exclusive fiftieth birthday weekend at Camp David with ten of his closest friends.

And then, in March of 2016, it was over.

"Honestly, it was a little bit of a shock," Goldsmith says. "But it was a hell of a run."

Back inside the rented estate in Topanga Canyon, at the commercial shoot for Luma, Goldsmith is in a dressing room on the first floor, being readied for his next scene. As the makeup artist touches up his face, the sound guy snakes a microphone cord around his torso. The wardrobe woman buttons a crisply ironed white shirt.

Goldsmith continues talking as the crew fusses, accustomed to the routine. He waves his unlit cigar for punctuation. He is warm and unguarded, accommodating even though I can tell it's a bit of a burden. Approaching his ninth decade, he is still vibrant. Later, though, between takes, I'll catch him in the chair fast asleep. But for the moment, he's feeling chatty. I've asked him about his Dos Equis commercial highlights—he's reminiscing about his various animal costars.

"They were fun, but they were dangerous," he says, sounding a little more like Woody Allen than Fernando Lamas. "Imagine being fifteen yards away from a wild rhinoceros. Or semi-wild, anyway. When they told me his name was Spike it didn't make me feel any better. The only thing between me and him was this kid with a little circus whip."

"Another time I worked with this puma," he continues. "He hated me. He had these big green eyes, and he just hissed at me and spit at me. But the one that frightened me the most was the barn owl. He would fly down and land on a gauntlet I had. He had these huge claws, and I could feel them clamping down. I worried that even if I moved wrong…"

Today, Goldsmith lives with his second wife, Barbara, the agent who got him the Dos Equis audition, on a rural property with views of the mountains near Manchester, Vermont, where he hunts, fishes, and chops his own wood, and where he still receives hundreds of letters from fans every month. When he's not there, he's either making public appearances or spending time visiting his five children (ages thirty-two to forty-seven), eleven grandchildren and seven great-grandchildren.

Last week, he introduced Jay Leno at a charity benefit. Next week, he's going to a ceremony on a Native American Indian reservation. This summer, he'll be hosting KAABOO, the high-end oldster music festival in Del Mar, California. He's spoken at Harvard twice. He's also a spokesman for the Make-A-Wish Foundation in Vermont and works closely with Hunger Free Vermont and other local charities. "Vermont is a very poor state," he says. "One out of five kids go to bed hungry. And we have a drug problem." He's active in politics as well, which is how he met Obama in the first place, during the former president's race for a second term.

While playing the Most Interesting Man in the World has made Goldsmith wealthy, beloved, and iconic, the effect goes much deeper. "When I was younger, I always felt slightly uncomfortable in a crowd," he says. "I never liked the party atmosphere, I never had the ability to laugh freely and wholeheartedly. I was always conscious of guarding myself, conscious of real or imagined insecurities. It was always like I was viewing life from a distance.

"So for me, playing him was amazingly liberating. He had facilities and ease that I didn't have. I enjoyed being that character. The reactions of people were astounding. Political figures. Sports figures. Celebrities. They all wanted to meet me. After I first met Obama I was driving home with my wife, and I said, 'This guy actually seems to like me. He's interested in me. How can that be?'"

It's like that thing they teach for self-improvement, I suggest. Becoming the person you project.

He looks at me earnestly. "I always knew I was a good person," he says, "but I never felt like I was a successful person. I do now. I feel a confidence that eluded me most of my life. There's a lot of wonderfully talented people in the world. Beautiful actresses, handsome actors, stars. But there's only one Most Interesting Man in the World."

GROWING ALMONDS IN THE DESERT

DESPITE A CRIPPLING DROUGHT, A FAMILY FARM IN CALIFORNIA'S CENTRAL VALLEY HARVESTS A BANNER CROP. HOW LONG WILL THEIR GOOD FORTUNE— AND THEIR WATER SUPPLY—LAST?

Six mornings a week, any time of the year, at the McDonald's restaurant off the Westley exit to California's Interstate 5, the owner-operators of Bays Ranch can be found at the same table by the window—two straw Stetsons and a gimme cap nursing cups of hot coffee, planning the upcoming day.

At five-thirty a full moon is still high in the western sky, illuminating the undulant folds of the dwarfish Coast Range, dirt dry in this third year of drought. At the foot of the mountains, red and white lights stream north and south along the great highway that traverses the length of the state, one of the many gargantuan projects—dams, bridges, tunnels, aqueducts—built to harness the rugged landscape during the last century, when America was keen on bending nature to its will. In California, state and federal water projects pump rivers uphill, transport salmon downstream, prevent spring floods, protect snail darters, hold back salty deltas from fields, and supply a large and thirsty southern populace with water from the north. Traveling the I-5, you can see clearly the California Aqueduct, an impressively large concrete canal, 130 feet across, that flows south past fertile green plots and cracked brown fields. If not for the ambitious machinations of politicians and engineers, the eternally green landscape of southern California would be coastal sage and desert. Despite the lack of rain, dire predictions, water rationing, hand-wringing—and a collection of regulations (and conflicting views) too complex for anyone but lawyers, biodiversity experts, and full-time farmers to clearly understand—the water continues to flow.

Beyond the artificial daylight of the highway-exit services stretches the darkness of the vast and fertile Central Valley. An oblong basin just east of the Pacific Ocean, protected on all sides by mountains, nourished by snowmelt and rushing streams and deep deposits of ancient water, the Valley is 60 miles wide and 450 miles long, ranging from the city of Redding south to Sacramento, Fresno, and Bakersfield, with San Francisco and Oakland at the western hip. Farms in the Central Valley produce 8 percent of the United States' total agricultural output on less than 1 percent of its total farmland. More than two hundred different crops are grown here; the Valley is the country's chief source of tomatoes, grapes, cotton, and apricots.

The Central Valley also produces about 80 percent of the world's almonds. A few years back, studies began to appear that made a strong case that almonds were, nutritionally, the single best food a person could eat, linked to all kinds of health benefits. A Harvard study found eating nuts decreased mortality rates by 20 percent.

Today, consumption of almonds is up more than 200 percent since 2005 (and nearly 1,000 percent since 1965). A thirsty crop, requiring water year-round, even when not producing, almonds are the Golden State's new gold—in 2013, the field price paid to farmers for almonds was about $2.50 a pound, up about 100 percent in the last decade. The 2013 crop was the second largest on record, 1.88 billion pounds, according to the Almond Board of California, down a bit from the previous year. For the fourth year, California exported more than 1 billion pounds of almonds, the second-largest export year on record. Prices for 2014 have not been tallied; like many commodities, the prices change over the year; farmers are paid averages in installments. Most agree the prices paid to farmers are likely to have been higher in 2014. Interestingly, in this time of Big Farma, 72 percent of the farms producing almonds in California are family owned; 51 percent are less than fifty acres in size. As of this season, nearly 50 percent of the 2,006 acres owned or leased by Bays Ranch is planted in almonds.

Sixty miles south of Oakland, the McDonald's is full of work boots and long-distance commuters; the city seems a world away. Business inside the restaurant is brisk, conducted in both Spanish and English. Every time the door opens, a loud overhead fan kicks on, blowing a strong curtain of air to the floor, a precaution against dust and flies. The Bays men wear zip hoodies over plaid shirts and blue jeans. They lean forward on their elbows, warming hands on Styrofoam cups, hat brims converging.

Gene Bays is eighty-eight. His father and grandfather were farmers. There is a fruit called a Bays cherimoya, pioneered by Gene's grandpa; only collectors eat or grow them anymore. Gene's grandpa owned ground near Ventura, California. Then suburban sprawl swept in like a desert haboob, leaving in its wake planned communities and malls and farmers with their pockets full.

Looking for a new piece, Gene and his wife, Eleanor, drove north in 1957. A real estate agent showed them a couple of places. They liked the one in Patterson. It was three hundred acres, $1,200 an acre. The land was planted in alfalfa. The house was there, the two sheds. The Bays couldn't afford to buy the entire plot; luckily, there was a neighbor who wanted some, too. Over the years, Bays has added ground when able—today, a family farm must be big enough to compete with the large corporations that are increasingly producing our food. Or find an expensive crop that pays the bills.

Ken Bays, fifty-five, is Gene and Eleanor's youngest, their only son, one of three children. He and his wife, Michele, a UCLA-trained nurse who teaches vocational nursing at a nearby trade school, live about a mile from the ranch, on their own piece of ground. Ken is an assistant fire chief at the Westley Volunteer Fire Department and a member of the board of the West Side Hulling Association, the cooperative where local farmers bring their nuts for processing. He is also chairman of the board of the West Stanislaus Irrigation District. Due to the complex regulations and the patchwork nature of the land they farm, Bays Ranch is located in three different irrigation districts. To water a field, Ken has to call the district two days in advance to order the water they've previously pumped from their wells into the federally built Delta Mendota Canal for storage in the San Luis Reservoir. The Bays have been banking water on and off since the seventies, when drought and high interest rates—and a heavy reliance on a single cash crop—threatened the future of the ranch. In essence, they're watering their crop with the water they've put away for just such a time as we're in. All of Bays's fields have drip systems or microsprinklers. (The times of flooding fields are over for most.) The sprinklers run for twelve to twenty-four hours. Last year, Bays Ranch used a lot of water, about three feet of water per acre, at a cost of about $115 an acre-foot (one acre-foot of water equals about 326,000 gallons), most of which reflects the price of electricity and fuel for pumping the water.

Aside from his time at California Polytechnic State University, two hundred miles away in San Luis Obispo, where he earned a bachelor's degree in ag business, Ken has never worked anywhere else but Bays Ranch, not even for a summer, which he sometimes regrets. He can take apart anything and fix it. He can weld. He can handle electricity. In the prefab barn beside his house are three combines, huge machines for harvesting grain crops. In front of the barn is a fifty-foot houseboat, up on blocks, undergoing renovation. When Ken was in high school, the whole family used to spend summer Sundays at Lake McClure, about an hour and a half east; a large group of local farmers and friends did the same. (In fact, that's the place Ken first got cozy with Michele, though they didn't date until college.) Years later, he and Michele would take their four kids to the lake, too. The primary function of the artificially created Lake McClure is to provide irrigation water to about two thousand farms in that area. As of July, the lake was down to 25 percent of its capacity; officials were racing to have 240 boat owners move their ungainly vessels. Ken continues to work on his; he figures he'll have it done this winter.

Ken crunches the numbers and handles all the ordering for Bays Ranch—fuel, pesticides, pipeline, gypsum for the orchard beds. It may be a family farm, but it's still a corporation that runs itself with an annual production loan of about $2 million. (Low interest rates keep the money cheap.) There is a year-round staff of fifteen to twenty laborers. Every single item of cost for every one of their twenty-eight different fields and dozens of pieces of heavy machinery must be broken down and recorded.

Ken's only son is Daniel Bays, twenty-eight. He's a fifth-generation California farmer. Like his dad, there is nothing else he ever wanted to do. Daniel is also a volunteer firefighter and an avid civic booster—the other day he spent five hours in the heat with a bunch of other men, baking sixteen hundred pounds of potatoes in a large propane-fired outdoor oven for a fundraiser at Patterson High School, which Ken, Michele, Daniel, and his three sisters all attended.

Besides the ground they own and lease (they pay an annual fee per acre and all the expenses and split the take with the lessor) and their interest in brush-shredding and custom-farming businesses (custom farming means being hired out by other farmers to harvest their crops), the Bays men also share three identical sets of bemused blue eyes, with happy crinkles at the corners, and a habit of punctuating conversations with a series of dry chuckles, *he he he*.

"They'll finish the almonds today, right?" Ken asks Daniel. Like most in these parts, he pronounces the word *ammonds*. The trees take three to four years of caretaking before a crop will grow. The nuts are harvested with a series of odd, ingenious machines created especially for their purpose. The first is a three-wheeler, low-slung (so as not to damage the branches of the trees as it prowls between the rows). It has an arm with a pincer grip, wrapped in vulcanized rubber, that grabs the trunk of each tree and shakes like the dickens, causing a heavy rain of nuts. Locals joke this is what happened to the pronunciation of the word *almond*—the *L* was shaken out of it.

"I think we're in pretty good shape," Daniel says. At Cal Poly, he departed from his father's path and studied agricultural engineering, worked at a different ranch or ag-related profession every summer. In the family corporation, you could say he's the chief operating officer.

He does the bulk of the heavy lifting on the ranch, hauling equipment around on a semitruck, working on machinery, and overseeing the Spanish-speaking crew, some of whom are from the same family and have been with Bays for as many as twenty-five years.

"Leonardo must have had to leave *early* yesterday," Grandpa Gene interjects, mentioning one of the most tenured workers; his eyebrows rise, raising the brim of his sweat-stained Stetson. In fact, Leonardo's absence was the reason the field wasn't finished yesterday. Nothing gets by Grandpa Gene, a spry man who survived polio and a broken back before he was old enough to get his driver's license. The last two times his wife insisted he see a doctor, he ended up in the hospital, once for an appendectomy, once for a triple bypass. Now he goes voluntarily for checkups. Each morning and evening, he and Eleanor walk a mile. Conveniently, they can do so without having to leave their own property, strolling down a dirt road between two orchards.

Gene still opens the bills and writes the checks. A former volunteer firefighter himself, he drives his white pickup to the fire station most afternoons at 4:00 p.m. for coffee with the guys at the Westley VFD. He's been on the board of the Del Puerto Water District for more than forty years; he's served as chairman for a decade. An hour from now, after his breakfast, he'll be inside the Bays Ranch office, an outbuilding behind his back patio. He and Ken have facing desks. Daniel's is against one wall. Their computers are all networked together; they have their own domain. They are beta-testing an iPad program that promises to save time.

"Leonardo had a doctor's appointment," Daniel explains.

"It's fine," Ken says. "He'll finish up there today before you guys do the walnuts at George's place?"

"There's about a quarter of the field left to pick up. Good thing we ain't had no rain," Daniel says ruefully.

"Good thing," says Ken.

They all chuckle, *he he he.*

It's been about three months since any measurable precipitation has fallen in the region, just a brief summer storm that did more harm than good—in fact, rain at the wrong time can ruin a crop, causing mold or other damage. In the newspapers it says that farmers have pumped so much water from their wells that the ground in the Central Valley is sinking. Federal irrigation water to the area's farmers was cut off in 2014. According to a University of California study, at least 5 percent of cropland is fallow and state agriculture has suffered $1.5 billion in losses. More than seventeen thousand farm jobs have disappeared.

Yet over the past month or so, it's become apparent that Bays Ranch is having a good harvest, as it has for the last several years. Last month, it took hundreds of contract workers with buckets and ladders more than three weeks to pick the entire Bays apricot crop by hand—Ken estimates they took four thousand tons from about eight hundred acres, bound for jars of Smucker's jelly and cans of Del Monte and S&W. According to the Apricot Producers of California, the final tonnage harvested for the 2014 season was greater than the previous year, which was greater than the year before that.

Hanging around Bays farm in October for the almond and walnut harvest, walking through Bays's orchards—which ripened about two weeks early this year due to the unusual summer heat, the men believe—it has been pretty clear from the amount of nuts on the ground and in the trailers headed to the huller, where huge dunes of processed nuts wait to be outshipped, that almond yields will be strong this year, as they have been the last five, according to the California Almond Association.

Amid the ringing of the fryer alarms and the dinging of the cash registers, the din of the customers, the roar of the passing traffic, the morning at McDonald's is cool and cacophonous. I point out the obvious: Despite dire predictions about water and weather and the future of the family farm, it seems like Bays Ranch is doing pretty well this season.

Three identical sets of blue eyes click my way.

Nobody's chuckling.

Daniel Bays pulls off the gravel road beside an almond orchard. On the back window of his pickup is a decal from Cal Poly and another from the Aircraft Owners and Pilots Association—in college, on a lark, he earned his license to fly. Daniel says he likes having that James Bond feeling of being able to handle any vehicle or piece of machinery put in his path—and being able to fix it, too. Part of being a pilot, he says, is knowing he can go anywhere he wants, even if he just prefers to stay here.

We have just crossed the Delta Mendota Canal, as we do several times a day on the way to and from the ranch and fields. Water policy allows Bays Ranch and others to pump well water into the canal, which flows into the "bank" at the San Luis Reservoir. After the payment of storage fees and a shrinkage charge to accommodate evaporation, the banked water can be sent to any of the Bays fields that are in proximity to the source well.

Bays Ranch has a "decent" supply of well water spread over a total of ten wells—it turns out asking a man about his well water is touchy business, akin to asking about the size of his harvest. But all the Bayses agree, and studies show, that groundwater in the Central Valley is at critical and historic lows. Grandpa remembers digging wells that struck water at fifty feet. Water diviners and well-drilling companies in the area are booked out nearly a year; neighbors are going down many hundreds of feet to find water. And the well water is saltier now than ever. Too much salt is bad for the plants; if it's too salty, the water cannot be pumped into the canal for banking. As we make our rounds, we pass other folks' orchards with leaves browned at the edges, a telltale sign of excess sodium. As it is, only two of the Bays wells can be used for banking water; the rest are too salty. Because the well pumps work at a relatively low capacity, in order to cover the banked water used this past spring and summer, Bays had to pump well water into the canal twenty-four hours a day, every day, from March through October. Last year their electric bill was $432,000.

Abutting the western side of Bays's properties is a stretch of the Governor Edmund G. Brown California Aqueduct, built in the 1960s during the administration of current governor Jerry Brown's father. The younger Brown has just muscled to passage a series of initiatives designed to add more capacity to the water system; part of the plan calls for the digging of huge tunnels beneath the Sacramento-San Joaquin Delta itself. As could be expected, the plan is controversial. If you wanted, you could stand on Bays ground and throw a bucket on a rope into the aqueduct. You could pull it up and water a tree. But the Bayses can't. The water is not theirs. It's going to southern California. Central Valley farmers who needed extra water this past summer could find it on the market for about $1,500 to $2,000 an acre-foot.

Daniel heads crossways through the rows of almonds, checking on the progress of his crew. Daniel has his mom's peaches-and-cream complexion and her gift for book learning; he was number four in his high school class of two hundred at Patterson High. He put off entering college for a year to serve as a state officer of Future Farmers of America, traveling around California and doing community outreach events to spread the gospel of farming. Grandma Eleanor always wanted Daniel to become a doctor. Her father was a farmer, too. She's lived through the Depression, recessions, a world war, droughts, times when interest rates were up past 18 percent. "What's so wrong with having a profession to fall back on?" she'd ask.

But Daniel grew up playing in the fields and orchards, watching the men work in the shop. By age ten he was driving a tractor during the apricot harvest. To this day there is rancor in his voice when he discusses Patterson High's refusal to allow him to take a welding class because it interfered with his college-prep classes. On a ranch, everything you can't do yourself means money paid to someone else.

When Daniel was young, this part of the San Joaquin Valley was known as the Apricot Capital of the World—there were signs everywhere. Then tastes and tariffs changed, NAFTA and the EU, and the Bayses ended up taking a shaker to their orchards and plowing under the fruit—the prices being offered were too low to pay for picking. The ranch was nearly ruined. According to Ken, they're still paying back loans from those years, which had to be refinanced because there was not enough income from their crops—operating loans are typically issued year to year and taken by the farmer in installments. Some of the loan money went to diversifying—planting a lot more almonds. And then, with the help of providence (the farmer's familiar friend and foe), came the nutritional and scientific findings.

Currently, Bays has about eight hundred acres of apricots, one hundred of walnuts, and one hundred of row crops—beans, Italian tomatoes for paste, and melons. Row crops like beans help enrich and rejuvenate the soil between plantings of orchards, which are typically pulled up and replanted every twenty-five years. (During the crisis of the nineties, Bays was forced to pull out apricot orchards that were only ten.) Seven hundred acres are planted with almonds. Besides the produce, the orchards provide a year-round panoply of simple beauty—the flurries of pink and white petals in the spring, the summer's fecundity, the winter's stark bare limbs, all of the trees planted so carefully in their soldier-straight lines. To make sure the rows are laid precisely, some tractors these days are equipped with GPS; if you have a problem with the onboard computer, the IT man drives his Toyota right into your field for a service call.

Bays almond trees are generally planted in rows twenty feet apart with sixteen feet between each tree. The largest two orchards are Field 16, 110 acres, also called Bondietti, after the family from whom they lease the ground, and Field 26, 90 acres, called Baldwin, after the road it's on. All of the property is located on the west side of Stanislaus County. The quilt of acreage—some of it owned, some of it leased—stretches in patches for nearly twenty miles. Daniel likes to joke about driving miles and miles every day and going nowhere. He has more than two hundred thousand on his F-150. A newer truck was totaled last spring when he was involved in a tragic fatal accident with a motorcycle rider one afternoon near the farm. Daniel was not charged by police with any offense. It was a deeply sorrowful event, he says.

Almond trees are actually two plants grafted together. First rootstock is planted; the varieties Bays uses have been crossbred to withstand various insects, viruses, molds, and wet conditions—Nemaguard, Lovell, and Hansen.

About a year later, once the root plant takes hold, the almond is grafted onto the top. Bays grows a large number of varieties—Nonpareil, Carmel, Wood Colony, Sonora, Butte, Padre, Fritz, Monterey, and Aldrich. Most almond strains require cross-pollination, meaning that in order for a flower to be pollinated, it must receive pollen from a different variety of flower from a different variety of tree. There have been some new varieties bred that are self-pollinating, but bees are still needed to move pollen from flower to flower. (The decline of a thriving bee population is another difficult issue.) With more varieties, which tend to bloom at different times, there is also a better chance for pollination. If there is rain and cold weather for several days, for instance, few bees will be out "working" the flowers. There are also different prices and markets for different varieties—growing different strains helps spread out risk. Finally, diverse tree strains mean a more prolonged harvest season, up to three months rather than three weeks. Bays has millions invested in harvest equipment. The more they can use the machines, the better, another reason for the custom work.

The shaker has already been through this section—a machine so delightfully purposeful you can't help but smile when you see it in action: One tree in the still and solemn line starts shaking like crazy, and then stops, and then the next one starts up, and then the next, all the way down the line, and all the nuts pelting down each time on the glass and metal (and air-conditioned) driver's cab like a sudden squall.

The sweeper comes next; it looks like a large orange four-wheeled armadillo with round brush legs. At the moment, a third machine is sucking up the nuts and spitting them into a trailing cart. When the cart is full, it will be pulled by tractor and dumped into the portable elevator; the nuts ride up a conveyor belt into a semitrailer. When that is full, Daniel will drive the short distance in the Bays semitruck to the huller.

All over the ranch—beside fields, inside various barns, on whole lots dedicated to storage—are uncounted tons of *stuff* needed for farming. Tractors and attachments and parts and irrigation pieces and specialized machines; behind Grandpa's house, in one of the garages, Bays has an entire hardware store of spare parts, all of them stored in cubbies and orderly rows, and an entire welding operation, the immediate atmosphere fragrant with a familiar agricultural musk—rust and oil, old grass and dust and time. There are huge tanks behind Ken's house for fuel and insecticides; it wasn't until after high school that Daniel filled up his truck at a gas station. Though much of what Bays buys is found at auction for good prices—the reason, for instance, Ken has *three* combines in his barn; you always need spare parts, right?—the sheer accumulation is staggering. The assumption, of course, is that all this stuff will be needed by the next generation ... and then the next.

The harvesting machine moves row by row at a fast clip, kicking up a smoke screen of red dust and diesel exhaust. Though it is October, the temperature is still over ninety; the sun feels intense on the skin. There is a distinct smell of ripe men in the air. The average yearly temperature in these parts is up about two degrees in the last hundred years, which could be due to greenhouse gases and global warming, or could be due to the clearing of land for agriculture. Or it could be due to human habitation—houses, buildings, cars, roads, factories. Or maybe it's happening as part of a larger cycle that humans can't fathom. As it is, the very ground of the Central Valley is receding as the water from the spongy aquifers is depleted. The longer the drought lasts, the more we rely on groundwater, which takes decades or centuries to replace.

The air in the Central Valley is historically bad two seasons of the year. During the summer months, emissions from fossil fuels are cooked into a thick soup of ozone by the sun. During the winter, fine particulate matter becomes the issue, the result of diesel fuel, fires, wood burning for heat, and other sources of combustion. (And then there's the methane from animal waste.) Back in the early sixties, California was a punchline for smog jokes. Over the years, with strong standards and expensive gas, the air was cleared again. But these dry times have created more temperature inversions (and more dust in the atmosphere); a layer of warmer air traps cooler air below, forcing the particulates and pollution to the ground. According to experts, heat and extreme drought have worsened smog in California in the past year, stalling decades of progress toward cleaner air. Usually rain helps to wash the air clean.

As Daniel walks through the rows of trees, he habitually reaches down and picks up a nut, or pulls one off a tree that was shaken but not released. Almonds are actually seeds. There is a green husk; inside is something that looks like a peach pit. Straight off the tree, the hull of the nut is easy to crack with your fingers. The meat is firm and delicious. It tastes like almond extract, but not so sweet.

"The drought years are what separate the men from the boys," Daniel says, stooping to pick up another *ammond*. "Believe it or not, sometimes, in a drought year, you'll make the best crops and have the most cash flow you'll have out of any other year."

I look at him. There's a crisis at hand, isn't there? Farmers are pulling up orchards; so much farmland fallow; billions in losses.

Yet in the coming weeks, Bays will get some final tallies and discover that its almond orchards yielded about two thousand pounds per acre this year. This is slightly down from last year but still considered a bumper crop, mirroring the statewide reports. (It is typical of trees that have been pumping out large harvests, as have Bays's over the past four or five years, to take a rest for a season or two and produce smaller yields, Ken says.) Bays Ranch will not know exactly how much money it made from the Fisher Nut Company, Stewart & Jasper, and Blue Diamond until the end of 2015. Like everything else in farming, the answer is... complicated. Prices are expected to be strong—higher demand, slightly smaller crop. As I write, a booth at my local farmers' market in San Diego is retailing Bays raw almonds for eleven bucks a pound.

"When there's no rain, we have more control over the growing conditions," Daniel explains. "Usually we have good sun. We have good warm weather. And right now we've got the water. We can control things. We know exactly what the crop needs to produce at an optimum level. If the crop gets rained on at the wrong times, you have a lot of different pest problems and moisture problems. You can lose a lot of your crop if the nuts are on the ground and it happens to rain."

So in a way, rain can be a detriment?

Daniel shrugs his shoulder, palms up. His fingernails are dirty from cracking almonds. He chuckles, *he he he.*

Most days, Daniel and Ken meet at home for lunch, the same house where Daniel and his three younger sisters grew up, the houseboat up on blocks in the driveway. If Michele is not off teaching a class, she still cooks the boys three meals a day. At the moment, Daniel has his own house in town, but he goes there only to sleep.

This afternoon, Daniel's eldest sister, Marie, is home, too. She's twenty-six, has a degree in ag management from UC Davis. Her job is similar to Daniel's—she oversees workers and fields of produce, makes decisions about watering, fertigation (liquid fertilizer released through the sprinkler systems), harvesting, and the like. Only she does it for a big nursery and receives a regular paycheck.

Marie is an attractive young woman with blond hair and a distinct resemblance to her kin—the blue eyes and wiry frame, the muddy shit kickers left by the door. She lives down the road in a house that's been in the family for years. Likewise, there's a big fancy house directly across the street from Michele and Ken's place that some people from the city built and then decided to sell. Ken wanted the land for orchards; the big house came with it. Now they rent it out for special occasions, and the relatives stay there during holiday visits. Marie's two sisters—Christine, twenty-two, and Theresa, twenty—are away at college.

Michele has made sandwiches—avocado, tomato, and cheese with pesto. We share an oval table. Before anyone eats, we join hands in prayer.

Daniel reports the morning's good news. Earlier he'd met the county extension agent at one of the fields, a fifty-acre plot where they'd just harvested melons. He'd asked if Bays would be part of a University of California study on fumigants.

Fumigants are used to rid the soil of pests and disease. Prior to planting, the chemicals are injected about eighteen inches under the ground by a tractor with big shanks, connected to large jugs of chemicals, one hundred to two hundred gallons each, which ride on the top of the rig. The chemicals they'll be injecting include chloropicrin, first manufactured during World War I for use as a chemical weapon. It helps farmers rid the soil of a broad spectrum of unwanted life, including fungi, insects, and rodents. Historically, chloropicrin has been found most effective when used in combination with methyl bromide, which has been found to be extremely harmful to the ozone layer. For this trial, the experimenters will be working with a combination of chloropicrin and Telone—thought to be more ecologically sound.

Scrubbing your ground of pests means better crop yields. And after the test is over, they'll be able to plant whatever they want. It's like winning a small-farm lottery. There is minor jubilation around the table.

"I just went to a training session and they talked all about chloropicrin and Telone," Marie says. "They like that combo best—well, methyl bromide is best if you can get it."

"Can you even get that anymore?" asks Michele; she grew up in town, but her dad was a field agent for Spreckels Sugar. And of course, she's been a farmer's wife for three decades. Ken also does a little farming with one of her brothers, primarily almonds for Blue Diamond.

"You can only get methyl if you're a strawberry grower," Marie says with a touch of pride. *Her* company grows strawberries.

"Maybe you wanna grow some strawberries on one of our other pieces?" asks Daniel, *he he he.*

"We can *say* we're gonna grow strawberries and then change our mind after it's fumigated," suggests Ken, *he he he.*

"That's why Joe wanted you to rent that piece of ground from him over there in Livingston," Daniel says, speaking of a neighbor.

"Get that field cleaned right up!" Ken says.

"And then he can plant ammonds in it," Daniel says.

"Oh yeah, I'm sure of that," Marie says ruefully.

It grows quiet around the table as we chew. I mention that a lot of people portray farmers these days as the bad guys—using harmful chemicals, injecting animals with hormones, releasing emissions into the air, pumping the aquifers dry, killing the environment.

"You're portrayed as someone who's just out here raping the dirt, trying to suck every last penny out," Daniel says. Everyone nods in agreement. "But if you're doing that, you're not going to be in business very long. How much more of an environmentalist can you be than making your living off the land and looking for the long-term betterment of it?"

"We want to have something to leave for the next generation," Ken says. "And hopefully they can carry it on, and hopefully it will be carried on after that."

I mention the drought, the climate. A lot of hope is needed.

"We've had droughts before," Daniel says. "Things cycle. If you look over a hundred-year period of your rain cycles and water cycles, we're not that far out of whack. I think a lot of it is the media hype, drumming up the shock factor. The big difference now compared to, say, 1977, when we had the last big drought, is the regulatory environment. We've been dealing with political droughts for the past five or six years—really the past twenty years—but the past five or six have been some of the worst. Let's face it, they're doing more to protect the snail darter and the salmon than they are to protect the food supply."

Marie frowns. "In the future, I think things are going to be even more regulation based—there are so many regulations and safety trainings and paperwork that are required of people who want to be in the farming industry nowadays. But I like to think positive. I think people are always going to have to eat, so the farming industry is a good place to be."

"There's always some type of crisis facing us, whether it's water or weather or markets," Daniel says. "If every time there was a crisis we just threw up our hands, we'd go out of business. Part of the balancing act is risk management over the long term."

Although there's been a lot of criticism this past year about permanent plantings and thirsty crops like almonds, Ken and Daniel insist that the water requirements are not that much different from cotton or tomatoes or an annual crop. Not to mention the record prices almonds and walnuts are bringing.

"With higher prices, you can afford to pay more for the water, more for fuel—it's all inflationary," Daniel says. "That's the kind of thing we get frustrated about. If we could have had these prices with the water we had eight years ago, we'd be rocking and rolling—but that's farming. Nothing's ever going to be 100 percent your way. If it was easy, everyone would do it."

"You know what farmers always say," Michele adds. "We don't need to go to Las Vegas. We gamble every single day."

Everybody cracks up.

Grandpa Gene and Grandma Eleanor are out for their morning walk. As always, they bring along Tweety, their white maltipoo. It's not unusual for people to drop off unwanted dogs out here in the country; that's how Tweety came to live with them. The Bays have seen a lot of strays over the years, but Tweety is different. "She's a real keeper," Eleanor says. Walking on their own property, they don't need a leash or a plastic bag.

At seven in the morning, the sun is low on the horizon, round and orange in the east; to the west the moon is still high, full and brightly extravagant, above the Coast Range—the fur of straw-brown vegetation glows warmly in the soft light. The couple moves at a decent pace down a dirt road, with almond orchards on both sides, the mountains visible to the west through the newly pruned trees. A half mile out, at the junction with a third orchard, they stop and turn around.

"You're doing pretty good this morning, Mama," Gene says, adjusting his Stetson.

"The morning's better than the evening," Eleanor says. "Sometimes I have to stop and catch my breath."

They were both raised in Ventura, which is now part of the suburban sprawl that flows northwest from Los Angeles. They've been married sixty-four years.

"Your dad grew beans and sugar beets," Gene says.

"And avocados and lemons," Eleanor adds.

"And we had avocados, almonds, walnuts, beans, tomatoes, different things," Gene says.

"Does that smell like smoke?" Eleanor asks.

"I smell a skunk," Gene says.

"*Tweety*," Eleanor calls. The dog scampers over. "You'd better stay right here so you don't get sprayed. Come on Tweets, 'cause you're a keeper."

We walk a little farther, eyes peeled.

"Gonna be another hot one today," Gene says.

"I liked it down there in Ventura," Eleanor says. "You didn't get the heat. The first year we moved up here, in '57, it was the hottest summer I think we ever had, and the foggiest winter. We used to get what they call tule fog. It was so thick in the mornings. And the kids had to go to school."

"You couldn't see your hand in front of your face," Gene says.

"You couldn't see your hand," Eleanor says. "But we haven't really had that kind of fog for several years now."

"Not for several years," Gene says.

"Not like it used to be."

"Nothin's like it used to be," Gene says.

What do you think about the drought and the weather, all that?

Grandpa Gene chews on the question for a few steps. "Everything repeats," he says. "You stick around long enough and everything goes around."

"The weather's the weather," Eleanor says. "There's nothing you can do to change it."

"Well, the weather ain't been bad this week," Gene says. "You should come when it's *really* hot" *he he he.*

We walk a bit farther in silence, back in the direction of the barns and the house. Gene gestures with his left hand toward an almond orchard. "This here is our home piece," he says. "That's what came with the house."

Eleanor nods in affirmation. This is where it all started. Three kids, thirteen grandchildren. Two thousand and six acres. A life.

"This is good dirt here," Gene says. "It's been good."

We stand a moment admiring the view of the mountains through the trees, the lightening sky, clear and cloudless.

"There's supposed to be a complete change in weather next week," Eleanor says.

WILL THE PUBLIC EVER GET TO SEE THE "DUELING DINOSAURS"?

AMERICA'S MOST SPECTACULAR FOSSIL, FOUND BY A PLUCKY MONTANA RANCHER, IS LOCKED UP IN A SECRET STORAGE ROOM.

The Dinosaur Cowboy sits behind an old desk in the dusty basement workshop of the ranch house where he grew up, wearing a denim shirt and blue jeans, his thinnish brown hair bearing the impression of his black Stetson, which he's left upstairs in the mudroom, along with his boots. Behind him, peering down over his shoulder from its perch atop an antique safe, is the fearsome, dragon-like head of a horned *Stygimoloch*, a replica of an important fossil he once found. The way it is mounted, jaws agape, it appears to be smiling, captured in a moment of prehistoric mirth.

The Dinosaur Cowboy is smiling, too. You could probably say it's an ironic smile, or a little bit of a grimace. His real name is Clayton Phipps. A wiry forty-four-year-old with a weathered yet impish face, he lives on the ranch with his wife, two sons, a few horses and eighty cows in the unincorporated community of Brusett, Montana. Located in the far north of the state, near the rim of the Missouri River Breaks, it is all but impassable during winter; the closest shopping mall is 180 miles southwest, in Billings. Of his spread, Phipps likes to say: "It's big enough to not starve to death on."

Phipps is the great-grandson of homesteaders—pioneers who were given the right to claim, improve, and buy land at bargain prices. Most became cattle ranchers, the only logical choice in this unforgiving region. Little did they know the land they'd claimed was sitting atop the Hell Creek Formation, a three-hundred-foot-thick bed of sandstone and mudstone that dates to a period between 66 million and 67.5 million years ago, the time just before dinosaurs went extinct. Stretching across the Dakotas and Montana (in Wyoming, it's known as Lance), the formation—one of the richest fossil troves in the world—is the remnant of great rivers that once flowed eastward toward an inland sea.

Before his father died, and the homestead was divided among four descendant families, including Phipps and his two siblings, Phipps scraped by as a ranch hand on a neighboring ranch. He and his wife, Lisa, a teacher's aide at the local school, lived in a cabin on the rancher's property. One day in 1998, Phipps says, a man showed up and asked the landowner's permission to hunt fossils. Given consent to roam the property for a weekend, the man returned Monday morning and showed Phipps a piece of triceratops frill—part of the shield-like structure that grew around the massive plant-eater's head.

"He told me: 'This piece is worth about $500,'" Phipps recalls. "And I was like, 'The heck it is! You found that just walking around?'"

From that day on, whenever Phipps wasn't doing ranch work, he was out looking for fossils. What he found he prepared in his basement workshop, or consigned to others to prepare, for sale at trade shows and to museums and private collectors. In 2003, he unearthed the head of the horned *Stygimoloch*—from the Greek and Hebrew, roughly, for "demon from the river Styx"—a bipedal dinosaur, about the size of a bighorn sheep, prized by collectors for its highly ornamented skull. Phipps sold the fossil for more than $100,000 to a private collector, who placed the specimen in a museum in Long Island, New York.

Then, one hot day in 2006, Phipps and some partners made the discovery of a lifetime—experts say it might well be one of the greatest fossil specimens ever unearthed. Or, more accurately, two specimens. Jutting out from a desiccated hillside were the remains of a 22-foot-long theropod and a 28-foot-long ceratopsian. Locked in mortal combat when they were instantly buried in sandstone, perhaps along a sandy riverbed, the incredibly well-preserved pair is forever captured in a moment in time from more than 66 million years ago. "There's an entire skin envelope around both dinosaurs," Phipps says. "They're basically mummies. There could be soft tissue inside." If true, the specimen offers the possibility that scientists might recover tissue cells or even ancient DNA.

The exact species of the Montana Dueling Dinosaurs, as the specimens have become known, are still in contention. The larger of the two appears to be a ceratopsian, from the family of beaked and bird-hipped plant-eaters beloved by children for their horned faces. The existence of additional horns on the animal's faceplate, however, has led to some speculation that it may be a rare or new species. The smaller specimen appears to be either a juvenile *Tyrannosaurus rex* or a *Nanotyrannus*, a dwarf species, rarely documented, the very existence of which some scientists dispute.

Scott Sampson, a paleontologist and the president of Science World, a nonprofit education and research facility in Vancouver, is among the few academics, museum officials and commercial collectors who have viewed the specimen. "The Dueling Dinosaurs is one of the most remarkable fossil discoveries ever made," he says. "It is the closest thing I have ever seen to large-scale fighting dinosaurs. If it is what we think it is, it's ancient behavior caught in the fossil record. We've been digging for over one hundred years in the Americas, and no one's found a specimen quite like this one."

And yet there is a chance the public will never see it.

We may speculate romantically about how far into the past dinosaur fossils were collected by our hominin ancestors, but the study of dinosaurs is a relatively new science. Deep thinkers in ancient Greece and Rome recognized fossils as the remains of life-forms from earlier epochs. Leonardo da Vinci proposed that fossils of marine creatures like mollusks found in the Italian countryside must have been evidence of ancient seas that once covered the land. But for the most part, fossils were regarded as the remains of gods or devils. Many believed they had special powers of healing or destruction; others that they were left behind from Noah's flood, a notion still held by creationists, who deny evolution.

Dinosaurs inhabited much of the earth, but their fossils are not easily found in most places. The western United States is a treasure trove due to a combination of factors: We live during a sweet spot in time when the rock layers laid down during the end of the Cretaceous Period have become exposed after eons of erosion, a process accentuated by the stark environment, lack of plant life and extreme weather conditions that continually reveal ever new layers of ancient rock. As layers of the earth's surface erode, fossilized bones of dinosaurs, more solid than the sand and clay in which they are buried, peek through.

In the early twentieth century, universities and museums frequently commissioned commercial bone diggers to excavate dinosaur fossils. Many of the oldest specimens on display in museums in the United States and Europe were uncovered and harvested by these "professional amateurs." While federal land can only be prospected by accredited academics in possession of a permit, dinosaur bones found on private land are private property: anybody can dig with the permission of the owner.

In 1990, a group of paleontologists digging on the Cheyenne River Indian Reservation, in South Dakota, unearthed an enormous and incredibly well-preserved *T. rex*. Later named "Sue," it is to date the largest and most complete specimen ever found, with more than 90 percent of its bones recovered. Sue was auctioned in 1997 for $7.6 million to the Field Museum of Natural History in Chicago, the most ever paid for a dinosaur fossil.

The record sale was publicized around the world and kicked off a sort of dinosaur bone "gold rush." Scores of prospectors descended on Hell Creek and other fossil beds in the West, drawing the ire of academics, who contend that fossils should be extracted according to scientific protocols, not ripped from the ground by profit-seeking amateurs. To scientists, every site contains much more than fossil trophies—the plant, pollen, and mineral records, as well as the exact placement of the find, are critically important to understanding the history of our planet. Over the following decade, the mania for dinosaur bones was fueled by the popularity of movies like *Jurassic Park*, booming wealth in Asia, where fossils became ultra-chic for use in home décor, and the media's attention to celebrity collectors like Leonardo DiCaprio and Nicolas Cage. At the height of the bone rush, there were perhaps hundreds of prospectors conducting digs across hundreds of thousands of square miles, ranging from the Dakotas to Texas.

One of them was Cowboy Phipps.

It was a typical day in early June, clear with the mercury in the triple digits, when Phipps discovered the Dueling Dinosaurs.

He was prospecting with his cousin Chad O'Connor, forty-nine, and a friend and fellow commercial bone digger named Mark Eatman, forty-five. O'Connor, strong and good-humored, is partially disabled by cerebral palsy. This was his first time hunting for dinosaur bones. He'd later say he accompanied his cousin on the expedition in the hope he'd "find something that could change my life."

Eatman had been a full-time prospector for many years before falling demand and prices for fossils, along with a three-year stretch of bad luck, forced him to give up the game. "His wife told him it was time to get a real job," Phipps says.

Eatman found work selling carpet in Billings. On occasion, he'd join Phipps for an expedition, sometimes camping out for a few days at a time. Bone diggers across the spectrum—commercial, academic, amateur—would probably agree that the hunt is often as important as the find, an opportunity to get out into nature and to collaborate with like-minded people beneath the same ancient stars the dinosaurs stood under.

Phipps and his partners were checking out an area about sixty miles north of Phipps' ranch. Because he was using "a small map of a big area," Phipps says, he believed they were on land his brother was leasing, in the Judith River Formation, which predates Hell Creek by at least ten million years. Later, Phipps discovered they were actually prospecting about ten miles north of where he thought they were, in the area that Phipps, like most of the locals, calls *Hell Crik*. The land was part of a twenty-five thousand–acre ranch owned by Mary Ann and Lige Murray.

The men picked their way through the sunburnt environment, the ground a mix of eroded clay, shale and sand. The topography is riven with canyons, ravines, and gullies, interrupted by striated buttes, hunkered beneath the cloudless sky like silent messengers from the past. In the time of the dinosaurs, the Hell Creek area was subtropical, with a warm and humid climate. The swampy lowlands were rich with flowering plants, palmettos and ferns. At higher elevations were forests of shrubs and a variety of broad-leaved trees and conifers.

About sixty-six million years ago, an asteroid collided with the earth, leading to the extinction of the dinosaurs and much of the earth's fauna and paving the way for the evolution of mammals and modern plants. Today, Hell Creek is stark, hot, and seemingly deserted. The crew made its way around low-growing cactuses, through prickly and fragrant sage, over tuffs of wild grasses. Phipps was riding a small, off-road motorcycle. The other two men were on foot.

Along the way they encountered an occasional set of sunbleached bones, late of a grazing cow or other denizen: prairie dog, mule deer, antelope, coyote. Rarely is a skeleton found complete. In nature, when an animal is killed by prey or by natural causes, scavengers make a meal of the corpse; often a piece of carrion will be dragged away, separating, say, a leg from the torso—one reason a complete set of dinosaur bones is so rare.

At about 11 a.m. Eatman spotted what looked like a piece of massive bone sticking out of a sandstone bank. Phipps approached the hillside for closer inspection. Right away, he says, "We knew we had a pelvis, possibly of a ceratopsian. And we knew we had the femur articulated into the pelvis—we could see the head of the femur." What they didn't know was whether any more of the creature was buried beneath the sand, or whether the rest of the dinosaur had already been washed away from erosion.

Phipps marked the spot carefully in his mind's eye, and then he and the party headed home. The answers to these mysteries would have to wait for another time.

"I had 260 acres of hay to cut," he says.

Later that summer, after the hay was mowed, rolled and put up—feed for his cattle over the long winter—Phipps returned to the secret location, this time in the company of Lige Murray, the landowner.

Now Phipps found pieces of ceratops frill that had already weathered out of the bank. He could also see a line of vertebrae leading toward a skull. It seemed likely the dinosaur's back end was buried in the hill—meaning there was a good chance it was still intact.

Murray gave his approval, and Phipps began the painstaking process of excavating, starting with a brush and a penknife. Meanwhile, business partners were gathered; contracts were signed. A $150,000 loan was arranged. A road to the site was constructed.

Most of the arduous work of extraction was done by Phipps and O'Connor. "He doesn't get around very good, but he's got a great sense of humor," Phipps says of his cousin, who helped ease the burden of their long, hot days. Eatman came up on weekends to help, as did a small cast of confidants and colleagues, who lent elbow grease and expertise. The find was kept secret throughout the entire process. "I didn't even tell my family until just before we finished the excavation," Phipps says.

After two weeks, Phipps had established a perimeter around the ceratopsian from head to tail. "We had basically all the bones to his body mapped out at that point," he says. One day he was sitting in the cab of a backhoe he'd borrowed from his uncle, which he was using to remove the soil behind and around the specimen to prepare the area for the fossil's removal.

"I went to dump my bucket—as usual I was watching very carefully," Phipps recalls. "Suddenly I see these bone chips. The bones were easy to tell from the light-colored sand because they were dark in color, like dark chocolate."

Phipps clambered down off the backhoe and began to sift the contents of the bucket by hand. That's when he saw it: "There was a claw," he says. "And it was a carnivore claw. It's not any bone that goes with a ceratopsian."

Phipps smiles at the memory. "Man, my hat went in the air," he recalls. "And then I had to sit down and think, like, What's going on? Here is this meat-eater in with this plant-eater, and obviously they weren't friends. What are the odds of another dinosaur being there?"

It took Phipps and his partners three months to extract the specimens from the remote site. The sinewy Phipps lost fifteen pounds in the process. Railroad ties were inserted beneath the Dueling Dinosaurs to preserve their position and integrity. Plaster jackets were placed around the exposed bone, a standard procedure among paleontologists. In the end, there were four large sections and several smaller ones—all together they weighed nearly twenty tons. The section of earth containing the theropod alone was the size of a small car, weighing some twelve thousand pounds.

Phipps enlisted the help of friends at CK Preparations, run by a preparer named Chris Morrow and the paleoartist Katie Busch. The multi-ton blocks were transported to a facility in northeastern Montana, where Phipps and his partners carefully removed the jackets. Next the specimens were "cleaned down to the outline of the bones, so you could see everything that was there, how each animal is arranged," Phipps says. About 30 percent of the fossils were exposed, the bones shiny and dark.

In situ, Phipps explains, using a model he holds in his lap, the skeletons overlapped, with the tail of the theropod, which was about the size of a polar bear, resting beneath the back foot of the elephant-size ceratopsian. Both dinosaurs, buried in some seventeen feet of sand, are fully articulated, meaning their skeletons are intact from nose to tail.

Phipps speculates that on the day in question, scores of millions of years ago, one or more *Nanotyrannuses* attacked the ceratopsian. A number of theropod teeth were found around the site, and at least two were embedded in what were the ceratopsian's fleshy areas, one in the throat and one near the pelvis. Scientists believe that theropods shed teeth and quickly regrew them, like sharks. In this case, Phipps says, some of the theropod's teeth are broken in half, indicating a violent fight.

A pitched battle ensued. "The ceratopsian is almost ready to die," Phipps says, picking up the narration and growing animated. "He's hot, he's tired, he's whipped, he's bleeding from all the bite marks in him.

Just as the ceratopsian is about to tip over, he staggers around and steps on the nano's tail. Well that hurts, right? So the nano bites the ceratopsian's leg. And what's the ceratopsian gonna do? Instinctively he kicks the nano in the face. The nano's skull is actually cracked. When the ceratopsian caved in the side of the nano's head, the force slammed him into a loose sandbank—and the wall of sand came down," burying them both instantly.

"There's so much science in these dinosaurs!" Phipps exclaims, a rare show of emotion from a guy who likes to wear his black cowboy hat low on his brow. "There may be last meals, there may be eggs, there may be babies—we don't know."

Well aware he'd found something special, Phipps set out to alert the world.

There was only one problem: Nobody would listen. "We called every major American museum and told them what we had," Phipps says. "But I was a nobody. A lot of them probably thought, Yeah, right. This guy is crazy. Nobody sent anyone to verify what we'd found."

In time, though, word got out. Sampson, the Canadian paleontologist, then with the Denver Museum of Nature & Science, spent an hour with a group from the museum examining the fossils in a Quonset hut in eastern Montana. "We were blown away," Sampson says. "It's an amazing specimen."

Several other experts who've seen the Dueling Dinosaurs have come to the same conclusion. "It's exquisite," says Kirk Johnson, director of the Smithsonian's National Museum of Natural History. "It's one of the more beautiful fossils found in North America, ever." Tyler Lyson, a curator at the Denver Museum of Nature & Science, calls it a "spectacular discovery. Any museum would love to have it."

But not everyone agrees. "As far as I'm concerned, those specimens are scientifically useless," says Jack Horner, the pioneering and world-famous paleontologist who was the inspiration for the dinosaur expert played by Sam Neill in *Jurassic Park*. "Every single specimen collected by a commercial collector is useless, because they do not come with any of the data" that academically trained paleontologists are careful to collect, Horner says.

As time dragged on, Phipps tried everything he could think of to find a buyer for the Dueling Dinosaurs. "There were a few museums that were interested," he says. "We got close with one. I was negotiating with the director, and we actually came to an agreement on a price at one point. And then—nothing happened. They didn't get back to us. I don't know more than that."

In 2013, after seven years in the lab of CK Preparations, the Dueling Dinosaurs were brought to auction at Bonhams, in New York City. It was valued by appraisers as high as $9 million, according to Phipps.

To transport the specimens from Montana, custom crates had to be built for each section. A special semi-truck with an air-ride suspension was hired. Phipps and his party flew to New York.

Bonhams displayed the fossils in a large atrium room at its facility on Madison Avenue. The crowd at the event was a mix of "professorial baby boomers, wily prospectors, impeccably dressed collectors," according to an account of the event published by the website Gizmodo. Phipps, the website reported, "wore a rancher's vest, neckerchief and black cowboy hat."

The bidding on the Dueling Dinosaurs lasted just eighty-one seconds. The only offer was $5.5 million, which failed to meet the reserve. (Although the reserve price was not publicly announced, Phipps says it was closer to the appraised figure of around $9 million.) "I just felt that they were worth probably twice what we were offered," Phipps says. "We were expecting better, and we weren't willing to take that."

Perhaps reflecting the falling market for fossils, a number of other items failed to sell that day, including a triceratops skeleton, valued between $700,000 and $900,000, and a *Tyrannosaurus rex* valued at up to $2.2 million.

Three years later, sitting in his office, there is regret in his voice. "The reason they went to auction was sort of out of frustration on my part. And then it was over before it started. It was disappointing that we couldn't make a sale, but I guess I was half expecting it. My attitude is always the same: You don't count your chickens before they hatch."

Since then, the Dueling Dinosaurs have been housed in a storage facility at an undisclosed location in New York. They remain unstudied more than a decade after they were exhumed. In the meantime, Phipps has been regarded by some, however undeservedly, as a privateer devoted more to money than to science.

"I've never had any money, so money's never been all that important to me," he says. "But I'm not gonna just give them away. There were people that said I should just donate them. Well, no. I've got partners. I've put too much into the project. I was out there trying to make a living. It's just like them academics that come out every summer between classes to look for fossils—they're trying to make a living, too."

Johnson, of the Smithsonian, says there is tremendous value in the Dueling Dinosaurs, despite some of the criticisms leveled against how the specimens were excavated. "There's scientific value, there's display value, there's the novelty of the two of the dinosaurs being adjacent," he says. But, he adds, "the price tag is sort of out of reach of most museums, unless somebody comes along who wants to buy it and donate it. And that hasn't happened yet." Johnson says he viewed the Dueling Dinosaurs in the company of a wealthy museum supporter whom he invited, hoping the man might take an interest in the fossil. It turned out the donor had already seen it—with an official from another museum. "There really aren't that many buyers for something like this."

The sale of Sue, the *T. rex*, for more than $7 million, was a "high-water mark" for fossils, Johnson says, reflecting unprecedented donations by corporate sponsors like McDonald's and Disney. "Sue changed everything, because ranchers went kind of nuts when they realized that dinosaurs weren't just old bones, they were a source of money—and that screwed everything up."

Tyler Lyson, of the Denver Museum, says it would unquestionably be "a shame if it ultimately doesn't end up in a museum." A Yale-trained paleontologist who grew up about three hours southeast of Phipps, along the Montana-North Dakota border, Lyson got his start hunting fossils on ranch land homesteaded by his mother's family. Improbably, through a series of scholarships, his childhood hobby became his life's work.

"There's only a certain percentage of people on the planet who are interested in fossils to begin with," Lyson says. "We all share that common bond, even though we might be interested for different reasons."

At five o'clock, Phipps' wife rings the dinner bell. Phipps hoists himself out of the chair and gingerly climbs the stairs. Three months ago, he and his twelve-year-old son were cutting a calf from the herd when Phipps' horse slipped and rolled over on top of him. Phipps broke his leg in several places; his foot was turned the wrong way. His son, thinking he was dead, began to administer CPR. Last week the screws were removed from the leg; it looks like he will recover full use. Of course, during his convalescence, an entire prospecting season was lost, along with any hope of any income from fossils—revenue that over the years has accounted for two-thirds of his annual income, he says.

Besides her duties at the nearby one-room schoolhouse, Lisa Phipps has published two children's books. We are joined at the table by the couple's two boys, the younger of whom is ten. (Their eldest, a daughter, is in nursing school.) We eat a convivial supper of shredded chicken, potatoes and squash. The windows frame the rugged beauty of the surrounding countryside. The early evening sunlight creates an intimate glow. Beside my plate, in two little plastic bags, are a pair of triceratops teeth that Phipps has given me as a remembrance of my visit.

"The academics think what I'm doing is horrid," Phipps is saying. "They think I'm destroying fossils and selling them to the highest bidder. But that's not true," he says, anger rising in his voice. "I love fossils as much as they do. Granted, I'm self-taught. I'm just a cowpoke, I don't know everything. But I've had several paleontologists, even ones who don't exactly condone what I do, tell me I did a good job getting the fossils out. Maybe I didn't do the totally detailed scientific work like they do, but I don't have thirty college students under me working for nothing. When we found the Dueling Dinosaurs, I thought the academics would be big enough to bridge the gap. I figured they'd say, 'Okay, this is a once in a lifetime find.'"

Someday, Phipps hopes, the divide with the academic community will be bridged and whatever valuable scientific data the Dueling Dinosaurs retain will be reaped. "The dinosaurs have been removed," he says. "If we left them in the hill, the weather would have destroyed them in the last eight or ten years since we dug them out. We did the best we could with what we had at our disposal. You gotta make up your own mind if what I do is wrong or not. But to me, it's not."

After my visit, not long before this article went to press, Phipps told me that there have been renewed overtures from a museum interested in buying the Dueling Dinosaurs. "There are some things happening, but I'm not at liberty to discuss it," he said. But he did suggest that sufficient funds haven't yet been raised. "It's like anything in business, I guess. You want a fair price. I'm gonna wait and see what happens. I'm not in any hurry."

In the meantime, Phipps says, "I've paid back my debts, and I'm trying to build the ranch up a little more, and to get more cattle. I'm leasing more ground now, too. I'm trying to focus on that, because fossils aren't a guarantee, you know?"

THE BONE DIGGERS

EVERY SUMMER, GROUPS OF SCIENTISTS AND STUDENTS CONVERGE ON THE BADLANDS, SEARCHING FOR FOSSILS AND WORKING TO SOLVE THE RIDDLES OF THE EARTH'S HISTORY.

T he bone digger is unloading his truck when three of his teen volunteers come loping toward him, flush with excitement.

"I think we found a theropod hand!" says Isiah Newbins, seventeen.

The rising senior from Cherokee Trails High School in Aurora is dripping sweat; his clothes are muddied with the slippery, volcanic clay known hereabouts as gumbo. His face is alight with the glow of discovery—equal parts scientific interest and little-boy hope.

It's been a long day in the Hell Creek Formation, a three-hundred-foot-deep bed of shale and mudstone that dates back to a period between 65 and 67 million years ago, to a time before dinosaurs became extinct. Stretching across the Dakotas, Montana, and Wyoming, it is one of the richest fossil troves in the world, left behind by great rivers that once flowed eastward toward an inland sea.

Newbins has been hunting fossils in the August heat with a team from the Denver Museum of Nature and Science. Every summer the DMNS, in cooperation with the Marmarth Research Foundation, offers several weeks of programs and research opportunities for students, academics, and serious hobbyists. A sort of ultimate fantasy camp for would-be paleontologists, the age among the thirty-five attendees and staff this week ranges from fifteen to eighty.

Theropods were carnivorous dinosaurs, bipedal predators like the *T. rex*—perhaps the most fearsome and captivating of all the extinct species, at least to the general public. To Newbins, who'll be applying this fall to paleontology programs at colleges, finding the *possible* hand is "unbelievably surreal—kind of like a dream-come-true moment." As he will later say, echoing the sentiments of most in attendance at the gathering: "You know how everybody likes dinosaurs when they're kids? I never stopped."

The bone digger thumbs back the brim of his well-seasoned Aussie bush hat. "Theropods are rare," says Tyler Lyson, thirty-three. He's been prospecting these parts for fossils since he was young. He raises his eyebrows skeptically. "I mean, *very* rare."

Lyson is the founder of the MRF; he is employed as a curator with the Denver Museum. A Yale-trained PhD with a specialty in fossil vertebrates—more specifically dinosaurs and turtles—Lyson (pro-nounced Lee-sun) was born and raised here in Marmarth, population 143, a once-thriving railroad town in the far southwest corner of North Dakota.

Lyson was just sixteen—a year younger than Newbins—when he spotted his first serious fossil, a mummified hadrosaur, or duck-billed dinosaur, later nicknamed "Dakota." An extraordinary find, Dakota had apparently died near the bend of a river, where its body was rapidly bur-ied under accumulating sediment. The wet, mineral-rich environment protected the specimen from decay, leaving a detailed preservation of the dinosaur's skin, bones and soft tissue. Eventually, the fees Lyson collected for loaning Dakota to a Japanese exposition would help him build out his foundation's summer program, which he started as a col-lege sophomore with four attendees in 2003. (Dakota later found a permanent home at the North Dakota Heritage Center in Bismarck.)

"Were there multiple bones?" Lyson asks.

Jeremy Wyman, seventeen, pulls out his cell phone, searches for a photo. "It looked like multiple bones and multiple hand bones," he says. "But then again—" his voice trails off.

Wyman is also a rising high school senior. He hails from Atlanta, Georgia. He's a bit more experienced than Newbins. And a bit more skeptical. His interest in paleontology, he says, has been "pretty much an individual pursuit because it's not something they teach in classes." Besides seeking out all the books and movies he could find and traveling with his supportive family to museums, he's participated in three other digs during summers past. At home, when his schedule allows, he volunteers as a docent at the Fernbank Museum of Natural History, to which he has donated fossils he collected at private sites, including a cast of a *T. rex* tooth and trilobite burrow.

Lyson squints at the photo through his prescription aviator shades. With his scrubby beard and dirty, long sleeve shirt, he looks like a guy who's just spent the day hiking ten miles though the thorny, sage-scented territory in the 90 degree heat.

"Ian said he *thought* it might be a hand," says Newbins, pleading his case. Ian is Ian Miller, their chaperone in the field today, a specialist in fossil plants who heads the paleontology department at the Denver Museum, making him Lyson's boss. Miller is visiting this week, as he does annually. Later this evening, after a dinner of Chinese carryout (from restaurant twenty miles away, across the Montana state line) Miller will be giving a lecture about the Snowmastodon Project of 2010, when he helped to lead an effort to harvest an important site that had been found unexpectedly during the re-construction of a reservoir in the resort town of Snowmass, Colorado. During the six-month window they were allowed, the crew unearthed 4,826 bones from 26 different Ice Age vertebrates, including mammoths, mastodons, bisons, American camels, a Pleistocene horse, and the first ground sloth ever found in Colorado.

Lyson returns the phone to Wyman. "I kind of wanna go look at it *right now*," he says.

"I could go get my field stuff," Newbins says.

"If that's a theropod hand," Lyson says, "I'm gonna give you the biggest hug."

"I'm gonna give *myself* a huge hug," Newbins says.

The bone digger is digging.

Perched on a low shelf of rock at the bottom of a wash, Lyson scrapes gingerly with the three-inch blade of a Swiss Army knife. Now and then he uses a small hand broom to wisk away the dust. He scrapes some more.

The object of his attention is what appears to be a perfectly intact shell of an Axestemys, an extinct soft-shelled turtle that grew to three and a half feet in diameter. A cousin of the large sacred turtles found in various temples in Asia, it was the largest animal in North America to survive the great extinction. You might say turtles were Lyson's first paleontological love. Over time he has become one of the world's foremost experts on turtle evolution. His latest work solves the mystery of how the turtle got its shell. Earlier in the day, a couple of dozen volunteers from the MRF walked right past the fossilized shell without seeing it. Then Lyson caught sight of it—a brownish edge sticking out of the weathered ochre slope. Dropping his backpack on the spot, he got right to work.

At three thousand feet of elevation, the air is slightly thin; the sun's rays feel harsh against the skin. Prior to sixty-five million years ago, this part of the arid Badlands was at sea level. A moderately wet area, with lakes and streams, palms and ferns, it resembled the modern Gulf Coast. Today, along with the prickly pear cactus and desert grasses—and the slippery sheets of gumbo collected in low areas like so many ponds of ice (used by oil companies as a lubricant for oil drilling)—the ground is a trove of minerals and fossils, bits and pieces of larger chunks that have weathered out of the sides of the buttes, evidence of the eternal cycle of erosion, and of the treasures buried all around.

The group from the MRF is fanned out along the network of gullies and buttes within shouting distance of Lyson. By summer's end, more than one hundred will have passed through the program, including student teams from Yale University, Brooklyn College, and the Smithsonian Institution. This week's group includes a retired auditor who has traveled to forty-nine of the fifty states; a retired science teacher credited with the 1997 find of an important *T. rex* named Peck's Rex; a twenty-three year old whose grandfather employed Lyson, while still a teenager, to recover a triceratops; and the mother of a young grad student who just wanted to see what her daughter's chosen life is all about. One crew applies a plaster cast to a bone from a pterosaur, a flying reptile, a rare find. Another uses brushes, rock hammers, and awls to unearth the jawbone and partial skull of a champsasaur, an alligator-like animal with a thin snout. Up on top of a nearby butte, a third crew attends to a rich vein of fossil leaves.

Another crew is equipped with a portable GPS system. Over the past two years, Lyson and his collaborators have hiked hundreds of miles in an attempt to create a computerized map of the K/T Boundary. Known more formally as the Cretaceous–Tertiary Boundary (the German word *kreide*, meaning chalk, is the traditional abbreviation for the Cretaceous Period), the K/T Boundary is an iridium-rich sedimentary layer that scientists believe marks in geologic time the catastrophic event—an asteroid colliding with the earth—that led to the extinction of the dinosaurs and much of the earth's fauna, paving the way for the evolution of mammals and modern plants. By placing all of the readings on a map—and by adding locations where fossils have been found (including samples of leaves and pollen) over a hundred-year period by researchers from the Smithsonian, the Denver Museum, and other regional museums—Lyson and the others have created a three-dimensional image of the boundary that will aid in dating past and future finds. Simply put, if you're below the boundary, you're in the Cretaceous, the world of the dinosaurs. If you're above, you're in the Paleoscene, the world of the mammals. Lyson and the others hope this data will help them more accurately depict the sequence of events of the great extinction. Did it happen all at once? Was it gradual? What was the timing across the globe?

At the moment, Lyson has taken a break from mapping to do something he's had precious little time for this summer—collecting a fossil. While the abundance of volunteers makes the painstaking tasks of digging and preparing fossils more efficient—everything taken will go to the Denvery Museum—it means that Lyson spends a lot more time administrating... and mapping.

We are a few miles outside of Marmarth, founded in the early 1900s as a hub along a railroad line, leading from Chicago to Seattle, that was built to aid in settlement of the great northern plains. The town was named for the railroad owner's grandaughter, Margaret Martha Finch. Despite a boom in the 1930s, caused by the discovery of oil nearby, the population has continued to dwindle from its high of five thousand. These days, locals say, a large percentage of Marmarth residents are retirees, here for the modest cost of living. There is one bar/restaurant, a Classic Auto museum, a coffee-shop/tobacco store, and a former railroad bunkhouse that rents out rooms—during summers it serves as the MRF dorm.

Meanwhile, in various locations across the four-state area that encompasses the Hell Creek Formation, groups of students, scholars, commercial collectors, and volunteers—all of them, no doubt, wearing sunhats, bug spray, and long, protective clothing—are working in groups in the unforgiving environment, each of them doing his or her little piece to help solve the riddles of the earth's history. As odd as it may seem, the formal study of paleontology itself isn't very old, dating back on only to the 1800s. We've only just begun to understand, scientists say.

The land where Lyson is digging is owned by his uncle; Lyson's maternal family, the Sonsallas, have ranched here for three generations. An important factor in fossil hunting is land ownership. Permission is needed to dig on both private and public lands, the latter managed by the US Bureau of Land Management.

Lyson's dad, Ranse Lyson, hails from a farming family in Montana. After a stint as a nuclear submariner, he worked as a DJ at a small radio station in Baker, Montana, where he met the former Molly Sonsalla. The couple married and settled in Marmarth; Ranse went to work for the oil company. The couple had three boys. The Hell Creek Formation was their playground.

"My mom would drop us off and we'd run around and chase rabbits and look for fossils and arrowheads," Lyson says, scratch-scratch-scratching at the sand with his knife. "I was the youngest. My older brothers would constantly beat me up, and I always gave them a run for their money. One of the guys we'd go fishing with, his nickname was Bear—he was a big bear of a guy, everybody around here has nicknames. And one time he said to me, 'You're gonna be tough when you grow up.' I guess it stuck."

Tuffy Lyson was in fourth or fifth grade when he came across his first important find—a trove of giant turtle shells; he named it the Turtle Graveyard. Likely they had died together as a pond dried up, he hypothesized. The next year he found his first hadrosaur. (Dakota would come later, in high school.) When he'd finished unearthing it, Lyson remembers, he took a piece of the fossil in a shoebox down to the bunkhouse—only three blocks from his parents' place—where all the commercial prospectors and academics would stay every summer while doing their field work.

"I'd just hang around and I wouldn't leave until they'd take me out digging. You can imagine how annoying I was. They gave me a hard time but I was pretty resilient," Lyson says. From the spot where he's working on the turtle shell, the butte where he found his first hadrosaur is about one mile north. The locals call it Tuffy Butte.

"Look at the size of that thing," says Kirk Johnson, interrupting Lyson's story.

Johnson, fifty-five, is a Yale-trained paleobotanist and the director of the Smithsonian Institution's National Museum of Natural History. He's been doing field work in Marmarth since he was an undergrad. He met Lyson when he was about twelve; when he was a "little gumbo butte Sherpa," Johnson says. Lyson affectionately calls him "Dr. J." Johnson would be instrumental in helping to convince Lyson's parents—who lived in a town where most of the sons went to work for the oil company—that their son could make an actual, paying career in paleontology. Eventually Lyson would go on to scholarships at Swarthmore and Yale.

"He's that rarest of all rare things, a native paleontologist," Johnson says of Lyson. "He's remarkable in the field because he's trained his eye since he was small. He can see everything."

Johnson would go on to work at the Denver Museum, first as a lead scientist, then as chief curator and vice president of research and collections. In 2012, he was selected to lead the Museum of Natural History in Washington, DC, one of the Smithsonian Institution's most popular museums on the National Mall. Still, Johnson comes to MRF every year.

"At least twenty-five people strolled right past it and then I spotted it," Lyson says of his turtle shell find, pointing to the distinctive raindrop pattern of the markings on the surface of the shell. His face is alight with the glow of discovery—equal parts scientific interest and little-boy hope.

The bone digger is standing on stage, beside a podium. Wearing clean chinos and a button-down oxford shirt, he's waiting to deliver a lecture.

We are sixty miles southwest of Marmarth, in the town of Ekalaka (*Eee-ka-laka)*, Montana. With a population of three hundred, it's another close-knit, Badlands ranching community, rich in fossils. The audience is a diverse collection, two hundred academics, dinosaur enthusiasts, ranch owners, and community members who have gathered in the pews and folding chairs of the spacious sanctuary at the St. Elizabeth Lutheran Church to celebrate the fourth annual Ekalaka Shindig.

Part small-town fair, part open-door conference, the Shindig is a weekend-long celebration of Ekalaka's contribution to paleontology, with a lecture program, kids' activities, field expeditions, and live music. Central to the entire program is the Carter County Museum, the first of its kind in Montana, founded in 1936. The museum's guiding force was a local high school teacher named Marshall Lambert, who died in 2005 at the age of ninety. He taught science to some of the old-timers in the crowd—as part of his curriculum, he took his students into the field to collect fossils. Today many of those students are landowners. Their cooperation is key.

The Shindig lectures started at nine this morning. Right now it's almost noon. As can be expected—besides being hot and dusty, life is a little bit slower out here where some cell phones have no service—things are running a bit late. Standing on the stage next to Lyson, getting ready to introduce him, is another bone digger. His name is Nate Carroll, but everybody calls him Ekalaka Jones.

Carroll is twenty-eight years old with a mop of black hair, wearing his trademark blue denim overalls. As the curator of the museum, the Ekalaka Shindig is his creation.

Like Lyson, Carroll grew up with the Badlands as his playground; his family goes back four generations. At fifteen, after a *T. rex* was unearthed twenty minutes away from his family's ranch, Carroll volunteered to work on the dig, sponsored by the LA County Museum. He continued for the next several summers; by his senior year in high school, he'd landed a spot as a paid field assistant. Currently he's pursuing his PhD at the University of Southern California. As an undergrad he focused on pterosaurs. Lately he's been more fascinated with amber. The secret to becoming a successful academic is finding a unique area of study—you're not just out digging bones, you're trying to figure out a particular piece of history's puzzle.

In 2012, when Carroll was hired as curator, he decided to find a way to bring together all the different academics who come to the area to do fieldwork—and to make it more attractive for others to come. At the same time, the Shindig celebrates the community that supports the local museum, and the landowners who make fossil hunting possible. Last night was the annual Pitchfork Fondue, so named for the regulation, farmyard-sized pitchforks upon which steaks by the dozen are skewered and then lowered into fifty-gallon caldrons of boiling peanut oil... to delicious result. As a band played country music and beer flowed from the taps, the assembled academics, students, and locals danced and mingled and traded tall tales into the wee hours of the warm and buggy night.

Early this morning, a caravan of sleepy MRF volunteers and staffers returned to Ekalaka to catch the day-long slate of distinguished speakers, including Lyson and Kirk Johnson. In the audience, along with interested locals, are field-workers from, among others, the Burpee Museum of Rockford, Illinois; the LA County Museum; the University of California; Carthage College in Pennsylvania; and the University of Maryland.

In the moments of fidgeting between presentations—as Carroll and Lyson stand idle on stage waiting to begin—one of the teens from the MRF group gets up from his chair and moves to the side of the sanctuary.

I join Jeremy Wyman against the wall. He has his cell phone out; per their MRF assignments, all four of the teen interns are live-covering the Shindig on various social media platforms. By way of greeting, I ask him what he's up to.

"Resting my butt," he says with a respectful smirk.

I ask about the theropod hand. What happened? Was it real?

Wyman shrugs. "It was nothing but plant matter, all crumbled up and packed together. We kind of jumped to a conclusion because it would be so *cool* to find a theropod hand."

I ask if he's disappointed. Wyman shakes his head emphatically, *no way.*

"Being out here has actually changed my *entire* view on paleontology," he says. "At first I was *super* into dinosaurs. But then coming out here and seeing all these important paleontologists doing research into fossilized plants and pollen, I realize that paleontology is a lot more than just dinosaurs. I feel like I've been missing something."

THE FIRST FAMILY OF DILDOS

AT DOC JOHNSON, SEX TOYS ARE A FAMILY AFFAIR. HOW ONE SMALL LA BUSINESS SURVIVED THE DARK DAYS OF THE REAGAN/BUSH WAR ON PORN.

C had Braverman is leading a tour of his family business, the oldest and largest sex-toy manufacturer in America.

"Dongs, dildos, masturbators, and butt plugs—that's 99 percent of what we do here," Chad says matter-of-factly, traversing the noisy expanse of the factory floor, part of a six-acre compound of white-washed buildings in a light-industrial district in North Hollywood that's been catering to sexual tastes for forty-one years.

As he goes, he waves here and there to employees he knows by name, most of them middle-aged Hispanic women with beauty-shop hairdos and gold crosses around their necks. They work along various assembly lines, bringing to mind Rosie the Riveter, or the chocolate factory episode of *I Love Lucy*. Many keep the exact nature of their jobs secret from their families. A good number have been here twenty years or more; in honor of their service, their names are inscribed on two plaques outside reception.

Depending upon the season, Doc Johnson employs three hundred to five hundred nonunion workers, who churn out an average of seventy-five thousand sex toys a month, or nearly a million a year, for sale online and in adult shops around the world. And some 15 percent of Doc Johnson products—most of them electronic, like the TRYST Multi Erogenous Zone Massager or the WonderLand series Kinky Kat 10 Function Silicone Massager (with a head resembling that of the Chesire Cat)—are manufactured to their specifications in China.

The print catalog, produced in-house, is 308 pages, a companion to the tricked-out website. There's the White Rabbit clitoral stimulator, with a soft, velvet-touch finish; the MILF in a Box Pocket Pussy; the Yumi Asian Anime Doll with Three-Hole Design; the Wendy Williams Three-Step Anal Trainer for men; and Triple Duty Fist, Fuck & Jack-Off Cream, in an eight-ounce pump bottle. (Clearly, three is a big number in sex toys.)

The company's strongest new line is called Kink, featuring "authentic fetish items, suitable for long-term practitioners and new initiates alike." Accessories dedicated to butt play are selling well—according to **family** the company's market research, "pegging" is the rage among hetero couples. (The woman wears the strap on, the business end of which looks more like a tapered peg than an actual penis; the sleek design seems to sit easier with the average straight guy.) The company even sells Doc Johnson brand batteries.

Chad, thirty-five, is a cool guy with a gym bod and a product-enhanced pompadour, the sides cut high and tight. He keeps his beard sculpted with the help of Doc Johnson-brand chamomile-infused So Smooth Shaving Cream, from their OptiMALE line of products and toiletries, which can be purchased in a six-item travel pack with deodorant powder, erection-enhancing lotion and a vibrating silicone cock ring.

A business management and marketing major who attended the University of Miami, Chad has worked at Doc Johnson since eighth grade—shortly after he learned what exactly his father did for a living. Since then, he's done time in just about every department—shipping, production, packaging, art and purchasing. Now, as chief operating officer and chief compliance officer, he's basically in charge.

Wearing vintage pink lace-up Vans and a Rolex Daytona watch—his Tesla X, which he hates and is trying to return, is in the parking lot—Braverman has about him the casually expensive sheen of a native Angeleno, a La La Land local who's attended the same schools, dined at the same restaurants and lived in the same neighborhoods as the bold names of Hollywood and their children. "It's like, one degree of separation to just about anyone," says his twenty-nine-year-old sister, Erica Braverman.

At the moment, Erica is in her office in another building, working with her team on the company's consumer education program, the School of Doc. Together with their father Ron, seventy, who founded the place and fought for its survival during the bleak years of the Meese Commission and the Republican war on pornography, they're taking Doc Johnson into its second generation.

The factory is cacophonous and retro, people working together with machines, like something from the 1950s, not a computer in sight. There's the clank of antique metal machinery, the whoosh of pressurized air, the gurgle of running water, the hum and squeak of conveyor belts. The cement floor seems to shudder beneath your feet. The atmosphere is thick with the (more or less) familiar aroma of ULTRASKYN, a proprietary, thermoplastic elastomer—the material that makes the dildos feel somewhat realistic. The company has been perfecting it for forty years. In liquid form, ULTRASKYN pours out of faucets at 250 to 300 degrees in three color choices: chocolate, caramel, and vanilla.

"I know it's a smell some people find off-putting, but I love it," Chad says whimsically, his voice projecting over the din. "I always wanted to put out a novelty fragrance called Dildo—not to sell, just to give out to friends as a gag gift."

At one station, women use common kitchen pots to pour the hot, viscous liquid into copper penis molds. (According to a company handout, Doc Johnson molds six tons of ULTRASKYN and other silicone products daily.) At another station, women paint veins onto the shafts of six-, eight- and ten-inch rubber penises. At a third, they paint pink the glans of the vanilla penises (the two other colors don't get this treatment). At a fourth, they smooth out imperfections in a run of magenta, double-headed dongs with small, rectangular irons. At a fifth, they trim with scissors the excess rubber around the life-like testicles of dildos. (Dildos have balls; dongs do not, which means there's no such thing as a double-headed dildo.)

Growing up a baseball-mad private school kid with divorced parents, Chad was kept in the dark about the details of the family business. "You have to remember I was born during the Reagan administration," he says of the 1980s, a moralistic era that coincided with the beginning of the AIDS and crack epidemics, the intensifying of the War on Drugs and the rise of the religious right.

"My parents never told me what my father did. They didn't want anyone to know," Chad says. "Back then, sex toys were considered part of porn. And my dad was considered like a porn mogul. The government was going after people like him. I went to this private school. My parents didn't want me to be ostracized, or judged by kids—or by kids' parents. They told everyone his business involved the manufacture of health and beauty products. That was back when you could lie to your kids about stuff, before the Internet."

In some ways, he adds, "I felt like it had to do with my parent's divorce. I was like most boys, I wanted to come to work with my dad. Because my friends were going to work with their dads. They were going to like, take-your-son-to-work day. And I never went with my dad. And I wanted to. I was also kind of like, sad that I wasn't asked, you know? It became part of the whole idea that we didn't live together anymore."

One afternoon, when he was about thirteen, Chad was at his dad's house in Beverly Hills. His dad was married to wife number two at the time. The new wife had a son who was sixteen. He, Chad and a friend were hanging out playing video games. Looking around Ron Braverman's well-appointed digs, Chad's friend asked, "What does your father do for a living?"

Chad repeated what he knew: "Health and beauty products, import-export, that kind of stuff."

The stepbrother made a face. "That's not what your dad does," he sneered.

"Then what does he do?" Chad asked.

"He makes fake dicks, you idiot."

The Porn Mogul is in.

Ron Braverman is sitting behind his desk in a pale lime shirt with the Doc Johnson logo embroidered over his heart. An extra-large man with a soft voice, meaty hands, and slicked-back hair, he looks like he could be comfortable drinking espresso at a back table in a restaurant in Little Italy.

As it is, he's sitting behind his executive desk in an office befitting the CEO and founder of a company he's built from the ground up—a substantial space with a wet bar, private bathroom and oak paneling. A cabinet behind his desk holds his collection of Daum crystal—there's an elephant, a tiger, and a dragon. Also displayed prominently is a photo he took with Arnold Schwarzenegger and Nancy Reagan at a ceremony at the Ronald Reagan Presidential Library. For years Ron was a member of Schwarzenegger's regular Sunday motorcycle and brunch gang. Funny how things go. During the two decades that made up the Reagan/Bush years, Ron Braverman had been a target of the Reagan administration's war on porn. Now here he was was rubbing elbows with Nancy.

Ron was born in Cleveland, the grandson of Russian Jewish immigrants. His mother was strong-willed and outgoing. His father was a CPA; his uncles were all salesmen. "I grew up in a family with a gift for gab," he says. "It was only natural that I went into sales, too."

At first, Ron sold appliances. Then he went Northeast to work for another Cleveland native, Reuben Sturman. Also a child of Russian Jewish immigrants, Sturman had started his business out of the trunk of his car, selling tobacco and magazines. After discovering the kind of money he could make on "girly magazines" and explicit books, his course was set. By 1960, Sturman was living in a sixteen-room mansion overlooking a swan-stocked lake. An exercise fanatic who shopped at Bijan, a trendy clothier, and attended the Cannes Film Festival every year, he owned an empire of an estimated two hundred adult businesses, according to published reports and court papers.

In the beginning, Ron says, Sturman had him selling adult books and magazines over a six-state area in New England. The hours and miles were long. "I would pull out Monday morning, and I didn't come home until Saturday night," he says. With a trunk full of adult products, things could get dicey, especially on dark nights in the vicinity of small towns. "Sometimes the cops just wanted a few magazines. Sometimes I ended up getting hauled down to the station," Ron remembers.

In 1972, Ron moved to Amsterdam to open and manage three adult bookstores there. Four years later, he came back to the States and purchased a fifteen-hundred-square-foot rubber molding business on Lankershim Boulevard in LA called Marche Manufacturing. "Marche made some adult toys, and maybe ten different dongs that came in several sizes," Ron says. "They also made rubber animals and insects, fishing lures and creepy stuff for Halloween, like those severed hands. They were using a very simplistic formula, a PVC, a material no different than what Disney was using at the time to make figurines."

According to some news reports, Sturman was suspected of being the initial owner of Doc Johnson and Ron was the operator. The Bravermans, however, dispute this version. "Ron started Doc Johnson," Chad says. "Reuben was a guy who was basically the godfather of the industry. He set a lot of people up in different areas—they owned stores, distribution, different things. Reuben wasn't a partner. But he was a very, very close friend, mentor, and sort of a father figure in my dad's life," Chad says. "They spent a lot of time together. They knew each other for many years. Their wives and families were close."

After his sojourn in Europe, where public morals were less inhibited, and where couples shopped openly together for a range of sex toys, Ron was convinced he could bring a different product and attitude to the American consumer, too. "Basically, all they were selling in the States in those days were a seven-inch vibrator, a four-and-half-inch vibrator, a seven-inch dildo and a second seven-inch dildo that had a wire inside—they called it The Bender. They were packaged in these nondescript poly bags and nobody really knew what to do with them," Ron says.

"I wanted to package the items in glossy cardboard," he continues. "I wanted to give them names. I wanted to give them descriptions. I wanted to make them into something more mainstream."

Before he could do that, though, he needed a brand name. "I needed a name people could be comfortable with. After Lee, Johnson was the second-largest surname in the world," he says.

For the logo, "I put him in a white jacket, and he was a hip-looking guy with a [mustache]. I called him 'Doc' because when you saw him, he looked a little like a pharmacist. Or Doc could be a nickname. Or it could mean that he was really a doctor. It wasn't clear. But I wanted him to have credibility so people thought they were buying something of substance."

Two years later, Ron began assembling the 215,000-square-feet facility that is Doc Johnson today. Just as he hit a groove, Reagan was elected president. Shortly thereafter, Reagan authorized something called the Attorney General's Commission on Pornography, which had wide-ranging powers to investigate.

In 1986, the attorney general's office released the document that came to be called the Meese Report. The 1,096-page tome identified Reuben Sturman as the biggest distributor of hardcore pornography in the nation. The report also documented what were found to be the harmful effects of pornography and connections between pornographers and organized crime. The report was criticized by many inside and outside the porn industry, who called it biased and inaccurate. Nevertheless, a wave of prosecutions and convictions followed. Hundreds of producers, distributors, and retailers in the sex industry were indicted and convicted. Better known men in the industry like Larry Flynt and Hugh Hefner fought similar charges and pressures. Many were driven from the business.

While Sturman had already been arrested many times, in the past he'd been successful at evading convictions on sex charges. Unlike others in his business, who often plea bargained when they were arrested, Sturman became a hero among his peers for fighting back. When one of his Detroit warehouses was raided by local police in 1963 and twenty thousand nudist magazines were seized, Sturman sued the department for $200,000, and the case was dropped. When the FBI raided another of his warehouses a year later, Sturman sued J. Edgar Hoover. Indicted on charges of receiving lewd books, he won a US Supreme Court ruling that the material was not obscene.

Twenty years later, however, the government was taking a different approach. As they had done successfully with Chicago crime kingpin Al Capone—and as they would continue to do later with drug dealers—investigators followed Sturman's money. His indictment, by a Cleveland grand jury, was announced by Attorney General Meese himself. Bail was set at $3 million.

"To his defenders in the sex industry, Sturman was a marketing genius and a champion of free speech, an entrepreneur whose toughness, intelligence, and boundless self-confidence were responsible for his successes," wrote the journalist Eric Schlosser in *U.S. News & World Report.* "But to anti-porn activists and Justice Department officials, Sturman was the head of a vast criminal organization whose companies enjoyed an unfair competitive advantage: protection and support from the highest levels of the Cosa Nostra."

A colorful character, Sturman often chatted with news reporters covering his various trials, during which many of the X-rated films he allegedly distributed became evidence and were screened for the juries—a fact he found hilarious. Somewhat camera shy, Sturman often wore a cowboy hat and white surgical mask on his way to court. Another time, he was photographed in a Groucho Marx-style fake nose-and-glasses combo.

In 1988, after additional investigation by the Meese Commission, Ron Braverman was convicted of perjury stemming from his relationship with Sturman. Sentenced to a year and one day in federal prison, he served six months. In 1996, the federal government again indicted Ron, charging him with tax evasion, based on alleged financial transactions connected to his close friend. Convicted a second time, Ron served five months in prison and another five under house arrest.

Sturman, meanwhile, was sentenced to twenty-nine years in jail and made to pay a $2.5 million fine. Nineteen years of the sentence were the result of his conviction for trying to influence a male juror in one of his trials. According to testimony, the agent of influence was Sturman's young wife, the former Naomi Delgado. A half-Venezuelan, half-Japanese beauty raised in Pasadena, Delgado was a singer popular in Spanish-language venues around California. According to published reports, Delgado asked the young man to meet her for a meal. Partway through, he started to question her intentions and left the restaurant.

Two years later Sturman escaped from the minimum security Federal Prison Camp in Boron, California, stopping at an In-N-Out for lunch before disappearing. After several months on the lam, US marshals tracked him to an apartment in Anaheim. Years later, when asked why he didn't leave the country after his escape, the then-seventy-two-year-old said, "I figured if I stayed away from everybody I knew there, I'd be fine. But I couldn't stay away from my wife and child." Eventually, he was transferred to F.C.I Manchester, a medium security prison in Lexington, Kentucky.

As Schlosser points out in his book *Reefer Madness: Sex, Drugs, and Cheap Labor in the American Black Market*, the Republican war on porn ended up coinciding with an exponential increase in America's consumption of porn. "According to *Adult Video News*, from 1985 to 1992—from the appointment of the Meese Commission to the close of George H. W. Bush's presidency—the number of hardcore video rentals each year in the United States *rose* from 79 million to 490 million," Schlosser writes.

As went the fortunes of porn, so went Doc Johnson. Though fate had drawn a dark cloud over Ron's early days in the industry, the future was bright. Following sixteen years of Republican rule, the Clinton administration abandoned efforts to enforce the nation's obscenity laws and porn quickly became widely available mainstream entertainment.

"A lot changed when *Cosmopolitan* and Helen Gurley Brown started to talk about women masturbating and women having orgasms and using vibrators," Ron says. "Then when VHS went to DVD, it freed up a lot more space on the shelves in adult stores. And unfortunately, the AIDS crisis kind of favored sex toys because a lot of people who were doing things that maybe they shouldn't have been doing started looking for alternative sources of enjoyment."

From there came *Sex and the City*, toys designed with women in mind and adult stores having women's nights and couple's nights.

And now pegging.

About the time Ron was getting off house arrest, in 1997, Sturman died in a prison hospital in Lexington, Kentucky. He was seventy-three. He left behind Delgado, by then his ex-wife, and a nine-year-old daughter.

A spokeswomen for the prison said the cause of death was "heart and kidney failure." After a traditional Jewish funeral, attended by a handful of family members, he was buried in a town south of San Francisco.

A few years later, as luck would have it, Ron bumped into Naomi at a gym in Sherman Oaks. By now he also was divorced, from wife number three. Their friendship was rekindled, and they began dating.

In 2001, they married, and Ron adopted Naomi's daughter, Erica.

Today, Erica Braverman is twenty-nine. After majoring in English lit and psychology—at the University of Miami, like Chad—and trying her hand at an LA PR firm, Sturman's biological daughter joined the Doc Johnson family about six years ago. For her work on the company's yearlong campaign commemorating Doc Johnson's fortieth anniversary, Erica was named "Marketing Executive of the Year" by the adult industry news source XBIZ.

With Erica's help, the company has moved heavily into social media, with behind-the-scenes video content at the factory, interviews with porn stars, product sneak peeks, customer forums, and giveaways. "Since she started here, Erica has absolutely grabbed ahold of it with her teeth and become a force in social marketing and PR," Ron says proudly. "I'm thrilled that both of my kids want to be here. They've done an amazing job." Together, he says, they "deal with the day-to-day. I'm just here to get coffee and bring doughnuts."

Now Erica pushes back from her screen, dressed in all black: Black tee, black Rag & Bone jeans and black Maison Martin Margiela ankle boots with a clunky heel. She has the dark hair and eyes of her mother; people say she has Sturman's smile. She loves going to concerts (Kanye was the last) and finding new restaurants. She went to Citizen in Beverly Hills twice last week: "Their salmon is bomb, it's like butter." When not at work or networking events, she spends a lot of time taking classes at General Assembly in Santa Monica—HTML, Java, digital marketing, graphic design.

"Reuben is my biological dad. And Ron is my second dad. Reuben died when I was so young that I don't remember that much about him—aside from the amazing things people tell me. He belonged to Mensa.

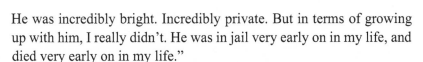

He was incredibly bright. Incredibly private. But in terms of growing up with him, I really didn't. He was in jail very early on in my life, and died very early on in my life."

How does that make you feel? I ask.

"That's what my therapist asks me," she deadpans. "I think a lot of society is backwards, even to this day. I don't have like a tragic wound from the fact that my father was taken away from me. But at the same time, yeah, it upsets me. It's like he was part of this big societal penitence. Our country is so screwed up. We can put violence on TV, but we still have a problem with seeing a vibrator or a sex toy. It doesn't make sense to me; it never has."

"It's funny how life works out," she continues. "But I feel blessed too, because it's all a part of my history, and it's a very rich story. A lot of people think Reuben was a hero. And Ron has been there for me literally since he came into the picture. He went to every recital, every game, every performance. He was always there, right next to my mom. I feel really lucky to have him.

"And I feel lucky now that Chad and I are here and we're able to make our mark. The industry is only two generations old. Because it's so new, there's a lot of room to take it into the future. We're both psyched to make that happen."

Almost on cue, Chad wanders in. As he's wont to do, he picks up one of the fancy vibrators arrayed on one of the several desks in the room, this one pink. Absently, he toys with the buttons.

"Growing up as an only child," he says, "before Erica was part of my life, I had this feeling that if I didn't take over the company, then no one would, and then the company would be gone. It made me feel really sad."

"Well, now there's both of us," Erica says.

WILL RON POPEIL'S FINAL PRODUCT BE HIS MASTERPIECE?

IT BOILS EGGS! IT STEAMS CLAMS AND LOBSTERS! IT BAKES BREAD! AND BEST OF ALL, IT CAN FRY A FIFTEEN-POUND TURKEY IN FORTY-SIX MINUTES!

After fourteen years, $4 million, thirty-five thousand pounds of fried turkey and uncounted thousands of pounds of potatoes, fish, bacon, and other fried delicacies—much of it consumed by firefighters at station houses in Beverly Hills and Coldwater Canyon—Ron Popeil is ready to bring to market his greatest invention.

You've seen him on late night TV, hawking his revolutionary products. The blue eyes blazing with entrepreneurial zeal. The helmet of shoe-polish black hair. The meaty, sensual, Brando-esque lips formed into a broad, porcelain-veneered smile. The stentorian voice, like a boardwalk huckster's.

But wait! There's more!

Popeil has been called the Einstein of the Infomercial. The Hemingway of Home Shopping. The Salesman of the Century. He's played himself on *The Simpsons* and has been parodied on *Saturday Night Live*. Weird Al Yankovic even produced a song about him, on which Popeil's half-sister sang all the backup parts. Since he made his first commercial, in the early 1950s for the Chop-O-Matic hand food processor ("Ladies and gentlemen, I'm going to show you the greatest kitchen appliance ever made."), he's been copied by every television pitchman and woman who has plied the airwaves.

Popeil has brought us such enduring products as Mr. Microphone, the Smokeless Ashtray, the Popeil Pocket Fisherman, the Ronco Electric Food Dehydrator and his spray-on remedy for bald spots, GLH Formula #9. (The GLH stands for Great Looking Hair. Like all the rest, he came up with the name himself.

His most lucrative product to date, the Ronco Showtime Rotisserie & BBQ, has earned more than $1.4 billion worldwide. Maybe you've seen the infomercial: The charismatic salesman demonstrating from the pulpit of his in-studio kitchen. The rapt audience in folding chairs. The call and response.

Just set it…

AND FORGET IT!

Popeil began selling as a thirteen-year-old, pushing Chop-O-Matics for $3.95—"All your onions chopped to perfection without shedding a single tear"—on Chicago's Maxwell Street, a bustling city bazaar catering to tastes both high and low.

Now, on a sunny afternoon more than sixty years later, he is found in the spacious kitchen-cum-R&D center of his art-filled home in Beverly Hills. Wearing a blue apron and an air of crotchety determination, the eighty-year-old Popeil is readying himself for yet another demo of his most amazing product yet. He's hoping it could be the last.

In two hours, a wealthy investor from China will be walking through the door with a trusted advisor. Her name is Sue, or maybe it's Hsu. He should have done more research, but he just hasn't had the time. Popeil has been told by an intermediary that Hsu is "a real estate mogul billionaire who's very into health and well-being." She wants to find a product she can purchase, own, brand, and sell in China, Europe, the United States, and South America.

It just so happens that Popeil has exactly the thing she needs.

He gestures with a meaty hand, the nails perfectly manicured, toward the object sitting before him on the butcher-block counter, Ron Popeil'sTM 5in1 FryerTM.

Manufactured in China to exacting standards—one of the reasons for all the years and expense—the 5in1 FryerTM cooks a fifteen-pound turkey in forty-six minutes, or two full pounds of thick bacon in ten minutes. It steams, it boils, it makes rice. It can even bake bread, cakes, or muffins in a fraction of the normal time. That it seems to do four things and not five is beside the point. What's most important is this: due to new regulations for home fryers that have recently gone into effect around the world, there is nothing like Popeil's fryer on the market today. Yes folks, Ron Popeil'sTM 5in1 FryerTM is the only product available on the planet that can cook an entire turkey using only five liters of cooking oil, the mandated safe limit.

Over the past five years, Popeil says, the most popular fryer in the world, the Butterball Turkey Fryer, has sold two hundred thousand units on QVC. It has been available in twenty thousand stores nationwide.

But unfortunately for Butterball, even the smallest model requires eight liters of cooking oil. The product has been discontinued.

Leaving only one option, according to Popeil: Ron Popeil'sTM 5in1 FryerTM.

"If each of the twenty thousand stores sells twenty-four pieces in twelve months, you make over $12 million pure profit," Popeil says in his practiced cadence, warming up for his pitch. "That's every year. Because Thanksgiving is not going away! And every day people make bacon, people fry chicken and french fries, people steam vegetables and clams and lobster. People boil eggs—thirty-six hardboiled eggs in eight minutes. It boils pasta, and strains it. It also bakes bread. Make a pizza bread or a whole-wheat nut bread in an hour and twenty minutes."

How much would you expect to pay for this once-in-a-lifetime value?

If ever a man needed to make a place for himself in the world it was Ron Popeil.

Born in May 1935 in the Bronx, his parents divorced when he was three. "Neither of them wanted me or my older brother Jerry, so they dumped us and sent us off to a boarding school in upstate New York," Popeil says. "We were a liability they chose not to accept. Most of the early years were so painful that I blocked much of it out."

He does have one vivid memory of that era, he says. It was parents' visiting day. All the other kids had visitors. "I stood in the middle of this straight road that seemed to go on for an eternity, hoping to see a speck of a car coming in my direction, thinking that my family would come to visit us, but they never did." To this day he can remember the feeling, "just sitting on the road, crying, waiting for my mother and father."

When Popeil was eight, his paternal grandparents "suddenly showed up one day, unannounced," and took the boys to Miami. The family lived frugally on a "poor people's diet" of chicken feet, bean soup, and potatoes. "My grandmother was the kind who would take advantage of coupons and sales, and walk miles to save fifty cents." His grandfather, Isadore, a Polish immigrant, was unemployed, "a mean, unhappy man who didn't believe in anybody or anything," Popeil says. "I never called him grandpa or even Isadore. He never had a name as far as I was concerned."

Five years later, the grandparents packed up the boys and moved to Chicago, where their son and Ron's father, Sam Popeil, ran a company with his brother Raymond that manufactured kitchen products. The boys lived with their grandparents. Sam Popeil lived in a hotel. On weekends, the grandparents would take the boys down to the Popeil Brothers factory and everybody would go to work. The boys did a lot of cleaning up and packaging. "I didn't even get a chance to see my father because he was never there on the weekends," Popeil says.

When he was thirteen, in 1948, Popeil begged his father to allow him to go to Maxwell Street and try his hand at sales.

The Maxwell Street Market was established in the late nineteenth century by newly arrived Jewish immigrants from Eastern Europe. Over the years, other races and cultures were attracted to the Market; it was sometimes called the Ellis Island of the Midwest. An economic hub for poor people looking to get ahead, almost anything was available at deep discounts—new or secondhand, pirated or hijacked, few questions were asked about the provenance of items for sale, even though the old Chicago Police Academy was just adjacent on O'Brien Street.

"The first time I went there," Popeil says, "the proverbial light bulb went on over my head. I saw all these people selling products, pocketing money, and my mind went racing."

Popeil gathered up a number of kitchen products from his father's factory—"he sold them to me at wholesale, so he made a full profit"— and went down to Maxwell Street at five o'clock one Sunday morning.

"I pushed. I yelled. I hawked. And it worked! I was stuffing money into my pockets, more money than I had ever seen in my life."

At that moment, Popeil says, he realized he'd found his calling.

"I figured out that sales could help me escape from the poverty and the miserable existence I had with my grandparents. I had lived for thirteen years in homes without love. Now I finally found a form of affection—and a human connection—through sales."

From then on, the course of his life was set.

On days he didn't go to school, young Popeil would be at the Market at the crack of dawn to prepare fifty pounds each of onions, cabbages, and carrots, and one hundred pounds of potatoes to use in his demonstrations. He'd work the crowds all day long, bringing in as much as $500, a fortune at the time. In his late teens, he began traveling to state and county fairs; eventually he got himself a prime spot inside the Woolworth's department store in Chicago's Loop, the top-grossing Woolworth's location in the country.

When not working, Popeil lived the high life. He dined at the Pump Room, wore a Rolex, rented hotel suites. In pictures from the period, he carries himself like a matinee idol; eventually he moved his offices to the Playboy Building. Over the years, he'd count among his friends such titans of industry as hotelier Steve Wynn. "He was mesmerizing," says Mel Korey, Popeil's college friend and first business partner. "There were secretaries who would take their lunch break at Woolworth's to watch him because he was so good-looking."

In summer 1964, after the Veg-O-Matic was introduced, Popeil founded Ronco. Already aware what television could do for his products, he shot a two-minute commercial for the handy dandy kitchen appliance, a descendant of the Chop-O-Matic, which sliced and diced fruits and vegetables. Then he set out across the Midwest to persuade local stores to carry the product. Once that was accomplished, Popeil and Korey visited local TV stations and bought the cheapest airtime they could find—often late at night. The cost to Popeil for a Veg-O-Matic was $3.42. They sold it to the stores for $7.46. The retail price was $9.95.

Once the commercials ran, stores could hardly keep the product on the shelves. Popeil never looked back.

In his piece on Popeil, "The Pitchman," written at the turn of the century, the New Yorker's Malcolm Gladwell sums up beautifully the nut of Popeil's success:

"Why did the Veg-O-Matic sell so well? Doubtless, Americans were eager for a better way of slicing vegetables. But it was more than that: the Veg-O-Matic represented a perfect marriage between the medium (television) and the message (the gadget).... More specifically, you could train the camera on the machine and compel viewers to pay total attention to the product you were selling. TV allowed you to do even more effectively what the best pitchmen strove to do in live demonstrations—make the product the star."

In his Beverly Hills kitchen, surrounded by his collection of olive oil bottles from around the world, Popeil readies the raw materials for his demonstration. According to the Guinness Book of World Records, the oil collection, more than twenty-four hundred bottles—displayed in glass-front cabinets and in every available nook and cranny—is the world's largest, one of his few personal indulgences, he says, along with his forty-three-foot custom-made, gunmetal gray Almar fishing boat, the Pocket Fisherman. (He has no idea how many gallons of canola oil he has used in the fourteen years developing Ron Popeil'sTM 5in1 FryerTM. "No doubt it could float my boat," Popeil muses.)

As he has done since he was a youngster, Popeil has gone to the market himself to carefully select each piece of food for the demo.

There are onions for chopping and tomatoes for slicing—each one as large and as perfect in appearance as he could find. There are turkeys, chicken parts, bacon slices, and a whole fish to fry.

And, because the potential investor is Chinese, there are boxes of fried squid and frozen wontons.

"The thing is this," he says, pulling the guts out of one of the turkeys, "my goal here is to sell the project to somebody, not to go back into business. There's *nothing* that will get me to go back into business. That's what I don't want to do anymore! What a headache! How many employees do you have? Do you have insurance? Where's your warehouse? How many secretaries? Who's running customer service? What's your lease like where you are? That's running a business. And that's what I no longer want to do.

"What I want to do is continue inventing more products. Because inventing isn't work. That's doing what I want, when I want to do it, which in my mind is the real secret to life, the true sign of success. It's not money. It's not power. It's doing what you want, when you want to do it. That's the golden ticket, right? So here I've created a situation that's quite interesting."

The kitchen grows quiet as he thrusts the turkey's pale carcass beneath the faucet and gives it a warm bath. At fifteen pounds, the turkey is about the size of a ten-week-old infant.

"George Foreman got $138 million of stock and cash for the rights to his grill," Popeil says thoughtfully. "Wolfgang Puck got $22 million for the rights to his soups. Those are both solid names. But neither of them have over fifty years in the business."

How much would you expect to pay for this once-in-a-lifetime value?

His blue eyes blaze. His voice rises in volume, like a carnival barker's.

"I'm not looking for $200 million. I'm not even looking for $100 million. Not even $50 million!"

Operators are standing by.

THE FIRST MALE SUPERMODEL WAS A CULT MEMBER

HOYT RICHARDS WAS ONE OF THE 1990S' MOST SUCCESSFUL MALE MODELS. NO ONE SUSPECTED HE WAS UNDER THE SWAY OF A DOOMSDAY CULT.

Heads turn as Hoyt Richards saunters through the low light and fashionable din inside the Petty Cash Taqueria, in Los Angeles' Fairfax District. Six foot one with a chiseled jaw and a dimple, a forelock of gray-blond hair cascading rakishly over one brow, he makes an immediate impression: That guy must be someone.

And he was. During the 1980s and '90s, Richards was one of fashion's most in-demand models. He traveled the world, appearing in campaigns for Versace, Valentino, Ralph Lauren, and Cartier and was a favorite subject for photographers like Bruce Weber, Richard Avedon, and Helmut Newton. In 1992, the Italian men's magazine *Mondo Uomo* gave him a fifty-eight-page spread, while *Vogue* named him one of the top twenty-five male models of all time. He worked and socialized with the era's A-list models, including Cindy Crawford, Linda Evangelista, Christy Turlington, and Naomi Campbell, and has a ribald story about being sandwiched between the latter two—they were nearly naked; Richards was sporting a bustier—at a birthday party for photographer Steven Meisel. He was, no doubt, the first male supermodel.

As successful as Richards was professionally, however, he harbored a harrowing secret. For years, he was enmeshed within a shadowy religious sect called Eternal Values, which kept him psychologically enslaved with convoluted forms of love and abuse, reassurance and disapproval.

Eventually he would save himself, but he would never be the same.

At the end of the summer between his junior and senior years at Princeton, Hoyt Richards was discovered by a modeling agent and cast in an ad campaign for Jeffrey Banks. He was John Richards Hoyt back then—the professional name change would happen later. "The pictures came out that fall and all of a sudden I was one of the 'new faces,'" he says now. "The agency was calling. They were like, 'We've got a job for you in Tokyo on Tuesday.' And I was like, 'Listen, sorry, I've got a test.'"

It was an intoxicating experience for an all-American kid who just months before counted Friday night football games as among the more exciting events in his life.

Richards was the fourth of six children, born in 1962 in Syracuse, New York. His father was a Lehigh University–trained engineer and his mom, Terry, a Mount Holyoke alumna. Both families claimed roots in the American Revolution. When Richards was two, the family moved to a wealthy enclave on Philadelphia's Main Line. Later on, at Princeton, he majored in economics and played varsity football.

Richards' mother, however, had a difficult upbringing that Richards says likely influenced how she related to her own children. When her mother, an alcoholic, died at an early age, Terry Richards had assumed full care for her younger siblings. "When you come from that background," Richards says, "you try to control everything because you don't want to ever get hurt again. You develop this kind of bubble that you live in where it's never your fault, and if anything goes wrong, you're the victim." As a child and teen, he tried very hard to please her. "[My mother] was very clear about what she expected me to be," he says. "In order to get the love I wanted from her, I felt I had to try to become the thing she wanted me to be, even though that didn't feel necessarily like who I really was."

A gifted athlete from an early age, Richards gravitated to sports. "I was always drawn toward things that would have a crowd; with sports, you had that stadium," he says. "All those eyes on me felt like maybe it would heal something. It's the same reason I think I ended up modeling."

Like many affluent families, the Hoyts summered in Nantucket, in an area called Shimmo and in a house his mom named Shimmo the Merrier. One day during the summer before his junior year of high school, Richards was at Nobadeer Beach—a kids' hangout referred to by locals as "No Brassiere Beach"—when he encountered an older but still youthful-looking man drawing a yin and yang diagram in the sand.

Frederick von Mierers was full of ideas. Tall, gaunt, and handsome, he spoke about Eastern philosophy, Hinduism, and reincarnation. The attention he paid to the young Richards was invigorating. At the time, Richards was being forced by his parents to transfer out of his public school to attend the prestigious Haverford School, and he was not, he says now, in a particularly good place. "I was sixteen, he was in his thirties," Richards says. "When you're that age, having an adult who will talk to you like an adult gets your attention."

Von Mierers invited a bunch of the underage kids from the beach back to his place for beer. "I remember arriving there and knowing very quickly that this was clearly the cheapest beer you could buy," Richards says. "I was not very impressed." But the next summer von Mierers was back, and again the summer after that, and Richards continued to be drawn to him for reasons he can't really explain. Freddy, as he came to be called, did Richards' astrological chart and Richards, in turn, began reading Hindu texts and other books von Mierers suggested. He went from unimpressed to infatuated. "One year I was going to England. He told me the experience would really change my life— which it absolutely did, but it doesn't take a rocket scientist to figure that out," Richards says today. "I remember thinking, when stuff was happening to me, Freddy really is clairvoyant!"

While he was at Princeton, and in the early days of his modeling career, Richards began visiting Freddy in Manhattan on the weekends. He and other young acolytes would go with Freddy to Studio 54, where it was impossible to get in without connections. Once inside, the group would see clubbers having sex on the dance floor and doing cocaine in the bathrooms, but Richards and his coterie had nobler pursuits. Freddy was against drinking and drugs. He thought the body was God's temple. In the wee hours, the group would return to Freddy's ornately decorated apartment to discuss Eastern philosophy.

"In my mind I was thinking that I was working him," Richards says. "I was bringing up a couple friends with me from school, and we knew he could get us into Studio 54 and we could crash at his apartment. I was looking at it like I was taking advantage of this guy!"

By his senior year in college, Richards had signed with Ford Models and proudly paid for his last two semesters of college tuition himself. He graduated in the spring of 1985 and moved into an apartment in the same Manhattan building as Freddy's. But there was much more to it than being neighbors. Richards was becoming part of Eternal Values, a cult led by von Mierers that counted a number of the building's residents among its ranks. Starting then and for years after, Richards donated almost all of his earnings to the group, helping to cover the rent on the apartments Freddy kept in the building, as well as others he began to acquire as the group grew in number.

When he wasn't jetting off to a modeling or commercial job, Richards spent his days and nights doing menial tasks around the building or studying alongside Freddy and, despite his financial importance to the group, sleeping on a mat on the floor.

Eternal Values was founded in the early 1980s by von Mierers, himself a former model, interior decorator, and socialite. An astrologer and self-styled prophet, he claimed to be an alien reincarnated from the distant star Arcturus. He said he had come to Earth to warn people of an impending apocalypse to be triggered by a change in the planet's magnetic poles, and to train his students to become leaders in the aftermath.

Based out of von Mierers' apartment building on the east side of Manhattan—the group also kept a loft in the Bronx and, later, a large house in North Carolina—Eternal Values attracted young, intelligent, and often wealthy followers. Most were seeking a greater understanding of the universe; some were rewarded with a life of mind control and fanaticism. At its peak, there were perhaps one hundred active members. They spoke in New Age jargon, with much talk about "highly evolved personalities," "ego renunciation," "the white light and the violet light," and the coming apocalypse, which made personal wealth and relationships unnecessary. Astrological charts and life readings, performed by von Mierers or one of his acolytes, played a central role. Included was often a "gem prescription," adopted from Hindu belief in the healing properties of certain precious stones. "The gems are God's thoughts condensed," he told *Vanity Fair* in a 1990 interview.

Von Mierers told followers he had connections for great deals on stones, which he often sold to them for more than $100,000; payments were only accepted in cash or traveler's checks. "The gems were supposed to be the most pure forms of matter on our planet," says Richards, who bought a fortune's worth over the years. "They were supposed to strengthen your inherent weakness and enhance your strengths."

Within the group, the number of gems one possessed was treated as a sign of devoutness. "I spent over $150,000," Richards says. "The gems all came with bogus appraisals. When I sold them later, I found out they were worth less than $8,000."

When Freddy's story was included in a popular 1985 book, *Aliens Among Us*—"Dazzling true testimony that extraterrestrials are on earth," the book promised—Eternal Values became a national phenomenon. Thousands of hopefuls contacted Freddy for astrological readings at $350 per session. Hundreds were drawn into his gemstone scams. Richards, then in his modeling heyday, was trotted out for interviews and appearances.

But while von Mierers was getting rich, Richards found in Eternal Values something more grounding. "The economy was kicking ass, there was opulence everywhere: a lot of drugs, a lot of cocaine," says Richards. "Being in [Eternal Values], you had this sense that there was an alternative to all that. The message was, don't be attached to this wealth and decadence because there's really a higher meaning to it all. Freddy was basically saying, 'Get your head out of your ass because the world is coming to an end—you better get your shit together because you've spent lifetimes preparing for this opportunity.'"

Gilberto Picinich joined the group in 1981 after hearing Freddy speak on the radio. A lifelong seeker, Picinich remembers the sense of purpose Eternal Values gave him. "We all had the feeling that we were on this critical mission that would help save ourselves, friends, and family from the coming apocalypse," he says. "The message self-validated over the years. You started to fear that if you left, you might miss something important, something that you've sacrificed for."

Because Richards was the group's golden goose, some felt he was given special privileges, "like flying around the world fucking beautiful models," says Picinich. Yet while they lived off his money, the group felt that Richards' work was inherently evil.

"The fact that the world puts so much importance on someone who won a genetic lottery—to the point of putting a billboard in Times Square and paying that person hundreds of thousands of dollars—is the exact reason why the world needs to be destroyed," Richards says in an attempt to explain the cult's point of view.

He tried to downplay his secret life with the people he met as a model while making choices those colleagues didn't understand. "Everyone else was living it up. It was like, 'Hey, let's go to Madonna's for the weekend!'" Richards has said. "But I was like, 'No, no. I can't. The end of the world is coming.'"

As it was with his mother, so it was with the cult. Nothing he did was good enough, but Richards kept trying. "More than anything, I felt like I'd made a commitment and I couldn't give up," he says. "Freddy had told us that we were responsible for our own lives—which I could deal with—but we were also responsible for the millions of people we were supposed to help, and that was a heavy trip that I couldn't screw up."

The hold Eternal Values had on him became so strong that he stayed on even after von Mierers' death in 1990 from AIDS-related causes. According to Richards, the Manhattan district attorney's office was investigating von Mierers' gemstone scams at the time of his death, but discontinued after he died, when it was discovered that the self-proclaimed alien's real name was Freddie Miers. He'd been raised Jewish in Brooklyn.

After Freddy died, there was a power struggle within Eternal Values. Freddy's successors were even more extreme. As the years passed and the group relocated to a big house on Lake Lure, North Carolina, Richards continued to earn money and fame but the group became increasingly hateful toward him. He was often interrogated for hours on end about what they called his "ego lapses."

"He was a good guy and a bit of a people pleaser," Picinich recalls. "After Freddy's death, the [new] leader was pretty cruel to him. You could see the toll it took." Richards recalls some truly terrible behavior: "They said I was resistant and resentful of my chores, and that I was guilty of vanity and looking in the mirror—for that offense they shaved my head," he says. "Mostly I would do menial jobs like scrubbing toilets and vacuuming. Any job they could think of that was a pain in the ass, they'd get me to do it."

The abuse was also emotional. "My nickname was Dipshit. When I wasn't in trouble, they'd call me Dippy, but generally I was just called Dipshit," Richards says. "And this was after I'd been financing this thing for fifteen years. Sometimes I would have to go out to the end of the dock and do belly flops as a form of self-punishment."

Finally, on the night of July 3, 1999—after two previous unsuccessful attempts to leave the cult—Richards escaped, having tithed to Eternal Values the majority of his earnings, estimated at nearly $4.5 million dollars over almost two decades of work. He hadn't spoken to his parents in twelve years. He turned to an old friend from his modeling days: Fabio Lanzoni, the long-haired and pectorally gifted spokesmodel best known for gracing the covers of hundreds of romance novels.

"When the shit hit the fan, he knew I would help," Lanzoni says. "The other models used to make fun of him because he believed in aliens, but I'd tell them, 'Listen, you shouldn't make fun of him because there was something that happened in his life that put him in this situation.'" Richards lived in Lanzoni's house in Los Angeles—and drove one of his Porches—for nearly a year.

On a recent afternoon, Richards sits on the sofa in his West Los Angeles apartment. He's in bare feet and shorts; his forelock looks a bit limp. He recently wrote, produced and starred in a movie called *Dumbbells*, playing a guy who escapes from a cult and opens a gym. Another movie, *Invisible Prisons,* is in the works.

After he left Eternal Values, Richards says, he began doing a lot of reflection. As unbelievable as it sounds, never once during his two decades with the group did he ever consider he might be a member of a cult. In his mind, he was in a special group on an important mission; he believed he was one of the Chosen who would lead the earth into a new era of peace and prosperity. Like anyone suffering from Stockholm syndrome, he had no ability to objectify his experience. The reason he finally left the group, he says, was because he felt like a failure, unable to conform to their standards.

"And then one day I was doing some research, and it hit me," Richards says, unabashed. "I was like, Oh, my God! I'm a textbook cult victim."

In the years that followed, Richards has sought counseling and worked to build a film career. A civil lawsuit recouped some of his funds and effectively killed the remnants of Eternal Values. These days Richards feels that he's finally reached a place of peace within himself. "I've come to understand that all this didn't happen because there was something wrong with me," he says. "It wasn't because my mother didn't love me enough. I was able to forgive myself. It's how I was able to relieve myself of all that shame." His great hope is that his story will be useful to others, "to make it cool for others to talk about their abusive situations, their fuck-ups."

Likewise, he tries to make the best of his years with Eternal Values. "When you meet new people, you're never quite sure when to mention it," Richards says. "But I know one thing for sure: if I do bring it up, nobody ever finds my story boring."

ARABIAN PRINCE HAS NO REGRETZ

THE FORGOTTEN SIXTH FOUNDING MEMBER OF THE SEMINAL HIP-HOP GROUP N.W.A IS DOING JUST FINE. LIKE THE FIFTH BEATLE, HE'S THE ONE WHO WALKED AWAY.

A rabian Prince gallops the hardwood floor on a fast break and sets up on the left wing—a trim fifty-year-old in Kobe-brand high tops, therapeutic knee sleeves and a large pair of diamond stud earrings glinting beneath the lights.

We are at the YMCA in Torrance, California, a dozen miles southwest of Compton, the checkered neighborhood where he grew up. It's nearing noon. Sneakers squeak. Balls pound, echoing off the familiar ceramic brick walls. Arab is running his eighth pickup game in two hours. The players at this plush, suburban-style facility are a diverse lot—black, Asian, Hispanic, a few of them women. The point guard drives hard to the basket and kicks it out to the arc. Arab nails the trey for the win.

"People try to stop me because they know I'm a three-point threat," Arab says, picking up a half-gallon jug of water. In his last two games he'd shot seven for eight. "They're always like, 'Don't let him shoot! Don't let him shoot!' I always tell them: 'Y'all need to change my name to Don't Let Him Shoot.'"

Arabian Prince is a man of many handles. To his friends he's Arab or 'Rab. Until recently Wikipedia had him listed as Mik Lezan. His real name is Kim Renard Nazel. (Mik Lezan is the semordnilap.) The son of a music teacher and a noted writer, he was born and raised in South Central, the birthplace of gangsta rap and a once-thriving middle-class community that has been devastated by what one African American law professor has called "the crack plague and its festering aftermath."

As Arabian Prince, he's been rapping and producing for more than thirty years. As Professor X, he's a respected electro-funk DJ who often spins his Kraftwerk-inspired EDM in Europe. And at times he still performs as part of the pioneering early-eighties rap group Jimmy Bobby and the Critters, founded by Russ Parr, an early host at LA's first total hip-hop station. Known for minstrel-like antics (sometimes performed in blackface) and the clever, farcical style that characterized the early days of West Coast rappers, Jimmy Bobby rocked the charts with songs such as "Ugly Knuckle Butt," "Roaches," and "One Glove," a satire of Michael Jackson.

Arab's most significant role, however, has been largely forgotten.

Of all the rappers to come out of LA, none were more influential than the founding members of Niggaz Wit Attitudes. Check out the iconic cover photo of N.W.A's debut studio LP, *Straight Outta Compton*. The camera looks up from street level, into a huddle of hard young faces that would change forever the world's music—and culture, language and sense of style—with songs like "Fuck tha Police" and "Gangsta Gangsta."

There's Ice Cube at twelve o'clock high, issuing his characteristic scowl. Eazy-E, RIP, is posted up at three o'clock, pointing a gat into the lens. Dr. Dre is to his right, then M.C. Ren, then DJ Yella.

And at nine o'clock, with his trademark Jheri curl dripping fashionably from beneath his ballcap, is Arabian Prince.

Like the fifth Beatle, he's the one who walked away.

On a sparkling blue day along the California coastline, Arabian Prince pulls his silver AMG Mercedes into the double-long parking spot beneath his loft in Marina del Rey. He's lived here for three years. Before that, he says, he had a series of "show houses."

"There was big lawns and gardens, huge upkeep. And the taxes! It was just a waste. I'm always traveling, ain't got no kids, none of that. So I decided I'd rather spend it on stuff I like."

He pats the tail of his 2006 Mercedes. "This one's 700 horsepower," he says. When he's not touring as a rap artist or DJ, or doing special effects—he's worked on movies like the *Mighty Morphin Power Rangers* and *The Addams Family*, cartoon series like *Silver Surfer* and video games like *Crash Bandicoot* and *Lord of the Rings*— he likes to race his cars at Willow Springs International and the Auto Club Raceway at Pomona.

We take the elevator upstairs. The hip, utilitarian glass and concrete loft building provides a panoramic view of the other tall gems that line the marina. We pause to take a look.

Nobody has to remind Arab he's come a long way from the apartment on South Willow Avenue in Compton, across the street from the Immanuel Baptist Church, where he grew up with his mom and stepdad.

His mom played piano in church. His father was Joseph Nazel, a political activist and prolific author, whose books range from noirish blaxploitation novels to biographies of prominent African Americans. For a period Nazel served as editor of *Players*, known at the time as *Playboy* for black men. Nazel sported an afro; he'd come of age politically at the time of the Black Panthers. He lived in a series of book-crammed apartments around Inglewood, Crenshaw, and Watts that would later be described as resembling the "atelier of a hard-boiled pulp writer from the 1950s." Upon his death at sixty-two, the Los Angeles Times called him an "editor and author of incalculable importance to LA's African American community, particularly to the readers, artists and writers he championed and served throughout his career."

Due to the pacifying influence of the church complex across the street, Arab's childhood apartment was located in a zone of relative calm amid the violence of the crack epidemic. But Arab also spent a lot of time at his grandmother's house, near the infamous Nickerson

Gardens and Ujima Village housing projects. At the time, the neighborhood was becoming increasingly violent. Gunshots rang out day and night. Ujima Village had a lake, a symbol of more hopeful times in the neighborhood. Arab remembers having seen bodies pulled from the muddy waters with some regularity.

Arab's parents did their best to shelter him. They sent him to Catholic schools; his maternal uncles pushed him hard in sports. "Other kids were in gangs and were acting a fool. They kept me out by making me a football player. My uncles were ex-military. They would fill up duffle bags with clothes, tie 'em to a tree. They'd be like, 'You gonna hit this tree until the leaves fall off.' It was a little crazy, but it made me tough, you know? And I'm glad it kept me out of the gang thing."

When Arab was in middle school, his father had a radio show at KACE in Inglewood, a top urban station at the time. While his dad was on air, spinning jazz and interviewing artists and writers, Arab would hang out in the production room. "I'd spend my time making mixtapes. Before long I was selling them at school and I was like, 'Oh, this is cool. I wanna be a DJ!'" He and his friend Termite began DJing school parties.

"I called myself DJ Prince at first; back in the day, I always used to dress like Prince. That was the thing in the early eighties—either you dressed like Prince or you dressed like Michael Jackson. I used to wear the tight parachute pants, and I had the trim moustache, the whole thing.

"One day I was DJing at a skating rink. I was with Egyptian Lover, that was my boy, still is. This girl comes up to us and asks us our names. And he's like, 'I'm Egyptian Lover.' And I'm like, 'I'm DJ Prince.' She looks at me and goes, 'I always see you two together. You should call yourself Arabian Prince.' And I guess that just stuck." The two still tour together.

Arab's work on the turntables—he was among the first in South Central to add a simple drum machine to his home-built DJ's coffin—eventually led to a gig as a house DJ at the Cave, a popular spot on Lennox Avenue that helped usher in the rap scene and bring together local artists like Arab, Egypt, and Uncle Jam's Army.

With financial backing from the owner of the Cave, Arab—by then eighteen and a recent graduate of Junipero Serra High School in Gardena—went to Macola Record Company to record a song.

Macola distributed records for early groups like the World Class Wreckin' Cru, Jimmy Bobby and the Critters and the LA Dream Team. But the LA company made its greatest mark as a sort of self-publishing house for hopefuls—anybody could pay for studio time and make a record. Five hundred and forty-five vinyls cost $1,000, cash and carry. As it happened, hip-hop's early business model depended heavily on sales out of the trunks of cars.

Arab's first record was called "Strange Life." The sound, he says, was influenced by the work of his favorite artists at the time—Prince, Devo, Parliament-Funkadelic, and Kraftwerk. Soon after, Arab met Dr. Dre. Dre was a member of the World Class Wreckin' Cru, known for their electro funk sound and their purple leather sequined suits. The future billionaire entrepreneur was also doing a lot of producing and DJing, as was Arab, who was working with a girl group called JJ FAD that would eventually score a big hit with "Supersonic."

Arab and Dre did a few DJ gigs together in skating rinks. One Sunday in 1984, Dre and Arab were attending the Roadium swap meet in Gardena, where a lot of artists and DJs bought and sold records. There was a guy named Steve Yano whose booth served as a gathering place and clearing house for the latest musicians and artists. Yano approached Dre and Arab with a proposition: There was this dude, Eazy-E. He might have been a crack dealer at one time. Maybe he still was. In either case, he wanted to get into the music game.

"Yano was like, 'Listen. Eazy got some money, he wants to get into this. He don't rap, he don't do nothing, he just wants in,'" Arab remembers. At the time, Arab says, Dre was driving an RX7 with no back window. "We were like, 'Hey, if he got some money, maybe we can get together and do something cool.'"

And so it was that the original sextet was assembled. Eazy brought his friend MC Ren. Dre brought Yella from the Wreckin' Cru. Ice Cube was the youngest, clearly a prodigy.

"We started working on all this new stuff," Arab remembers. "We were sittin' in my mom's living room one day, trying to come up with names. And I remember I had said something stupid. I was like, 'Hey man, we should call the album, "From Compton With Love" and have a bunch of dudes with guns on the cover.' But everybody was like, 'Nah, nah, that's wack.'

"I know everybody who was there probably got their own interpretation of what happened next, but this is what I remember. Nobody just came out and said, 'Hey, let's call it N.W.A.' What happened was, somebody had said, 'I feel like a nigga with an attitude.' And we all kind of agreed. And that's when it hit. It was like, 'Oh shit! Let's call it that! We were all niggaz wit attitudes."

In 1987, N.W.A released its first single, "Panic Zone," on Eazy-E's Ruthless Records label. An EP called N.W.A came next; then, a bootleg issued by Macola titled N.W.A and the Posse.

NWA's debut studio album, *Straight Outta Compton*, dropped in 1988. The record was a revelation and a clarion call, employing gut-rattling beats and raw, journalistic detail. Realistic sound effects like gunshots and squealing tires added a riveting you-are-there quality.

The audacity of the headline song, "Fuck Tha Police," revealed a bitter social and racial animosity that was bubbling beneath the surface some twenty years after the Civil Rights Act. Rodney King's beating by police was still three years away. Michael Brown's murder in Missouri—and the ensuing public outcry—was still a quarter century off. The economic hardships that had led to the thriving outlaw economy of the street gangs—and the thriving military-industrial economy of the government's War on Drugs—had to be addressed. The streets had become a war zone, complete with motorized battering rams. Everybody in the hood knew somebody in jail. There seemed no way out. "There was a lotta niggas with attitudes all over the country," Arab says. "We was just the ones laying it down in the most naked terms."

For their first national tour, the group hit the road in a fifteen-passenger van. ("Everybody drove but Cube. I don't think we ever let Cube drive," Arab says.) The shitstorm that followed is well-documented. There were letters from the FBI, arrests by local law enforcement, concerts canceled or shut down mid-note. "It was crazy. It's still a blur. I can't remember which city was which," Arab says. "I think it was in

Detroit where the cops came up on stage and threw flash-bang gre-
nades because they told us we weren't supposed to perform 'Fuck Tha
Police.' And I remember flying into this airport and the police were
waiting for us. They took Dre away. They took Ice T away—he was on
tour with us. They said they had a report that somebody on the plane
had a gun. And it was like, Ice T had this gold chain with a little gun on
it. It was like some science-fiction shit."

Straight Outta Compton was one of the first albums to carry a
parental warning label. Despite a resulting moratorium on airplay, the
outraged headlines and frenzied media coverage shot the album to double platinum.

The thuggish behavior of early rap moguls like Eazy-E and Suge
Knight—who employed business practices learned in the streets as drug
dealers—is no secret. Also well-known are the details of the partnership
between Eazy-E and music manager Gerald E. "Jerry" Heller, a longtime
industry insider who'd stewarded Elton John and Pink Floyd on their
first American tours. He recently sued the producers for his portrayal in
the hit biopic *Straight Outta Compton*. Eventually, financial disagree-
ments brought the group to an end in a hail of diss-tracks and lawsuits.

"It was like the old Cadillac Records thing, man. Bottom line, we
weren't getting paid," Arab says. "We were selling like two to three
million records, and all we was getting was a little check for like thirty
grand and a Suzuki Samurai. See, I had my own solo records before
N.W.A. I had an apartment and a car. I was producing. I knew how stuff
worked. I knew what royalties were; I knew that if I sold this many
records, I'm supposed to get this much money. And I knew that every
quarter that was supposed to happen again. But it wasn't happening. I
would go to Eazy and say, 'Can I get paid?' And he'd be like, 'Talk to
Jerry.' So I'd go talk to Jerry, and he'd say, 'Talk to Eazy.' It was just
that back-and-forth thing. Finally, I was like fuck it, you know what
I'm saying? I bounced."

When he told Cube he was leaving, Arab remembers, "At first he
was like, 'Man, you stupid for leaving.' But I told him, 'It ain't no hard
feelings. It's about business. We out here getting chased by police and
getting arrested, and getting in fights with fools, and I'm not getting
money. I got bills. I got stuff I need to do. I'm tired, I don't need to beg.'

"It was sketchy, man," Arab says. "I wish it could've gone a different way."

Seagulls screech and soar in the air above the outside terrace at Killer Shrimp in Marina del Rey. Million-dollar boats bob along the docks.

Years ago, when N.W.A first went out on tour, Arab brought along the latest object of his fascination—an early laptop. His first was a Texas Instruments T199. After that, he bought a Tandy from RadioShack, then a Commodore 64, and so on. In his spare time, he taught himself code. As the computer revolution came to the entertainment business, Arab used his hip-hop connections to get in on the ground floor.

After working for a time on computerized special effects for movies, Arab eventually scored a job at Fox Interactive. "I worked on thirty, forty video games," he says. "At one point I was heading up some of the Barbie titles. I would have all this Barbie stuff sitting on my desk— like a Barbie boat and a Barbie car. "People would walk by and look at me. I'd get all hard and be like, 'What? You got something to say about my Barbies?'"

At the moment, Arab says, he's involved with a startup that will provide content for virtual-reality programs and 3-D games. His apartment is stacked with boxes of hardware that will enable him to design software to go with the new VR goggles and other applications that are quickly coming to the market.

"I have a game on my phone right now," he says, holding it up. "Someday, you'll be able to play it on this table, a 3-D game. We could be shooting at holographic zombies and all that... And it looks real. You can use these special glasses, or someday you will just be able to use your handheld or wrist device. That's gonna be the future.

As our bowls of killer shrimp slowly empty, I go ahead and ask the obvious: "Are you ever sorry you left N.W.A?"

Arab's answer is immediate. "My mom always taught me to be humble, so I know what I accomplished with the group, I know what we did. If there's a lot of people who don't know what I did, well, they just don't know. But it seems like even in the group, some of the cats, they trying to change history a little bit. To make it more favorable, you know what I'm sayin'? To reinvent who they are. I don't care that

I dressed like Prince back in the day, or that Dre dressed in his glitter stuff with the Wreckin' Cru. That's what we did. If it wasn't for those things, we wouldn't be here.

"I've never wanted to be the guy over all these years to be like, 'Oh he's whining. He's complaining. He's got sour grapes.' Because I'm successful. I've always been successful, I was making records before any of them. I've always done my own thing."

Arab admits he was a bit taken aback by the particular version of history put forth in the movie *Straight Outta Compton*, a biopic which documented the group's rise. "They left me totally out," he says incredulously, after seeing the movie twice. "I think I was there in real life for more than half of the scenes. I kept wondering, 'Did I go to the bathroom during this scene? Was I behind the couch picking up popcorn?'"

Arab laughs at his own riff. "It is what it is," he says. "I am still cool with everybody in the group. When I left, I never had no beef with nobody."

Arab says he still hangs out with Yella. "I actually helped Yella—I helped him get back into the DJ thing because he was doing that porn thing for a while, then he got married and his wife was like, 'Nah, you can't do this.' So I talked to Yella. I said, 'Man, you need to get back out there and start DJing again.' I took him through the conventions, hooked him up with some of the companies, so he's back out there."

He talks to Ren all the time, he says. "We cool. I don't talk to Dre as much, or Cube as much. Over the years, I might have bumped into them or talked to them every now and then. We don't keep in contact. They're doing their thing, but we still cool. I'm still cool with everybody. I'm even still cool with freakin' Jerry Heller. I don't care. I've done my thing. As a grown man you've got to accept the ways certain things happen and then move on, you know what I mean? I wouldn't change nothing."

Sometimes, Arab says, he'll be walking down the street and people look at him funny. They're like, "Did I go to school with you? You look familiar."

Arab holds a palm up in the air, the universal symbol for "stop."

"I ain't going there, you know what I'm sayin? That shit is over."

LIVING OFF THE GRID IN SUBURBIA

PART HENRY DAVID THOREAU, PART ROBINSON CRUSOE, THIS FORMER MARKETING MAN CHUCKED IT ALL TO LIVE ON A UTOPIAN ISLAND IN THE MIDDLE A SAN DIEGO SUBURB.

B ehind a tall row of hedges, on a steep hillside terraced with million-dollar houses in an oceanside suburb of San Diego, Rob Greenfield hops up on a hay bale, one of three arranged around a fire pit. He peers over the simple wooden privacy fence that surrounds his encampment, searching the Pacific sky expectantly for signs of a storm.

His balding head is deeply tanned; the soles of his feet are black and calloused. He always goes barefoot. Not long ago, when he discovered he needed shoes to travel on a commercial flight, he went down to the beach and foraged a pair of flip-flops from a trash can. There's a fresh scar where surgeons recently reattached the fourth toe on his right foot after a bicycle mishap, and yellow dust on the tip of his nose—the telltale remnants of his daily dose of turmeric, a natural anti-inflammatory he believes is also good for his general health.

Part Henry David Thoreau, part Robinson Crusoe, Greenfield, twenty-nine, is a former marketing man who suffered his own Don Draper moment a few years ago and chucked it all for an eco-mindful lifestyle. He has purposefully shipwrecked himself on a utopian island in the middle of suburbia, a haven from the forces of waste and consumerism that have come to rule our daily lives.

Greenfield doesn't own a cell phone or a car. He gets around on a bamboo bike he has ridden across the country twice; with the help of donors, dumpsters, and extreme conservation techniques. He shits into a five-gallon bucket and composts his own waste with the leaves from a spreading pepper tree that also provides his shade. The end product is called *humanure*; there's surprisingly little smell, although he tolerates a minor plague of flies around his humble encampment. He waters his wicking-bed garden with his urine and his dirty dishwater. The trash he generated last month fits into the space of a large Ziploc bag.

He retires at 10 p.m. every evening and sleeps nine hours on a futon on the floor of a fifty-square-foot house. The structure is a prototype of a DIY emergency shelter designed by a local contractor. It has wheels and cost $950, but it isn't tall enough inside for Greenfield to stand. He charges his computer with solar panels and uses the Internet at a library or cafe. He tries not to use public utilities, unless he's away from home and has no other option. Social media is his largest concession to modernity—he has more than fifteen thousand Facebook friends and twenty-eight thousand followers on Twitter. He calls himself a Dude Making a Difference. With or without the attention, he figures he does, in his own small way, just by trying.

Turning in place, wearing the perpetual smile of the fervently engaged, Greenfield surveys with pride his environmentally friendly kingdom, roughly 750 square feet of dirt and leaf mulch in a pricey part of San Diego called Point Loma, near the quirky seaside town of Ocean Beach. The houses across the street cling to the hillside above. Looking up from Greenfield's plot below, you can see, through large picture windows, the treadmills, telescopes, and big-screen TVs that dominate the front rooms.

Greenfield's place has a kitchen area with a small sink connected to a water collector. Nonperishable items are kept in an insulated locker made of plastic. To one side he's set up his own little outdoor privy, with bamboo walls and a little mirror. Due to the high hedges and the canopy of the pepper tree, nobody in the neighborhood suspects he is here, living off the grid in suburbia. The landlord, a follower of his blog he had never previously met, has given Greenfield the space in exchange for his improvements, which include the fence around the property and a rain-gathering system that utilizes the sloped asphalt roof of the landlord's house, hunkered on a terrace below.

Greenfield is wearing a T-shirt and quick-dry Patagonia shorts. He hasn't taken a proper shower since April 2013, preferring instead to bathe in the ocean, lakes, rivers, downpours or leaky fire hydrants—one such hydrant, encountered in Brooklyn, was, by his own careful measure, leaking two gallons a minute. In Africa, he says, there are billions of people living on two to five gallons a day. The average American consumes eighty to one hundred gallons of water a day. Greenfield consumes less than two gallons a day. Using five-gallon buckets, it takes him two hours to haul enough water uphill from the collector below to fill his water tank.

"The idea of living here is to simplify," he says. "Though in a sense, my life is more complex because I have to pay attention. I don't turn on the faucet and have an infinite supply of water; I have to harvest my water, ration it, and finally dispose of it properly. I can't flush my poo down a toilet; I have to turn it into soil. What I've learned is that every time something is easy in our modern life, typically that means you've just outsourced the burden to someone else. The reason flushing a toilet is easy is because there are people dealing with your poo somewhere else. The reason driving is easy is because fossil fuels were pumped from the earth, and pollution is being caused—or wars or price gouging—and that's why you can go from sixty to eight miles per hour just by changing the angle of your foot. Whereas running or biking is hard because you're generating the energy.

"A lot of people work hard to have a lot of money so they don't have to work when they're not at work," Greenfield says in his loopy but thoughtful style. "They pay maids and gardeners and construction workers. They pay food stores. They pay for people to work them out at a gym. They pay for water and sewage, for electricity to run their things."

He hops down off the hay bale, absently waving away a pesky black house fly. "Try carrying 165 gallons of water up the hill," he says. "You won't need a gym membership."

Greenfield and his three siblings were raised in Ashland, Wisconsin, by a single mother. Coming from a family of modest means, he says, "I was extremely money-oriented. One of my hobbies as a kid was collecting coins, collecting things to hold coins in, just counting coins—like every time I went to a friend's house I would count his piggy bank. I just loved money. I thought I wanted to be a banker."

After his freshman year at the University of Wisconsin, La Crosse, Greenfield spent his summer selling educational books door-to-door. "I worked like eighty or ninety hours a week. My first summer I made $18,000. And then I was hooked. I did about the same the next few summers. I loved that feeling of amassing the numbers. It was, in a very real way, a security blanket for me."

After graduating with a degree in science and suffering a bad breakup with a girlfriend, Greenfield put Wisconsin in his rearview mirror. In 2011, after a brief sojourn in Florida, he landed in San Diego, where he and several partners started a marketing company that sold advertising on shopping carts and cash register tapes.

"The company did OK, but nobody ever made their money back from what we were selling," Greenfield says. "It was like: The most important thing is making the sale. You did whatever it took. It didn't matter that the product you were selling was bogus."

Greenfield left the company to start his own. His main product was hotel key card advertising. At the business's peak, he says, he had twenty salespeople. The money was great, but the management was a nightmare. All these personalities, every one of them grabbing for the kind of numbers that gave them self-worth. And the products they were pushing—hotel key card advertising! At last, he says, he'd had enough of his "soulless existence devoted to selling little pieces of plastic. I had to get out of there."

He shuttered the company and left the marketing business forever.

Since then, Greenfield has lived full-time as an eco-pioneer, carrying on his personal crusade as a learning experience and as an example, part of a small but committed worldwide movement of people who believe that less is more, not only for the benefit of the besieged planet and its depleted natural resources, but because why in the hell do we need all the stuff with which modern life has presented us?

In his bicycle trips across the country, Greenfield promoted aware-ness of water use and food waste, getting attention from news outlets along the way. Soon he will embark on his most challenging feat of eco-adventurism: a barefoot sojourn across South America, from Rio de Janeiro to the Panama Canal, with no money.

He looks up toward the sky. The sun is getting stronger. The storm clouds in the middle distance seem to be receding. Three weeks ago there was a heavy mist overnight. He collected about 10 gallons of water off the roof. There hasn't been anything since.

"I'm gonna be a little bummed if it pours over there and doesn't rain here," he says. As it turns out, there will be flash-flood warnings several miles north away in Pacific Beach, where his girlfriend lives; she, too, is avidly eco-conscious, down to three showers a week.

But Greenfield knows better than to get too upset about the weather: To live closer to nature is to learn to surrender. Plus, the next challenge is already upon him: to free himself from the tyranny of money.

"I've been learning that I prefer a life that's less based around money. Without money, I follow my truest desires and my truest ethics. Money makes it too easy to complicate your life with things that don't matter, that nobody needs.

"At the beginning of the year I was down to like $10,000. Now I have about $5,000. I think the money will run out in January. I'm look-ing forward to that day."

PEACE OUT

AT SAN FRANCISCO'S ZEN HOSPICE PROJECT, DEATH IS A CREATIVE ACT, NOT A TRAGEDY—THE ENDING OF ONE BEAUTIFUL THING AND THE BEGINNING OF ANOTHER.

On a foggy hilltop in San Francisco, beyond the ocean-blue front doors of a cheerfully restored Victorian house, twenty strangers sit in chairs in two large circles, speaking intimately about death.

The air in the parlor is fragrant with baked goods and coffee, fraught with quiet emotions. Dusk filters through the sheer curtains on the bay window; the furnishings are a mixture of antiques, original works of art, and pieces you might find in your grandma's apartment. On the wall is a large canvas of an ensō, a Zen circle, which symbolizes absolute enlightenment—strength, elegance, the universe, and *mu* (the void). It's also the logo of the Zen Hospice Project (ZHP), a nonprofit residential care facility where death is treated less like a catastrophic medical event and more like a natural part of life.

"I feel like death is always there," says a twenty-something with a ponytail and a beard. "It can be paralyzing. I don't know what to do with it."

"Knowing I'm going to die, knowing we're all going to die, makes things feel kind of futile," says a woman in her thirties. "I try to be upbeat with my kids, but I'm walking around experiencing a kind of pregrief. My parents are going to die. My husband is going to die. I'm going to die. It's going to happen, you just don't know when."

"I worry that I will die and my son will need me," says a fortyish father.

As the sharing continues, the diverse crowd appears to draw closer together, leaning into the conversation. Most of them have come here, to the Zen Hospice Project Guest House in San Francisco's Lower Haight, in response to a public announcement of this meeting, one in a series that's been billed as an "Open Death Conversation," a forum for discussing the many aspects of death and dying. That most in attendance found news of the meeting online conjures a wrenching montage—so many diverse people, each on his or her solitary screen, searching for answers to deep personal fears, Googling words like death and dying.

"I don't want to be a burden on my family," says a well-put-together older woman with snow-white hair.

"Who's going to even know I was here?" asks a woman with a nose ring.

One floor above, death is less abstract.

In five spartan rooms decorated with personal items, five residents of the Guest House are spending their final days, attended in round-the-clock shifts by more than one hundred trained volunteers and staff, who take a Zen Buddhist approach to helping people die mindfully—to savor their last days, to view death not as a tragedy, but as an ending of one beautiful thing and the beginning of another.

Last year, forty-five people departed our earthly realm from this whisper-quiet transit station. During their final days, the residents— the word "patient" is discouraged—watched their favorite movies and TV shows, engaged in preferred activities of which they were still capable, shared silent or intensely personal moments with volunteers, spent comfortable quality time with family, all of it with minimal invasive treatment (though pain medications and other drugs are freely used), away from the institutional setting of a hospital. The residents ate their favorite foods, prepared to order by a noted chef and a staff of kitchen volunteers, who keep a whiteboard of everyone's likes and dislikes—they'll even cook whole meals or special cookies for people who are no longer eating, just because they love the smell. Those who wished, and were able, could go out to the beautiful garden terrace—bamboo and orchids and fresh herbs for the kitchen—to smoke cigarettes or medical marijuana, or to share a good bottle of wine with visiting loved ones.

After each passing, the entire staff, and the families and residents who so desired, returned to the terrace for the Flower Petal Ritual, a ceremony in which petals are sprinkled over the carefully washed and dressed body of the departed loved one before it's taken to a waiting hearse.

Though people become technically "hospice eligible" when their doctors determine they have only six months to live, the average stay at the Guest House is about three weeks (one notable resident enjoyed her stay so much that she recovered and is still alive and thriving at a long-term care facility). Compared to the average of $6,000 a day for hospital-based hospice care, the Guest House charges residents about $800. There's a sliding scale to accommodate the less fortunate; much of the ZHP budget relies on charitable donations. A cooperative agreement with the University of California, San Francisco, health system also helps meet the bottom line. Unlike home hospice services, where people are allowed to die in their own houses, attended by their bereaved (and often unprepared) families, residential health care, like that provided at the Guest House, isn't covered by Medicare or private health insurance.

In both practical and philosophical ways, the ZHP is trying to change the way our society approaches death. The program originated in the late 1980s, under the auspices of the San Francisco Zen Center, as a response to the epidemic of AIDS deaths in the city and the nation at that time. Since then, ZHP has grown into an independent nonprofit organization that provides bedside care for people (and their loved ones) facing advanced terminal illness. Their larger mission is to train and support a new wave of volunteer and professional caregivers adept in the principles of Zen Buddhism and palliative care, a growing medical field that stresses a multidisciplinary approach to caring for the dying—employing a range of medical, philosophical, and sensory therapies to provide relief from symptoms, pain, and the extreme mental stress of one's impending and often painful death, whatever the diagnosis.

ZHP opened the Guest House officially in 1990. In 2010, after a six-year renovation and reorganization, the Guest House was reopened as a licensed residential care facility for the chronically ill with twenty-four-hour nursing staff, all of whom are trained in its Zen approach. Including ongoing service at nearby Laguna Honda Hospital, one of the largest public long-term care facilities in the United States, Zen Hospice workers have served more than thirty-one thousand people in the Bay Area.

In time, the staff and supporters of ZHP hope their approach will become more standard around the country and the world, revolutionizing the way we look at death, and removing some of the fear and angst that so many carry around silently every day.

"We can't solve for death, but we can design toward it," says BJ Miller, a hands-on physician who specializes in palliative care, and who also serves as the senior director and advocate for ZHP.

A handsome and charismatic triple amputee—who goes everywhere with his dog and has started a successful company that makes hip shoes for prosthesis wearers—Miller lost both legs below the knee and his left hand below the wrist in 1990, when he was a sophomore at Princeton, the result of a free-spirited but inadvisable urge to climb to the top of an idle New Jersey Transit commuter train. Eleven thousand volts surged through his body; he spent months thereafter in excruciating pain in a burn unit. It was there that Miller began his long and personal relationship with the notion of suffering and death.

Since his wildly popular TED talk last fall, titled "What Really Matters at the End of Life," Miller has been in high demand as a speaker at a time when the national conversation about death and dying are undergoing a shift. In recent times, there has been renewed debate over assisted suicide; several best-selling books and viral videos have made the rounds. In more than twenty countries, thousands of people have gotten together to discuss dying through a project called Death Over Dinner.

What Miller and the ZHP are talking about, he says, is drawing a distinction between models of care that are "disease-centered" and ones that are more "patient-centered"—designed to usher a person more easily into death. In this model, the type of care offered, says Miller, "becomes a creative, generative, even playful act. 'Play' may sound like a funny word here. But it is also one of our highest forms of adaptation. Consider every major compulsory effort it takes to be human. The need for food has birthed cuisine. The need for shelter has given rise to architecture. The need for cover, fashion. And for being subjected to the clock, well, we invented music. So, since dying is a necessary part of life, what might we create with this fact?"

Instead of a sterile environment with expensive machines and invasive treatments, asks Miller and the ZHP, why not allow life to play itself out in a different fashion? Instead of going out with a fearful whimper or a valiant but vain fight, Miller says, "aging and dying can become a process of crescendo through to the end."

Maybe, he says, "we can learn to live well—not in spite of death, but because of it. Let death be what takes us, not lack of imagination."

On another afternoon in the Guest House, Celeyce Matthews is sitting in the parlor. The cook has been making cornbread; the down-home smell wafts around the first floor. Four of the residents upstairs are comatose. The fifth is not eating. Either way, the kitchen staff tries to keep if fragrant and cheery. Volunteers snack on the muffins.

Matthews is forty-six, born in Berkeley. Her parents, who she calls "lefty do-gooders" made up her name unusual first name. Nearly two decades ago, Matthews says, she had her first experience with death; her grandmother was dying of pancreatic cancer in hospice care at home. "As she breathed her last breaths, we were all around her, we all got to say goodbye. And then afterwards my mother, aunt, and I, we cleaned and dressed her and we put a little makeup on her and we covered her in my great-great-grandmother's beautiful linen sheet. Then we all sat around and ate spaghetti. We had a meal around her body. And I remember feeling proud of her because it was such a process to let go of life."

Over the ensuing years, Matthews worked as a teacher and artist and as a mindfulness coach, but the resonance of her grandmother's death was never far away from her thoughts. She was at a meditation retreat when she heard about the Guest House and the volunteer program. "I read about it, and it was suddenly very clear. I said, 'That's it! That's what I want to do!'" She took the training; she's been volunteering now for more than a year—doing everything from bathing people to feeding them to just sitting there and watching TV with them. "I love sitting quietly with a resident and paying attention to them, noticing the way they look, the way they're breathing—just being present with the knowledge that they're dying, that these are their final days, and that this also will happen to me in some form."

Recently, she completed her certified nursing assistant training and will soon begin working at the Guest House with an eye toward becoming a registered nurse to provide care to the fatally ill who are too sick to do much at all. "One woman I think a lot about. She was bedridden. She may have had some dementia happening, but she was in this amazing state of gratitude. We had this ritual together where I'd be feeding her brownies, and she'd say, 'I'm so grateful for brownies!' and I'd repeat, 'I'm so grateful for brownies.'" Another man died during one of Matthews's shifts. "[He] was ninety-four years old. It was such an honor to be with his body and to clean it and care for it, just as I had done for my grandmother.

"What was so amazing was that his limbs were cold, but as we rolled him to his side, his back was still warm. And the thing that struck me was: this is literally the last of his life's energy. I got to feel that."

Dedan Gills had always hoped to die in his beloved Mendocino, surrounded by the redwoods, the ravens, and the ocean, his books and poems-in-progress, all the things that he loved, most especially his wife, Belvie Rooks.

A writer, poet, and civil-rights activist, Gills' most recent project had been undertaken together with Rooks, a writer, educator, and producer whose work weaves the worlds of spirituality, feminism, ecology, and social justice. The project was called Growing a Global Heart. The mission: to plant one million trees along the routes of both the Transatlantic Slave Trade in West Africa and the Underground Railroad in the United States "to honor and remember the millions of unnamed, unheralded and unremembered souls who were lost during the slave trade" and "to help combat the ravaging effects of global warming and catastrophic climate change."

Then, in March 2012, Gills was diagnosed with liver cancer. He had 70 percent of his liver removed. The surgery went well; the cancer went into remission. Gills and Rooks went on with their lives' work, spending time in Ghana and Senegal, as part of an ongoing exploration into the intergenerational impact of the slave trade.

A year ago, the cancer returned. Though the couple made an effort to carry out Gills' wishes and stay at home in Mendocino, as he became more incapacitated, as the disease became more painful, it became obvious that they needed to change their plans. They made the difficult decision to move him to the ZHP Guest House.

Over the next four and a half months, if it could be said that a man could thrive even as he was dying a painful death, Gills did. He went around and introduced himself to every patient who came and went during his time on the second floor. A learned and impressive man with a deep spirit and a full complement of exciting stories and experiences to tell, and much wisdom to impart, Gills became a popular and valued fixture in the Guest House, beloved by all the staff and volunteers. Rooks herself took the volunteer training course. When he was up to it, Gills was asked to address some of the classes. Last August, they celebrated his seventieth birthday and their eighth wedding anniversary there.

"I never really expected in hospice to find a family of people that I feel in touch with," Rooks says. "I never expected to find community. I just expected there would be clinical services, pain would be managed, and that would be it. But it became powerfully transformative for both of us."

One Sunday afternoon, Gills and Rooks learned from a nurse that another one of the residents, call him Bob, was celebrating his eighty-fifth birthday. A small crowd of relatives came and went throughout the day, paying respects to the family's dying patriarch.

At some point in the afternoon, Rooks remembers, "Dedan said to me, 'I'm going to go down and wish Bob a happy birthday.'"

Gills left the room. Two steps out, he turned around and came back, grabbed a stuffed animal someone had given him.

"I'm gonna pass this forward," Gills told his wife.

The following Tuesday night, Bob died.

When Gills and Rooks went down to the garden terrace for the Flower Petal Ritual, they found Bob on the gurney. The stuffed animal had been laid upon his heart, his arms wrapped around it.

Bob's wife came up to them.

"I just wanted to thank your husband so much," Rooks remembers her saying. "That little toy he gave to Bob was his only birthday gift." Because Bob was dying, nobody thought about gifts.

Dedan Gills died about fifteen weeks later, a long stay by hospice standards. His Flower Petal Ritual was perhaps the most crowded in Guest House history.

PERMISSIONS

The following stories were first published in a shorter form in *Esquire:*
    "Growing Almonds in the Desert," February, 2015
    "The Life of a Clown," June, 2015
    "The Day Peter Dinklage Watched Someone Die," April, 2016
    "The Golden Child," December, 2016
    "The Lonely Hedonist," November, 2016

The following stories were first published in a shorter form in *Mel Magazine:*
    "Living Off the Grid in Suburbia," January 9, 2016
    "Arabian Prince Left N.W.A and He's Doing Just Fine," January 16, 2016
    "Will Ron Popeil's Final Product Be His Masterpiece?" February 20, 2016
    "Peace Out," March 12, 2016
    "The First Family of Dildos," May 8, 2017
    "The Most Interesting Man in the World, In Retirement," June 5, 2017

The following story was first published in a shorter form on MadeMan.com:
    "The Pot Doctor Will See You Now," October 14, 2016

The following story was first published in a shorter form in *Smithsonian:*
    "Will the Public Ever Get to See the "Dueling Dinosaurs?" July 2017

The following stories were first published in a shorter form in *California Sunday:*
    "The Samoan Pipeline," November 19, 2015
    "Dab Artists," May 3, 2015.

The following story was first published in a shorter form in *DuJour:*
    "The First Male Supermodel Was a Cult Member," September 2016.

The following story was never before published:
    "The Bone Diggers."

ABOUT THE AUTHOR

Mike Sager is a best-selling author and award-winning reporter. A former *Washington Post* staff writer under Watergate investigator Bob Woodward, he worked closely, during his years as a contributing editor to *Rolling Stone*, with gonzo journalist Hunter S. Thompson. Sager is the author of more than ten books, including anthologies, novels, biography, and textbooks. He has served for two decades as a writer at large for *Esquire*. In 2010 he won the National Magazine Award for profile writing. Several of his stories have inspired films and documentaries; he is the editor and publisher of The Sager Group LLC. For more information, please see www.MikeSager.com

ABOUT THE PUBLISHER

The Sager Group was founded in 1984. In 2012 it was chartered as a multimedia artists' and writers' consortium, with the intent of empowering those who create art—an umbrella beneath which makers can pursue, and profit from, their craft directly, without gatekeepers. TSG publishes books; ministers to artists and provides modest grants; and produces documentary, feature, and commercial films. By harnessing the means of production, The Sager Group helps artists help themselves. For more information, please see www.TheSagerGroup.net.

53431933R00140

Made in the USA
San Bernardino, CA
16 September 2017